If only *The Victorious Mind* had been written ten years ago... It would have saved me a lot of frustration and self-blame in failing to keep up my regular meditation practice. Now I not only know why I struggled so much, but what to do instead.

— SEPH FONTANE Pennock, Co-founder, PositivePsychology.com

In *The Victorious Mind*, Anthony Metivier brings his terrifying experience of mental illness together with his depth of knowledge of memory systems to show how using mnemonics systematically can ease a troubled mind and replace terror with joy. This is a unique book from an author who speaks from a lifetime of experience beyond anything I could have imagined.

— LYNNE KELLY, author of *The Memory Code* and *Memory Craft*

Anthony Metivier has a compelling personal story and a remarkable, practical methodology of helping us move beyond our stories and into the living truth. With one foot planted firmly in the relative and the other rooted in the Absolute, Anthony has hit the sweet spot that combines the two - which is authentic nonduality.

— FRED DAVIS, author of *Awaken Now* and *The Book of Undoing*

With so many memory books out there, this is really the first I've ever seen that heavily intertwines the ideas of meditation and memory. I've always felt the two go hand in hand and Anthony really does an amazing job at showing that! I highly recommend this book!

— NELSON DELLIS, 4x USA Memory Champion and author of *Remember It!*

The Victorious Mind is a masterful book written by a master of the field. Anthony Metivier has written an invaluable resource to anyone who wants to learn to fully utilize their cognitive capabilities to build a sharper mind and a better life.

— NIR EYAL, bestselling author of *Hooked* and *Indistractable*

At last, someone has remembered the true purpose and potential of the Art of Memory. In times past, it was seen as a path of self development. Using its methods you could bring health, harmony and excellence into your mind and thus your life. Sadly, this beautiful, beneficial art has been all but forgotten, until now. In this dynamic book, Anthony Metivier teaches you this ancient wisdom with a modern slant. Written from his own experience this is a book that will show you how to develop a "magnetic" memory that holds the information you wish but also attracts the influences you want into your life.

— MARTIN FAULKS, author of *Enlightened Living*

Anthony Metivier is a Warrior of the Mind!

— TONY BUZAN, author of *Mind Map Mastery* and
Co-Founder of the World Memory Championships

Dr. Metivier is a master of his craft and experienced teacher of the bridge between memory and meditation. In *The Victorious Mind*, you're learning from the best!

— JONATHAN LEVI, author of *The Only Skill that Matters* and
creator of SuperLearner

I now remember whole chunks of passages in another language. I'm learning with such ease that I often think it can't be this easy. The real "work" has been to calm my anxieties, and in this, Anthony is a very wise and effective guide and teacher. I am very grateful to him.

— JEANNIE KOH

I am usually a bit of an anxious person – not always suffering, but just someone with a very chatty mind, I'm always thinking, and being able to direct this energy in a productive way is very appealing to me. You have helped me direct my anxiety better.

— DANIELLA LOPEZ

I have made a lot of progress using this meditation technique to improve my spatial awareness and to see things clearer!

— JEFF JANSSON

Anthony's writing always triggers major moments of insight. *The Victorious Mind* goes deep and far beyond your typical "3 step method." Highly recommended.

— JIMMY NARAINE, motivational speaker

I've witnessed first-hand Anthony's ability to channel his mind into overcoming challenges that would destroy most people. Extraordinary and inspiring.

— OLLY RICHARDS, iwillteachyoualanguage.com

The Victorious Mind is unlike any book I've ever read about memory and the human mind. Anthony shares his personal experiences with mental health, advanced memory practices and various types of meditation. He uses engaging personal transformation stories that stayed with me long after I read the book. It's meticulously researched and contains many practices I'd never tried. I'm already working on my vision statement.

— BRYAN COLLINS, Becomeawritertoday.com

Anthony has spent a lifetime bringing useful information to light on the subject of memory. In his latest work, *The Victorious Mind*, he opens an amazing door into the world of the human mind, blending ancient memory techniques with captivating meditative experiences. If you want a personal adventure into peace of mind, this is the read for you.

— JIM SAMUELS, author of *Re-mind Yourself: Better Memory, Lower Stress*

In one word... Wow! In this highly engaging and worthwhile book, Anthony shares his personal story... sometimes some very raw and vulnerable moments. I have completed masters studies in neuroscience and thought I knew a fair bit about memory. I even believed my memory capacity was reasonably good. I wasn't even close! After reading *The Victorious Mind*, I realised there is so much more to embedding and remembering information successfully, which makes our lives more fulfilling.

— Josie Thomson, MCC and author of *The Wise Advocate: The Inner Voice of Strategic Leadership* (with Jeffrey M. Schwartz and Art Kleiner)

I've never read a memory book so visceral, yet so practical. Anthony holds nothing back in *The Victorious Mind* as he tells of his life-long struggle with mental illness in a manner both touching and humorous. I even learned things that I look forward to applying in my own memory training! I can't recommend this book enough for anyone out there looking to improve their mental fitness.

— Braden Adams, 2x Canadian Mind Sports Association National Memory Champion

I consider Anthony Metivier a personal mentor. If there is someone who thinks about and uses memory techniques as often as he does, I haven't found that person. He connects the dots better than anyone I know and will teach you how to use mnemonics to enhance the quality of your life.

— John Graham, 2018 USA Memory Champion

As a neuroscientist, I study the underlying mechanism of memory techniques and I am very interested in their widespread application. Because Anthony is such an expert in this field, having him uncover the use of mnemonics for mental health is fantastic and will help many readers!

— Boris Konrad, Guinness Record Holder and Memory Competitor, Award-Winning Speaker, and Neuroscientist

THE VICTORIOUS MIND

How to Master Memory,

Meditation and Mental Well-Being

ANTHONY METIVIER

MAGNETIC
MEMORY
METHOD

Published by Advanced Education Methodologies Pty Ltd

Website: *magneticmemorymethod.com*

ISBN: 978-0-6487519-8-4 *paperback*
          978-0-6487519-0-8 *hardcover*
          978-0-6487519-1-5 *ebook*

To the memory of Tony Buzan,

#WarrioroftheMind.

I still hear his voice,

"Floreant Dendritae!

May your brain cells flourish!"

*"If you don't become the ocean,
you'll be seasick every day."*

— LEONARD COHEN

*"You are not controlling the storm, and
you are not lost in it. You are the storm."*

— SAM HARRIS

*"O mind, remember, that which was done,
remember!"*

— ISHA UPANISHAD

TABLE OF CONTENTS

Preface: CAUGHT IN A STORM

A STRANGER PULLED *THIS* BODY back from the platform edge as a dirty sub-way train raced into the station.

"What the hell are you doing?" he yelled as he pulled me back from the edge. My entire frame was hyper-charged with mania and my mind streaming with voices. When I caught my breath in the ambulance, and when I think about his question now through the diverse and strange lenses of human memory...

I didn't know. I seem to have had no choice in the matter.

Few people outside of doctor's offices have heard this episode from my younger days. I spent years in waiting rooms and consulting rooms, desperately coping with immense mental suffering. I still use some of those spaces as "Memory Palaces." Their walls and corners, furniture and bookcases, and even the doctors themselves help me memorize far better "medicine" than they ever prescribed. But back then I followed their advice, often without question, and many pharmacies around the world now serve as Memory Palaces too.

Good medicine, bad medicine. Every pill has its place in the story of how this "self" assembles with people around the world to joyously teach, mostly for free, the memory techniques that saved my life and *keep* saving it. And none of it would have happened if a stranger hadn't tackled a confused mental patient who was about to "commit suicide."

As I remember it, I wasn't actually *committed* to suicide. Rather, a phantasmal blitzkrieg of impulses bombarded me—fuelled by self-destructive notions that had been pummelling me for years, and would pound even harder for many more.

It was spring. I had just been released from the Clarke Institute for Mental Health and I was a *mess*. As I stood in the humid Bloor station that evening in Toronto, my head was pulsing and warm with angelic voices telling me that every-one would understand because everyone wanted me to do it. An auditory version of Michelangelo's Sistine Chapel ceiling besieged me. I couldn't see them, but I heard floating in space around me *everyone* in the world, people known and unknown, gently urging me to the end. The bridge, cars crossing the bridge, the subway.

Whatever it takes, said a voice I *felt* more than heard, a synaesthesia signal that seemed to come straight from the pages of a William S. Burroughs novel. *Just get it done.*

My nerves were shattered from a massive manic episode. I had spent three months in the hospital, where most of my time had been devoted to arguing that I didn't need to take their pills, not lithium and certainly not Risperdal. As I explained with boundless, manic energy during my "incarceration," I had discovered a secret relationship between the Latinate alphabet and the Arabic symbols for one and zero. One built the other, and provided the code for finally unveiling the ultimate truth of reality as a kind of language. When the doctors succeeded in (briefly) convincing me my enhanced state and jumbled ideas were a "problem," I gave them long, rambling lectures about how only a Marxist psychotherapist could possibly cure me because clearly capitalism was the true source of schizophrenia.

These medical professionals repaid my willingness to engage in philosophical debates about my condition by handing me a diagnosis of "bipolar disorder with psychosis." They followed this death sentence, or so it felt for many years, with hours of "occupational counselling." But rather than develop my resume or work on matching my skills with a suitable job, these sessions involved instructions on finding lodging in a boarding home and securing welfare. According to these wizards devoted to helping people re-enter society, I would never return to university or be employable. Indeed, the myriad of professionals I saw every day in the hospital seemed devoted to fulfilling this dark outcome because they practically married me to disaster as if to ice the cake of my diagnosis. As soon as they released me, I took up residence with another patient with whom I'd started an unusual affair. We not only had the blessing of our doctors, but also their institutional prediction that everything *should* be fine. "Some patients are very successful in supporting each other," we were told.

Things weren't fine and we two patients had the mutual-support skills of mice caring for cats in a small cage. I found myself in an eighteenth-floor apartment compelled by ceaseless urges to jump out the window. While my manic partner scrubbed dishes and the kitchen walls for hours on end with glee, I obsessively imagined myself as Spider-Man leaping from balcony to balcony, wondering when my webbing would run dry. I woke up startled from medicated sleep dreaming about acrobatic powers I didn't want, only to find the nightmare was real and the next pill in the bottle offered no cure.

To escape these height-induced urges, I wandered the streets and listened to the spirits in the sky. I played mental chess to keep my body from pouncing into traffic and eventually wound up in a McDonald's on Yonge Street. My hands shook so badly, I couldn't get my new, child-proofed pill bottles open. I felt nauseous from the lithium and terrified by warnings from the doctors about lithium toxicity. If I missed a dose, I was told, there would be horrible consequences. I was okay *now*, they told me, "a high-functioning manic depressive," but they took pains to show me examples of others in the mental ward who had failed to "comply." These were unkempt zombies mumbling conspiratorial poetry whose battle-worn faces were scarred by self-induced wounds. In the smoking room, one woman blew on the cherry of her cigarette to maximize its heat before taking out her eye. They stopped her in time, but you couldn't have arranged a better haunted house on a Hollywood budget if you wanted to film Dante walking the circles of past, present and future hell. These were the tortures I could expect for failing to take my pills on time— *every* time, for the rest of my life.

I don't remember what I told the stranger that night after he tackled me on the platform... I don't even remember *how* I got there. But I do remember that after this kind stranger hauled me back from the platform edge, I was soon on my way back to the hospital—this time for a long sleep on the floor. They didn't have a bed for me this time around, but they did have a pill. It was the biggest, whitest pill I'd ever swallowed. Later, they gave me more.

I remember noticing the aroma of a burger and fries in my backpack as the new pill took hold. It was the barely eaten "meal" from McDonald's I could hardly get down my lithium-sick throat. But I was too poor and trained by years of hunger to waste food, so I'd shoved it into my bag along with a copy of Don Delillo's *Underworld* and a course kit packed with enough French Critical Theory to start a revolution. But not that night. Nurses took my belt and my shoelaces, leaving me with trembling hands in empty pockets. Strangely, they let me keep the twin garrottes of my backpack, two straps perfect for hanging myself using the door handle to hold the makeshift noose in place. Fortunately, I was too doped to move. I woke to the smell of rancid meat slathered in sugary ketchup, my mind already rambling through what felt like a thousand devious plans to die. Later, a nurse rifled through my belongings and asked if I still wanted to eat the garbage she found. Groggy, I shook my head and accepted another pill instead. Later, I wept over the grease stain now marring the beautiful reading materials I couldn't have concentrated no matter how hard my love of reading tried to cut through the medicinal fog in my head.

I was 22 and this is what my life had become: stints in mental institutions, perilous episodes outside them. I wasn't getting better, and under the half-interested watch of Canada's medical system, this third circle of hell (*or was it the fifth?*) was just the beginning.

What this book is really about

This is a book about how I did manage to get better—how I dragged myself back to stable ground following the Toronto subway incident and how I've done it again many times since. In the end, the reason I got better was that I got sick—sick of seeking peace through pills and hospitals. Instead, I found solace in two secondary regimes of treatment I'd been exploring for years: memory training and meditation primarily, with some "biohacking" thrown in for good measure. "Biohacking"—still a relatively new term—refers to science-guided self-experimentation to improve one's body. And that mind you experience in your head? There's good reason to believe it's produced by your body too—through the brain. Improve your body and you stand a good chance of freeing yourself from the kind of mental suffering that nearly took my life.

The more I made memory and meditation practices my primary source of stability, and then began to biohack, the more life improved. In retrospect, I recognize these techniques had been healing me incrementally all along. In fact, consistent meditation practice combined with memory training has done more for me than any medication—legal or not—that I've tried. Far more than I ever could have imagined when I began exploring.

Am I cured—am I entirely well? Well, no, but I did complete the BA that drove me to the subway platform edge, and I have gone on to finish two MAs and a PhD. I've written more than 15 books, started two online businesses and essentially given manic depression the boot. My mind is at peace; my body is healthy and fit; my relationships are strong and stable; I do my favorite things every day—play music, read and write and share what I've learned with others through teaching. By experimenting with and developing the tools and techniques I'll describe throughout this book, I learned to sustain a positive process of self-transformation and ongoing maintenance leading to consistent personal growth.

I've learned to separate myself from the mental chaos that used to rule my mind. This book is about my journey, before and after applying a meditation and memory-focused program described by Gary Weber in *Happiness Beyond Thought*. But this book you're reading now has a dual purpose: to share both my journey through the storm and the techniques that enabled me to sail to calm waters. By telling the story and detailing the techniques that enabled me to thrive, I hope to help others learn to find peace and even victory in life, every day.

What does meditation have to do with memory? Their combination is the key: memory and cognitive functioning in general are inhibited when we're feeling stressed, nervous, or anxious, and relaxation can counter this effect and help us remember more and better. Since writing my first book on memory training for learning German vocabulary, I've understood how to calm my mind and generate states of deep concentration and creativity through meditation. Relaxation techniques have helped me both learn and use memory techniques and accomplish so much with earning degrees and learning languages—including teaching others the techniques.

I only recently realized that this understanding of the connections among the techniques, learning, and medication for mental well-being needed more explanation—especially so others can benefit from them as I have. As the author of thousands of articles, podcasts and videos about memory techniques and language learning, I've received tens of thousands of emails from people struggling to focus and concentrate. Most would take to memory techniques like ducks to water if they could just calm their mental noise. Even if these people could achieve only temporary release from what Sam Harris refers to as the "committee" chewing up so much mental space, they could begin creating the mnemonics that would drive their learning dreams. This book is my attempt to help you, if you're anything like these people, and perhaps you'll find benefit even if you're not. I only hope you're not starting as far down in the jaws of an illness as I did.

As you'll also find throughout the book, I am a proponent of using a *variety* of tools and techniques to enhance well-being. Why use only an Allen wrench when you have a whole toolbox at your disposal? The benefits compound when you use a range of the fantastic mental gizmos you'll discover in this book, to work on one project—yourself—from different angles, including the mental, physical, and even spiritual (though you'll find no religion in my kit even if I espouse the memorization of scripture from a variety of traditions).

Before continuing, we need to talk about the main word we'll be using throughout our journey. You see, one of the many quirks of English is how "memory" seems singular, when it is in fact many things.

Our autobiographical memory is subject to change. We often remember things that either did not happen, or happened differently than we remember. Some scientists think this happens because the brain changes the location and character of our memories each time we recall them. Then we have our personal preferences, illustrated by the revealing line in David Lynch's Lost Highway. As Fred Madison tells his wife, *"I like to remember things my own way. How I remembered them, not necessarily the way they happened."* Aren't we all like that from time to time? On top of these issues, we have quirks specific to episodic memory, figural memory, semantic memory and more terms than we need to list in these pages.

Memory techniques, on the other hand, demonstrate that the brain can remember some things perfectly and keep them intact. The techniques in this book make it possible to remember certain kinds of information (vocabulary, numbers, names, playing cards) with stunning accuracy. For this reason, it is important not to confuse malleable content with information that does not change. The techniques that help us accurately lock down useful types of information can override the stories we tell about ourselves, leading to incorruptible recall of simple things that set you free—on demand. Some of the best is both ancient *and* new every time you use it, but always the same.

What matters is that you follow the rules. When you do, "the rules will set you free." This is what Tony Buzan, co-founder of the World Memory Championships and proponent of "radiant thinking" told me. I've thought a lot about what these rules might be, and they boil down to something that really will set you F.R.E.E.

Frequent practice while...
Relaxed and focused on relevant information in a state of...
Experimentation and...
Entertainment.

How exactly to implement the techniques will unfold in stages as you read and begin to apply them. More than applying them as such, we need to follow these rules consistently. If you make yourself a student of the rules (not any particular teacher of them), their logic really will set you free. Although not a perfect circle, this F.R.E.E. acronym will soon reinforce itself, and you will experience how the benefits deepen the more you practice. Please write it down and remember it.

Story time and suggestion time

As much as this book tells the story of my own redemption, it is an instructional guide too. Like many such programs, the main points could be compressed onto a few index cards. Some readers will question why I've used so many pages. For those readers, the exercises will serve, and you can skip directly to them.

Most of us, however, need space and context—and often stories—to percolate abstract ideas and isolated instructions.

- Some learners need to know about techniques in great detail. This need will be served.

- Others gain understanding through narrative and context. For these readers, I share my story.

- Some need to know the reasons why and how certain techniques work. While it is not always clear, whenever possible, I share the brain science I'm aware of and a wide variety of sources they can follow up.

I've included stories from my own life for a few reasons. First, many people have loved *Moonwalking with Einstein*, Joshua Foer's incredible study of the memory competition world and how he rose through its ranks. Readers new to memory techniques, though, have complained that he doesn't do much teaching. That's understandable. It's hard to perceive the great wisdom he shares about memory techniques when you've never used them before. Similar complaints have arisen regarding Lynne Kelly's *The Memory Code*, a book which doesn't even express the teaching of memory techniques as its purpose. Rather, it's a (very good) book focused on the role of memory strategies in the survival of cultures deep into history. If you already use memory techniques, you'll perceive many wonderful angles that supplement and improve your practice because previous experience allows you to see more. She's recently followed it up with *Memory Craft*, which dives deeper into the techniques themselves and includes stories of her own (highly recommended).

The Victorious Mind is different from these recent entries into the long canon of memory training books because it combines personal history with science-based technical instruction for *both* memory *and* meditation focused on helping people cope with, and potentially resolve, mental health issues. I have done my best to serve every reading preference simultaneously. I always explain what these exercises and techniques are, how they work, and why they are useful, along with suggested steps to take. This means I tell stories, present scientific evidence in support of claims, take you on a few theoretical odysseys and guide you step-by-step through what Lynne Kelly might call the "crafting" of procedures that will help you remember more and enjoy peace of mind.

Nonetheless, memory techniques *are* technical. Theory about them is pivotal in the same way knowledge of scales enables good musicians to make great music. The hundreds of thousands of discussion posts on the Internet about using memory techniques well testify to the value of these theoretical ins-and-outs for serious practitioners. The same is true of meditation techniques, and my hope is that using stories as entry points will help more people engage in applying the exercises, as well as make the technical aspects more interesting and accessible.

How this book is different

This book differs from other memory books because I've come to believe memory training and meditation go hand in hand. By taking up a memory training practice, you may well receive many of the same benefits meditation can bring. My discussion differs from many meditation books, as well, because it offers instruction and personal stories that contextualize the techniques. Many authors of meditation books leave out personal stories because they claim to have scrubbed out their egos. Other writers make useful reference to biographical matters in ways readers might miss. None of these authors is wrong in thinking that too much biography creates precisely the attachments they're trying to help people avoid. Other times there's a great deal of storytelling but little guidance. I've found James Swartz a refreshing alternative to these styles. In *Mystic by Default*, Swartz shares his personal story of how he came to be a teacher and guardian of the Vedanta school of Hindu philosophy. If you know his other books and other teachings on this tradition, then by reading *Mystic by Default*, you are richly rewarded with insights into Vedanta. If you don't, you are richly rewarded by a well-written narrative.

My experiences with these books—and many others like them—led me to the hybrid approach used here. For some readers, this fusion of styles will work gangbusters. Others, who just want the details of instruction, will find these too. But stories have power—including the power to heal. As Brené Brown points out, "When we deny our stories, they define us. When we own our stories, we get to write a brave new ending." If my stories of overcoming major limitations help you own your stories, perhaps you'll be encouraged to take action. Perhaps you'll rise to meet the challenges of these techniques and, thus, experience the rich rewards they offer. The uncomfortable parts of life have taught me the most. I'm not going to leave anything out retelling them here.

This is also a self-improvement book more broadly

In contextualizing the techniques in stories about my life, however, I want to avoid the standard "do as I do" nature of self-improvement books. As Chin-Ning Chu rightfully observes about the self-help industry in *Thick Face, Black Heart*:

> In these books, the author prescribes a course of action that will lead to the desired result. Typically, it is a plan that has worked for the author and for some of his students. But it doesn't necessarily work well for many readers, even though they carefully follow the author's instructions. For example, two people can read the same book on lion-taming.

They can enter the lion's cage dressed identically. They can use identical gestures and words to command the lion. But the results will not be the same. One of them will get the lion to jump through the hoop, and the other will end up as a gruesome mess on the floor of the lion's cage.

Overall, I believe self-help teachers do more good than harm. Whereas some are more conceptual than others and speak in riddles, others teach well through story or a combination of direct step-by-step instruction with concrete examples. The real trick is in creating contexts in which student and teacher meet each other halfway and the teacher has one major outcome in mind: *to free the student from the teacher as quickly as possible*. This is sometimes called "teaching by abandonment," an approach I admire in Gary Weber, even if it can seem especially challenging for the student. It works because, if anything, it is the cleaving to teachers that explains why so many people find themselves torn apart by the lions. A lion tamer has dressed, taught and equipped them as lion tamers, yet they have not made *themselves* into lion tamers. And the lion knows it.

The three types of reader this book is for

1. Those struggling to learn and implement memory techniques because they do not have enough calm to focus for long enough. Even the simplest mnemonic strategies can be difficult to understand and practice if your mind is occupied by unhelpful noise and distraction.

2. Those I've already helped but who want to experience even greater benefits from memory techniques. Adding dedicated meditation practice that draws upon existing memory skills is tremendously rewarding.

3. Those who already meditate who want to add memory techniques to their practice. They will likely also be delighted by new perspectives on old favorites and perhaps pick up a few new meditation techniques along the way.

Trigger warning and how to navigate this book

These days, trigger warnings seem to be a necessity. So, for those sensitive to gritty descriptions of mental illness, suicidal ideation, drug use and violent impulses: STOP READING NOW (if you haven't already).

I cannot help you reproduce the maps that led me out of hell without frank honesty about what my hell was like. I was scared the first time I shared these struggles on the Magnetic Memory Method podcast and my YouTube channel. But I'm glad I did—gory details and all—because in response, people shared their own stories of hope and transformation. Lives have been saved. I will keep sharing these struggles in ways I hope respects the suffering while also giving people courage to navigate and free themselves from similar states.

A note about terms: over the years of teaching and writing about memory techniques, I've developed or modified terms from the vast lexicon of memory enhancement strategies bequeathed to us from historical and contemporary explorers in this field. I provide a glossary in the back, and the techniques themselves are detailed in the third part of the book. Throughout, I refer to "Memory Palaces" (not a term I invented—it was used by Augustine of Hippo and many memory artists since). You might be more familiar with the notion of keeping a "Mind Palace," "Roman Rooms," or even "Memory Castles." Whatever you call them, these mental creations are places in the mind—based on actual places you know well or other sources like movies and games—to "store" the images and information you are trying to memorize. Any information can be memorized, from vocabulary and phrases to complex formulas in math and science. For the purposes of this book, the ancient information I'll suggest you memorize is wonderful medicine.

For some, memorization with Memory Palaces is difficult, but the learning curve is worth the challenge. I found it difficult to conceive how it was possible for such a weird technique to work when learning it during a dark depression. Yet, the practice soon helped me *feel* better as my memory improved, and it turns out there's a good reason why it boosted my mood. As researcher Dr. Tim Dalgleish has shown, this style of using memory can help people with a history of depression and other mental health issues experience relief. Amongst several of his studies, one in particular stands out: "Method-of-loci as a mnemonic device to facilitate access to self-affirming personal memories for individuals with depression." Note that "method of loci" is another term for "Memory Palace." You might also encounter the term "Journey Method" as you explore these techniques, or even "apartments with compartments," as one of my first students preferred to call it. No matter what term you use for the technique, relief from mental distress is made possible because this mental tool helps us remember and rapidly access positive affirmations and memories quickly and accurately, even during times of distress. These higher quality memories can help dissolve negative ones, both immediately and for the long term.

I also often refer to the "Magnetic Memory Method", which is the systematic, 21st-century approach I developed to memorizing foreign language vocabulary, dreams, names, music, poetry and much more, in ways that are easy, elegant, effective and fun. This process comes from years of research and practice based on an ancient methodology that humans have preserved, elaborated and continue to share via a vibrant international community. Although all the best instructors in this community must "teach by abandonment" because of the nature of the techniques, there is *never* any need to go it alone. Just search for either my name or Magnetic Memory Method on the Internet. You'll find us.

With or without our community, this book is structured intentionally to free you from teachers and help you find *victory* over your own mind through memory training and meditation. You are the only one who can. To this end, there are four parts:

Part I: In the Eye of the Storm
In Part I, I share the background of this book, which is the story of how I transformed my misery into peace by using the techniques taught in the rest of this book. Although I don't know you, chances are you've been drawn to this book because you're in the eye of your own storm and want to get out. Welcome. I'm confident that the entire Magnetic Memory Method community can help you.

Part II: Become the Storm
In Part II, you'll learn why meditation is so important for enhancing mindfulness and memory improvement and how memory improvement techniques can help you finally experience mindfulness. The title of the section, "Become the Storm," refers to Sam Harris's point that you are not influenced by the storms of external circumstances so much as "you are the storm." I take this further by arguing that you need to do more than recognize the wisdom of Harris' insight—you need to "become the storm." Becoming the storm and staging the dual games of memory and mindfulness practice will help you remain in a watchful state of becoming.

Part III: Calm the Storm
In Part III, we dig deep into the techniques. Here, I will help you build the mental gymnasium where the workouts needed for mental transformation will occur. There is no place other than your mind where this can happen. This is about *your* mind and *your* mind alone, a place where I will appear as a kind of Morpheus to your Neo. The difference is this: when you say, "I know kung fu," like Neo, I can't be there to say, "show me," like Morpheus. But this book will help you become your

own Morpheus so that you won't need me—or any teacher—ever again. Which isn't to say you won't *want* more teachers. But your understanding of the role of teachers will likely be changed.

Part IV: No More Storms?

Part IV fills a gap I see in so many books that aim to "set you free." The truth is you can experience all kinds of rewards in your brain and still get caught up in destruction. Blessings and bombshells can fire off simultaneously, especially if you have a brain structurally predisposed to impulsive thoughts and behaviors, *even if* you've been meditating for years. Everything you ever experience happens through a combination of luck, brain chemistry and a capacity for awareness that only you can sharpen. The final chapters of the book demonstrate how important it is to keep sharpening, keep working, keep cultivating—they are not a resounding declaration of freedom from the mind belted out from a higher plane but reflections on the kinds of freedom you can achieve through continual learning, practicing and teaching.

Are you ready?

I hope you said a resounding "yes!" either out loud or in your head because, one way or another, the next moment is coming. And there's really no compelling reason not to embrace it with a Victorious Mind.

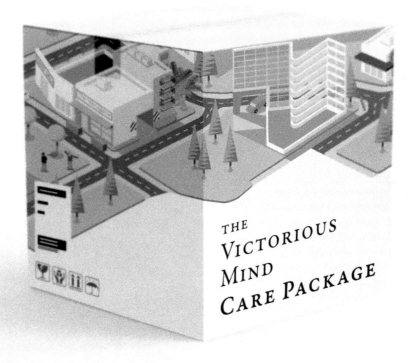

THE
VICTORIOUS
MIND
CARE PACKAGE

Visit *magneticmemorymethod.com/vmm*
now for all the additional care you need to fully implement
The Victorious Mind Methodology today.

Wait!

This book comes with...
THE VICTORIOUS MIND CARE PACKAGE *and* STUDY GUIDE

Would you like even more results and better memory and meditation success? It takes practice with both.

Download this multi-media supplement now and receive:

- Private discussion group for meditation memorizers

- Full Memory Palace Video Walkthrough with full color PDF map

- The Secret of Reusing any Memory Palace

- Self-inquiry Made Simple MP3

- Free Chapter from my forthcoming book *SMARTER The New Rules for Learning Faster In An Age of Overwhelm*

Part I

IN THE EYE
OF THE STORM

1 BEYOND THE BUDDHA SMILE TO BLISS

B EN FISHEL AND I sat in front of The Menagerie, my favorite cafe in Kelvin Grove, a district of Brisbane that shares many of the village-life characteristics I also enjoyed (when I wasn't hungover and depressed) for more than 10 years as a York University student in Toronto. The sun was shining, the coconut hot-chocolate tasted great and my favorite topics were on the table. Ben is the man behind projectmonkeymind.com, a site dedicated to meditation instruction and a variety of tools (like journaling) that can help you get out of your head and live a better life. As we talked, my experiences with meditation came up. I shared my first experience of the "Buddha Smile," which had happened about a decade before.

Ben and I originally met through Jon Morrow, an incredible entrepreneur who runs a group called Serious Bloggers Only, which helps individual bloggers with big missions stand a chance against the corporations and their massive budgets. With Jon's help, anyone can cut through the clutter and make it to page one of your favorite search engine. Jon's an inspiring guy too. Sometimes when I get caught up in my sob story, or hear someone else lost in theirs, I think of his epic, "7 Life Lessons from a Guy Who Can't Move Anything but His Face." Using speech rec-ognition technology, the power of practice and, as he told me during one of our advising sessions, "reverse engineering what works." Jon's pain, which sounds like it must have been immense, seems invisible next to his accomplishments. No wonder he calls one of his websites Unstoppable.me.

Thanks to Jon's group, there was Ben sitting across from me on that spring day in 2017. Assured by our co-membership in Jon's tribe, I told Ben my story, the same story you'll read in this book. This is the kind of thing you usually only talk about with fellow journeyers, especially those anxious to enter the realms of bliss promised by self-help gurus. The Buddha Smile I told Ben about was not a physical smile using the mouth. Instead, it was a sense of "bliss" that opened in my fore-head one day around an area some people rather un-scientifically call the "third eye." Depending on who you talk to, this notion refers either to the pineal gland or some portal that exists on this or that plane of extra-dimensional reality. As a skeptic-leaning scholar trained to sort, sift and screen for woo-woo, I was fascinated to finally experience something that I would describe as *rapturous* in the area just above my eyes.

I'd experienced the Buddha Smile often after that, but what Ben suggested that afternoon knocked my experience of this contained bit of "third eye" bliss permanently loose. Soon, half of my head would feel like it was beaming with light—and it still does (I'd knock on wood, but I'm not superstitious). I remember our meeting like a scene from the Joseph Campbell playbook, with a "call to adventure" that keeps on giving. Whereas I used to experience a gleam of pleasure at the center of my forehead, now I often feel my brain is floating on a cloud, particularly the right side. I regularly experience what some people call "non-duality" or what Jeffrey Martin has termed Persistent Non-Symbolic Experience (PNSE). I've even started to enjoy something I vehemently denied could be possible: the complete absence of thought—exquisite freedom from the source of the worst misery and suffering imaginable: my mind.

Martin describes PNSE in a paper called "Clusters of Individual Experiences Form a Continuum of Persistent Non-Symbolic Experiences in Adults." He describes "locations" along this continuum where some people might experience "no individualized sense of self, no self-related thoughts, no emotion, and no apparent sense of agency." Other people he studied claim to maintain a sense of individuality but also experience oneness or a sense of feeling "connected to everything." When I first read about these locations, it sounded like sci-fi or something out of Alejandro Jodorowsky's *El Topo*, a surreal cowboy movie in which the hero encounters gun masters who represent particular religions or philosophies, and acquires different skills from each before challenging them to a duel.

Now, I'm aware that what I'm describing might make PNSE seem like a fishing tale. I was skeptical too and still think it's all too-good-to-be-true from time to time—when there are thoughts at all. Sure, life presents challenges, sometimes several on any given day. Strangely enough, they soon feel like blessings, because I can see that only delusion turns most of them into "problems." Thanks to meditation and memory, I am quick to incorporate life's many situations into growth without self-delusion. Through experimentation, I feel I've arrived at something even better than PNSE, and as we'll see in the conclusion, Martin himself has recently updated that rather unwieldy terminology.

But before I get into the mission Ben gave me that made all this possible, I need to take you back to that original experience and my life at the time. My first Buddha Smile occurred while I was meditating on the floor of my home office in Saarbrücken, Germany, a city with many beautiful bridges, two hours from Paris by high-speed train. I was teaching Film Studies at the University of Saarland and completing my dissertation. Although I was busy watching dozens of movies and writing hundreds of pages of lecture notes—and my dissertation—I guzzled self-help audiobooks in an attempt to cope with my misery. This binge started after I heard Sam Harris speak on NPR. Harris is a well-known philosopher, neuroscientist, and meditator who writes and gives talks on the brain, spirituality without religion, consciousness, and mental well-being. That day, what hooked me was something he said about atheism: the fact that we have a word for the state of lacking belief in a god about whom few individuals and cultures can agree is so patently foolish. He joked that you might as well call yourself a "nonstrologist" if you're not convinced by astrology. Fuelled by this kindred thinking and other sparks of interest, I followed a chain of associations only the Internet of that era could allow. It might seem weird that a famous skeptic like Sam Harris would encourage me to drop the barriers between myself and a world of self-help filled with woo-woo. But even if I can't quite put my finger on it, it's perhaps the gift of curiosity he gives when, in his Ask Me Anything private podcast episodes, he intentionally neglected to mention what one might read for more on nonduality-focused meditation. So long as my "open mind" doesn't gape so wide that my brain falls out, following random chains of association has usually done me well, and I remain skeptical even of my current states of bliss. James Swartz warns of losing such experiences often in his books, and perhaps it is nothing more than the commitment to inward and outward skepticism that keeps my "bliss" glowing.

So I listened to a vast variety of audio books during long walks and bus commutes between the campus and the other important hub of my life: my psychotherapist's office. Why did I need a psychotherapist back when I had the Buddha Smile—even if was merely a flicker? Because, as I walked beautiful Saarbrücken, the city's layout made crossing its many bridges inevitable. "Saarbrücken" literally means "bridges over the river Saar," and, in addition to the dozen or so river bridges, there are numerous Autobahn overpasses. So, you can pick between plummeting into cold dark waters or smacking onto the hard tarmac of the A620. Endless fantasies of doing both kept me up late at night and woke me early. The avoidance strategies I undertook to keep me far away from the bridges took a terrible toll. Despite Wayne Dyer's advice to "give up all addictions" as I ploughed through his audio programs, I drank heavily to dull the impulses. But of course, binging only brought hangovers, depression and marital strife.

My brain was the problem, not the bridges. I knew this and sought help with a therapist who offered to take me to the nearest bridge to "desensitize" me. He didn't psychoanalyze my childhood memories or offer any pills. He felt certain that by confronting the fear, I would recognize it as just a feeling. By getting comfortable with the feeling, I would overcome the fear. Although I knew all about the *aggressive OCD* or (*harm OCD*) theory used to explain and treat violent impulses to self-harm that some people experience, I turned him down. The mere thought of walking with anyone to any bridge made me feel sick. So I kept avoiding bridges and walked like a madman across them when I had no other choice. I would get off the sidewalk and walk in the car laneways whenever an absence of traffic made it possible to get myself farther away from the railing. Worse, I would often remember my years of performing the same avoidance behavior over Toronto's bridges, which only compounded my anxiety. I was trapped in a self-replicating maze of impulses in the now and the past while facing a miserable future filled with more of the same.

The madness didn't stop with bridges. The rushing urge also gripped me when I was near windows. It was so bad, I eventually boarded up my home office window, closing off the view beyond. It was a real shame that I spent so many hours typing my dissertation without enjoying gazing out at that extraordinary landscape of forest, river and distant hills. The view was even better from the top of Himmelsleiter ("Heaven's Ladder"), a long concrete staircase that begins on Talstrasse and ends at the top of Philipinnenstrasse, which I took to get to my apartment and home office. But of course, eliminating the temptation to jump out of my office window only helped when I was in my office. Every time I walked up or down Himmelsleiter, my palms would sweat as a panicked urge to throw myself down the stairs quickened my pulse.

Although I turned down my therapist's suggestion to visit the bridge with him, I was determined to beat these tortuous mental impulses that unleashed surges of nervous energy through my body. I spent hours listening to Alan Watts, Eckhart Tolle, Tony Robbins and many other self-help figures. I consulted other programs constantly and used a wide array of materials to conduct experiments with a variety of meditation techniques. During my PhD, I had also learned hypnotherapy and so-called neuro-linguistic programming (NLP). These are other realms where you learn how far and low some people will go to make a buck (although you can find a few virtuous cats at play in these fields if you search long enough). You also learn how susceptible you'll always be to language patterns that can create states of trance. These patterns can be personally useful when you know how to induce them in the "Virtuous Scheme Laboratory" of your own mind.

Although I did not call my home office the "Virtuous Scheme Laboratory" back then, I've used the term often over the years after hearing a guy I sometimes think of as the "Buddha of Business" named Dean Jackson use a similar phrase.

Certainly, what I was doing in that office was "scheming" with the stubborn tenacity of Wile E. Coyote to find a way out of hell without sacrificing my intelligence or believing in some vapid god that couldn't possibly exist. It might seem weird to call your office something like this, but I think of it in terms of the "frame effect" in psychotherapy, which can be a safe, or even helpfully threatening space as you'll learn later, in which to try making changes. Now, I often give names to areas, missions and things to help my mind more fully engage with them and focus through memory on what I'm trying to accomplish and why. I don't know how to measure the precise impact treating my mind as a laboratory for running experiments has had, but I picked up the notion from the skeptic Ian Rowland in *The Full Facts Book of Cold Reading*, and mindset tricks like these do seem to help.

Especially maddening to me, though, were those in the spiritual marketplace claiming that thought can be escaped, people who seem happy to sell you a program promising such. The cruel thing is that some of these ideas about achieving "no mind" are not that far off the mark. The problem is the maps many popular gurus are teaching are bogged down by spiritual rubbish. But you usually only know how something will work out if you try and only my willingness to experiment and deep suffering can explain my ability to suspend disbelief for many of the tests I ran.

Throughout my trials, I thought intensely about the fields from which I was drawing upon, something which seems essential for substantial and lasting progress—even if your goal is to reduce thinking. As we'll see, thought can neutralize thought, just as comparison can reveal and weed out woo-woo. No matter how closely traces of the more reasonable elements of spiritual traditions like Advaita Vedanta might place Deepak Chopra next to Einstein and Sean Carrol, so much of Chopra's teaching feels like a violation of common sense. Worse, many self-help emperors actually appear *proud* to be caught with no clothes. When people can't stomach the unchecked woo-woo and flee, who can blame them?

If I sound snotty as I write about such people, it's not that I feel superior. It's mainly because I've lost patience with unnecessary shortcomings at this point in the 21st century and with a general absence of *truly* scientific living. Rest assured, I do have a healthy amount of humility when it comes to my own PhD, but I do happen to have one and was fortunate to have many science-based professors. It's in the Humanities and involved the history of science, religion and classical languages. I wrote my dissertation on friendship and later won a prestigious Mercator research grant from the DFG (Deutsche Forschungsgemeinschaft or German Research Foundation). This award enabled me to teach and research in Saarbrücken, where I brought a scientific focus to film as an industry, the nature of narrative and the special communities of collaboration that support the cinematic arts.

But much to the chagrin of my therapist, I put those accolades aside the instant I got them. He winced when I told him that PhD really stands for "Piled higher and Deeper." Although it seems clear in hindsight that diminishing my accomplishments was often the depression speaking, I wish more of my fellow laureled doctorates did more to recognize the relative insignificance of their degrees and focus on what their intelligence might enable outside of the world of academia where everyone is driven by the mandate: "publish or perish." As Smithonian.com has cited, a study demonstrated "as many as 50% of papers are never read by anyone other than their authors, referees and journal editors... 90% of papers are never cited." As if to drive the point home, the link to this study has been removed from Bloomington University's website with no reason given. "Piled higher and Deeper" has become "catch me if you can."

Throughout this time, I attempted to meditate, to stop my thoughts, to achieve "no mind" or at least temporarily escape my mind. And I kept following Sam Harris, who fanned the flames of my long-seated skepticism toward certain claims made by these spiritual gurus, which had also been bolstered by sleight-of-hand teachers I admired, like James Randi, Derren Brown, Penn Jillette, Banacek and Houdini. These were scientists and prestidigitators who swept off the veils of hokum others had woven around their craft. They had given me tools of discernment that enabled me to extract the real value in these spiritual programs—to milk the good stuff for all it was worth.

I came to see life and the world itself as the real university, in all its confusing and contradictory glory. We're all "graduating" each and every minute without the need of a guru's blessing, let alone "authority." Each time we pay attention to the present moment, we receive a reward far better than any degree. Like a diploma you can admire on your wall, your memory itself will serve as a certificate of accomplishment when you look back over a week, or a month or a year and remember how present you were during that time. You will *feel* the rewards.

None of which is to say that I didn't take study seriously while earning my degrees. Far from it. I found Alan Watts by being so studious. In the midst of "brute force learning" during hours of audiobook consumption that involved a vast spectrum of gurus-on-tape of every age, ethnicity, background and gender, the reasonableness, precision and clarity of Watts' thoughts and references to various traditions were a breath of fresh air. (I could have no idea that, as I listened to his languid, posh voice, I would later wind up consulting on a screenplay about his life with his son, Mark, which is a story for another time.) Watts answered my frustration with other gurus' woo-woo with something that rang true for me and my skepticism. Yet, for me, what I heard in Watts ultimately became both a launching pad and a trap; why this is so will become clear a bit later.

I still recall the day when the difference between Watts and the "woo-woo gurus" crystallized for me and opened a new path. It was fall. I was on the Philippinenstrasse, Watts' voice in my ears, my state of mind as painful as walking barefoot on a scalding hot frying pan. I kept listening as Watts asked his audience to consider a rock in a forest. I had to adjust my ear buds to make sure I was understanding correctly.

Why do you want no mind? I recall Watts asking. He went on: The forest is filled with rocks. They have no minds. But you've been blessed with a mind. So, meditation begins when you sit just to sit and learn to experience your mind for what it really is.

This teaching, so direct and filled with common sense, attracted me deeply. I had tried, with limited success, many kinds of breathing routines that are supposed to eliminate the mind by focusing on the nostrils. And here was Watts, this laughing Yoda, preserved for perpetuity through the magic of MP3 technology, calling this goal of "no mind" not only impossible, but *undesirable*!

After processing this notion that the mind was something to experience and not diminish or avoid, I put "sitting just to sit" into practice. Meditation changed for me completely for the next eight years. Although I continued to run experiments (and still do), I stopped making anything other than the study of sitting itself my goal. Other interesting and helpful suggestions came to my awareness and assisted this mission. For example, in *The Power of Now*, Eckhart Tolle teaches us to act like a cat perched in front of a mouse hole. Just as the cat anticipates the mouse that is going to emerge next, you can continually ask yourself, "what thoughts will I think next?" This kind of exercise not only teaches you a tremendous amount about the experience of thought, but also helps you see what thought *could* be like if you train it. Later in this book there are many direct exercises that will not only shift how you experience your mind, but also improve your memory.

Back in my home office with the boarded-up window in Saarbrücken, something profound happened. I do not know how long after hearing Watts speak of the rock in the forest that this took place, but it couldn't have been more than a few weeks. As I sat on the floor, meditating, I felt the center of my forehead "open." It was as if I could see light without seeing it and feel warmth in the absence of anything generating warmth. The feeling grew with alarming intensity. Before I knew it, I was swept into the kind of "celestial mental orgasm" so many gurus refer to. Instead of raising my skeptical hackles, I started weeping. On one of the dozens of programs I'd been listening to, the speaker described a state one could reach called the "Buddha Smile." Because this feeling forced me to smile with intense pleasure, I figured the name fit.

As I continued my meditation practices, the Buddha Smile came over me again and again. During these sessions, I would often start laughing. My mind would roll out one of its endless narratives or worries and then the very *thought* that there was a guy sitting in a basement *thinking thoughts* suddenly seemed like the funniest thing on the planet. I laughed so hard I broke into tears. Other times, tears would spill out as the pleasure pulsed in the center of my forehead like flames. It was as if a fire was trying to burn out "impurities." It didn't hurt, but it still felt alarming. Then I would perhaps laugh some more, wipe away the tears and return to the rest of my day feeling raw, but edified.

The only problem was that the pleasure wouldn't last long. As the weeks went by and I actively pursued more experiences like these, I felt completely worn out from their blissful rigors—not in the negative sense of being tired, but in that sense of "coming down" after an incredible LSD, mushroom or marijuana high. This was not just any old trip, however. It was a special mental state that created residual effects that lingered after the bliss for a very long time, even if the Buddha Smile blasts of intensity were short-lived. I felt more aware of the presence of thought without getting wrapped up in it. I no longer felt quite so closely tied to the contents of my mind, even if the destructive whips kept lashing and the binds of negative thinking did their best to hold tight with discomforting success.

Yet, heartened by the obvious benefits of experiencing better states of mind, I kept at it. Although I did not leap into bliss each and every time, the warm light opened in the center of my forehead often enough that I was hooked. I was not unaware of being like a lab rat pushing endlessly at the pleasure button and potentially starving myself to death based on an experience for which I could not properly account. I told my wife at the time about it. Although intrigued, Ingrid didn't seem particularly interested in pursuing the experiences for herself. No amount of pleading or presentation of evidence could convince her. Nor did my new mental states eliminate the friction in our shared life. They also did nothing to discourage me from guzzling epic amounts of excellent German beer and French wine, all while seeking more teachings. But in the midst of drunken arguments, I did experience a soft, new detachment that was helpful, even if only minutely. But if you're thinking "Aha! This is how Anthony fought off the bizarre suicidal urges," you'd be wrong. The Buddha Smiles had little effect on them. I couldn't make anything better or change the depressions and impulses, and I certainly couldn't change the character who dwelled on so many negative things. I hated the world and thought I could change everyone in it, and even though I understood the "self help" messages that I needed to change myself first, exactly *how* continued to evade me. But with the Buddha Smile, everything was sufficiently different and repeated exposure to the message that change starts within "the individual self to whom the world appears" kept chipping through.

In retrospect, it's possible the stage had been set for performing such meditation practices and receiving their benefits much earlier than my Saarbrücken days. I was first introduced to meditation in high school one afternoon by an English teacher. For years before that, prayer had been all around me in a variety of churches, primarily of the Methodist and Evangelical leaning. By the time I was teaching in Saarbrücken, I'd also earned certificates in hypnosis and created many self-hypnosis recordings designed to help with everything from getting my dissertation written to falling asleep at night. So, I had some experience with controlled states of consciousness, but nothing like the Buddha Smile had arrived until Alan Watts shifted my perception of what meditation could be. I believe all these experiences had created a contextual and practical field large enough to contain the next experiences that, years later, Ben unlocked for me on that fateful day in Kelvin Grove.

Before getting back to Ben, I want to note that as poisonous as so many things were for me (particularly my church experiences), I have to acknowledge that they brought some good. I mention this because the sooner you start with the techniques in this book, the sooner you'll start laying foundations for increasingly profound experiences that can only arrive in a brain that practices *multiple* techniques. These techniques include things that might structurally look like "prayer." If this notion brings up resistance in you, as it did for me, I ask you to consider the evidence of their benefits, so you might let science persuade you into giving them a secular try, even if you're a card-carrying... nonstrologist. I did, and haven't looked back since.

So...what exactly happened with Ben?

Ben is an accomplished freelance writer and long-time meditator. If he hadn't been, I probably wouldn't have gone from merely chatting about meditation to debating about it with him.

Despite Ben's obvious expertise with meditation practices, I raised a number of objections to his points—especially those concerning spirituality. I promoted the durability of Alan Watts' stripped-of-woo-woo, sitting-just-to-sit approach with levels of certainty approaching dogmatism. My routine was so deep in my procedural memory, I couldn't see an alternative. Plus, I'd "made it my own" by peppering in practices I'd learned from the Russian martial art Systema, Wim Hof's cold therapy, and breathing and stretching practices. Above all, I argued against *any* idea of meditation as spiritual practice due to the deep ethical problems inherent in all religions. More than ethically compromising oneself, I claimed, to even flirt with them is to be part of the problem in a criminal way that deserves swift punishment. In accordance with my then-militant atheism, I proclaimed that if a "belief system" doesn't gel with science according to the best definitions of this empirical tool we have, it *is* the enemy.

"You should read Gary Weber," Ben said calmly.

"Oh?" I said, completely prepared to dismiss what was coming up next.

As we sat in front of The Menagerie, Ben explained how Weber's *Happiness Beyond Thought* emerged from the author's insistence that if spiritual practices *could* create anything like the states of enduring bliss we've all heard described, then it *should* be achievable in a purely secular manner.

Game on, I thought. That may indeed provide reasonable grounds for launching an... experiment.

Among other points Ben raised, the one that hit me most was his suggestion to let go of the need for atheism to be right. This suggestion felt like a "check mate" moment where I knew that even if my King could move around the board perpetually to avoid losing the game, I was deliberately not exploring aspects of meditation due to prejudices that may have come from science, but were not necessarily scientific. Not if I weren't willing to run the experiments myself, as apparently Gary Weber and Ben had done.

Unlike many of my friends who purchase my book recommendations from their phones seconds after I've made them, I was "digital fasting" and had to memorize Weber's name and book title. Not a problem. As soon as I got home, I ordered my own copy of *Happiness Beyond Thought*. The book arrived with alarming speed, and I swallowed it in a few sittings. Shortly thereafter, its sequel, *Evolving Beyond Thought*, appeared on Amazon and I've been rereading both in frequent doses ever since.

But more importantly, I've been putting the teaching to work. *Every day since*, through memory. And these practices—combined with some other techniques I'll describe in this book—have massively enhanced my interior and exterior life.

Beyond thought?

Whether you order these volumes through your phone, laptop or local bookstore, please make time for them. I'm confident they'll be powerful additions to your mental life. Be cautious, however, about how easy it is to misinterpret Weber's description of the peaceful mental state of "happiness beyond thought." Although I feel his book titles, with the phrase "beyond thought," are perfectly appropriate, it is useful to pay close attention to what Weber is really saying and not let your mind make hasty conclusions. What Weber describes is not so much the *absence* of words in your mind. Rather, it is a reduction in I-centered cognition. I-thoughts can be gradually replaced through a process called self-inquiry, which for Weber is aided by the recitation of the vast amounts of Sanskrit he memorized.

Since I know how to memorize just about anything rapidly, I made it my mission to memorize the exact same Sanskrit texts. With his permission, I've included the first part of what I memorized in this book, along with a full description of how I used ancient memory tools to make the process fun and easy. I might be partial, but it seems that using these tools, which rely heavily on autobiographical reference, paradoxically breaks down the addiction to self-reference. We'll get to why I think this might be the case later, but for now, what is it that Weber says?

First, it's important to understand that Weber got into meditation and memorizing texts to assuage his own mental pain. A scholar himself, he was bombarded by endless reams of "blah blah blah." As a scholar, he seems to have also experienced a need for testable and verifiable methods that would work *regardless* of belief. After all, what use is "belief," when the thoughts that carry it create so much conflict and pain? By combining stretching, breathing and memorization of particular texts that train the mind to dispel and dissolve unhelpful thoughts, Weber says thought almost entirely disappeared one day while executing a move during yoga.

But not *all* thought—only the useless, self-referential, *me-me-me* thoughts. Obviously, "planning thoughts" seem to make events involving a guy named "Gary" happen, and as I watched all of his videos, he seemed perfectly capable of answering questions using words. But as I performed due diligence on his teaching and read his responses to forum posts all over the Internet, it seemed clear that many people were not reading him very closely, and worse, not reading between the lines by *being* between those lines through application of the techniques. Most of your opinions or questions can be silenced—or answered—only by practice.

The practices Weber describes are not Watts' sitting-just-to-sit. In fact, sitting to meditate is just one means of practicing these techniques, as you'll learn. Ultimately, if you can get yourself to train, these techniques are about rewiring the physical brain to experience fewer intrusive thoughts because the structures producing the thoughts have been changed.

As Weber explains—and his conclusions are based on a combination of his own experience and scientific literature—the practices seem to release us from past-present-future cognition taking place in the "default mode network" of the brain. Where do we go instead? Into the "task-positive network," where we exist "in the zone" or in a "state of flow." Except this state, once you get it, is far better than those words suggest: for me, with minimal practice, much suffering faded, fear strangely disappeared and memory improved merely by the present-moment living this approach accelerated. By following the instructions in *Happiness Beyond Thought*, what was formerly peanut-sized short-lived pleasure at the center of my forehead is now experienced as astonishingly enduring bliss that seems to blossom from exactly where this task-positive network is thought to reside in the brain. I've written this book in the hopes you too can achieve similar bliss, focus and clarity.

A lot of evidence from brain scans supports the likelihood of your enjoying this outcome. You can read some of the science in *How Enlightenment Changes Your Brain* by Andrew Newberg and Mark Waldman, to mention just one source. It would be misleading, however, to suggest that any single book will get you there. I believe there are several factors at play in how I achieved these enduring states of bliss:

1. As discussed, I have long experienced similar, albeit weaker, states of bliss in the center of my forehead—that is, the Buddha Smile.

2. I have spent many years exploring and practicing memory techniques. It's possible that I have unusually high levels of norepinephrine in my brain; this neurotransmitter heightens alertness and attention and is associated with the formation and retrieval of memories. In the absence of a research budget and access to machinery, I'm speculating here. Yet, plenty of research suggests that novel experiences create more of this chemical. When you're using the memory techniques you'll learn in this book daily, novel experiences will be a dime a dozen. Imagine visiting Disneyland on demand, and having it be a completely unique playground every time. That's what using memory techniques does for you.

3. I am aware of both the placebo effect and the expectation effect (in which what you think will happen colors your perception of what actually happens—also called the subject-expectancy effect). I do all I can to live free of self-delusion, and, as a consequence, must accept the possibility that I have completely hypnotized myself into a state of bliss by "assembling" with Weber's teachings.

By "assembling" I mean that nothing "new" happens until a student meets a teacher halfway. Think of is as the process of creating new meaning, complexity, or even harmony through acts of combination and integration. Ezra Pound, in one of his clearer moments, talked about the "luminous detail" that putting two lines of poetry together produces, where the meaning may not be in line A or in line B, but requires the two coming together to create a greater resonance. Consider his poem, "In a Station of the Metro":

> *The apparition of these faces in the crowd;*
> *Petals on a wet, black bough.*

Each line, absent the other or the title, is minimally evocative, but together they offer much more complexity and significance.

When you really start feeling the effects of "next level" meditation by putting teaching into practice, "assemble" is more than just a good word for what is happening. Weber uses terminology like "software" and "downloading," but brains and human knowledge are just as much like Lego pieces or Ikea furniture as anything else. Instructions plus acts of assemblage make the house or chair emerge from the pieces. And as you read and assimilate multiple teachings, the "luminous detail" of what it all means at an experiential level requires more than your expectation that things will change along the way. You must make it so.

This is an important point because the sitting-just-to-sit practice, no matter how well fed with a wide variety of muscle relaxation, breathing and cold exposure techniques, ultimately locked me into the prison I was trying to escape. That is, although I felt this tremendous bliss in the center of my forehead, my harmful thoughts and reckless impulses did not abate. The problem was that I was rigidly beholden to one teaching, which held me captive and unable to progress.

I recognize now that my practice of "sitting just to sit" was also undoubtedly increasing my ego. After all, the practice uses *thought* to convince oneself to sit. This mental overcoming of mental resistance is characteristic of Zen and features strongly in books like Philip Kapleau's *Three Pillars of Zen* and the works of Shun-ryu Suzuki. As great as these are, they include some masochistic advice that cannot help but make you feel chuffed if you can "master" sitting long enough to get a reward. As Suzuki advises in *Zen Mind, Beginner's Mind*:

> If you yourself have true practice, then everything else is practicing our way at the same time. That is why we should always address ourselves, checking up on ourselves like a doctor tapping himself. This kind of practice should be continued moment after moment, incessantly.

I acknowledge off the bat that it's easy to cherry-pick a quote like this one from a larger work. But with all due respect, this description of "true practice" based on endless self-policing sounds miserable. Isn't *consistent* practice towards an achievable outcome *true* enough? When Suzuki contradicts this doctor image with a tile-polishing metaphor a few sentences later, it sounds worse. So much training seems like maze creation by rats taking pride in pressing buttons for a bit of Zen hoping to realize though acts of mental force that the maze itself is made of Zen. The effect soon fades, and you've got to return to get another buzz—which keeps you locked in the thought needed to keep tapping. This is an example of a meditative practice locking you in the exact prison you're trying to escape—a kind I bought into for too long because not enough teachers and authors took pains to do the meta-analysis we're going through now.

Variety is the key

The alternative is simpler and more direct. It's transformation of the brain structures responsible for experiencing thought in the first place, which is made possible by the phenomenon of neuroplasticity—the ability to form new neuropathways, and thus, new mental habits—and a combination of different meditation approaches is more likely to do the trick. I'm not sure if Suzuki ever made it out of the maze, but he quips that his wife certainly never thought so.

I'm not entirely out either and don't fantasize that there is an out from thought so long as this brain keeps ticking. But I could not have experienced release from my imprisoned state and "thought addiction" without Gary Weber's teaching, which seems to assemble many others that have gone before. Obviously, my stubborn, self-hypnotized devotion to the sitting-just-sit technique has played a role in my own "assemblage," but the point is that masochistic devotion was not the way forward.

Rather, allowing a *variety* of *experiential* practices to work in parallel makes more sense. I am talking about practices that combine movement, sound and semantic content to expose the fleeting nature of thought in a way that dissolves thought. Seen and accepted as part of an ongoing evolution with no end point other than death, this approach has helped me the most. Perhaps there is nothing particularly new in what I'm about to say, but each of us has to *re-new* our awareness of our awareness by constantly refreshing through continued learning. If you haven't added memorization to your meditation yet, I predict from inside this Virtuous Scheme Laboratory that you're in for a wonderful ride.

Will the practices in this book lead to lasting victory over your mind and memory? It's entirely up to you. It's all based on your will to practice and your present mental state. To hit the ground running and help ensure success, you will want to describe what your mind is currently like using a Memory Journal.

A Memory Journal is nothing fancy, but to get the most out of this book you'll want to keep one. I recommend to my memory students that they:

1. **Use physical journals.** This helps ensure that you *actually* use it instead of forgetting it because it's locked inside a folder on your computer or lost in a sea of apps. By putting your journal in a prominent place that you see often, you trigger more consistent use of it.

2. **Decorate your journal.** I recommend you draw on the cover or create some kind of collage with images that symbolize or "frame" what you want to achieve. In my experience and research, such acts of personalization "deepen" the processing your brain performs related to goals as opposed to "shallow" processing of mental activities worked through on devices.

I've been recommending this approach to students since I started teaching memory techniques, and my hunch was confirmed by neuroscientist and philosopher Manfred Spitzer, who coined the term "digital dementia" in 2014 to help explain why more people are "forgetting" to complete goals they've set for themselves.

Since the teaching in this book involves both exercises and note taking, if you need more convincing, that "the pen is mightier than the keyboard," or tapping on a screen, please look up the article of this name by Pam A. Mueller and Daniel M. Oppenheimer for their data on the advantages of longhand over digital note taking.

Of course, it's entirely up to you, but I've included some lovely images from Magnetic Memory Method students who have followed this recommendation and reaped the rewards as a result. Their Magnetic Memory Journals are beautiful, a key driver of results and we'll talk more about why and how journaling works to transform us for the better throughout this book.

Exercise: Mental experience rating

Get out your Memory Journal now and answer this question on a scale from 1 to 10 (with 1 being "not at all" and 10 being "totally"):

How comfortable are you with your mental experience right now?

If it is a 1, you might be like I once was—not necessarily "suicidal" in the literal sense, but continually attacked by a mind looking for every opportunity to harm itself. Or maybe you've had some of the other tortures I haven't gotten around to mentioning yet. Perhaps it was an impulse to drive into opposing traffic, jump up and shout expletives in a crowded theater, smack loved ones in the face or worse... Whatever you do, be honest. Now is your chance.

I'm serious.

... and complete the exercise.

Okay, you're back. One of the key differences between those who succeed and those who continue to fail is *doing* the exercises. This point is important and the only reason I'm able to write this book: I am a victorious survivor *only* because I paused the recording or put down the book and completed the exercises on offer from many teachers. It makes sense because we transform ourselves *when* we use mental acts of symbolization (such as this exercise) to download better software into our operating systems. It really is like updating a computer. The computer simply won't update, defrag or reset itself unless you reset it. Likewise, the furniture won't assemble itself without your picking up the tools and using them. So...

Did you complete the exercise?

If so, great.

If not, rest assured: I'll be repeating this prompt to take action for the benefit of everyone throughout the book.

Next, I want you to choose a metaphor for your mental state. Doing so will have a few benefits. Now, you'll hear me express throughout the book my fondness for the maxim "if you measure it, you can improve it." Think of your mental metaphor as a piece of qualitative data you register at the beginning of your research; later, when you've gained more skills through practice and experimentation, you'll likely find yourself wanting to adopt a new mental metaphor, and the difference between these two pieces of data can serve as one way of marking your improvement. Another benefit, which is related, is that the image can serve as a touchstone and benchmark: after you've been testing out the techniques for a while, revisit your mental image and ask yourself if it still serves. A mental metaphor can also be aspirational. Maybe your current image is dark and chaotic, but you see in it glimmers of light as the stormy night passes, and you focus on that light as it grows.

I'll give you an example. When I first completed this exercise, I thought of my mental state as a Francis Bacon painting. If you've never seen one and you have the stomach for something shocking, look up his Pope series of paintings. They are nightmares committed to canvas. Over time, I've learned to make far better choices and moved away from those images of pure anguish. In fact, I've used many metaphors since I learned this simple technique. When it comes to my post-*Happiness Beyond Thought* existence, I've carefully chosen the metaphor of Victory and often use Poseidon—Ancient Greek god of the sea, earthquakes, storms and horses—as a guiding image.

I used to think guiding images and mental metaphors were silly. Once, while taking what was supposed to be a practical course for writing better resumes and getting more job interviews, the course instructor brought out a pile of magazines. The facilitator told us to cut out images that matched our vision for the future. We then were to paste these onto a sheet of paper that was somehow going to help guide us towards a better job. Some people selected yachts, expensive homes and fancy clothes. I stuck a mouth on an awkwardly angled black and white arm from a perfume ad, creating a surreal portrait of suffering like some poor beast in a Francis Bacon triptych.

However, I later warmed to the idea after remembering something from a lecture I'd heard on Nietzsche in a Fred Ulfers seminar: *Humans have always and will always create the myths that govern us. But who amongst us will self-consciously participate in the creation of the myths that hold us sovereign?* Since I've started creating vision boards with sincerity, I have images that help keep my focus on goals—and redirect focus back to my goals—and it has helped immensely. In fact, holding onto the image of Poseidon calming the ocean of endless distractions as I worked on this book has been a key part of getting it done, in addition to having a mind map (a kind of vision board) in sight throughout.

Nir Eyal bolsters this approach in *Indistractable: How to Control Your Attention and Choose Your Life* with what he calls "identity pacts" or "a precommitment to a self-image that helps us pursue what we really want" (177). He connects the use of such mental images to the establishment of "secular rituals" that lead to greater success in life. Ultimately, he concludes based on detailed research that our beliefs do not shape our behaviors. It is our behaviors, based on internal images of identity that shape what we believe about ourselves and others.

Gary Weber discusses his initial reluctance to having a guru, which is tanta-mount to creating a mental image. I imagine he was reluctant for the same reason I tried to avoid any attachments to creating an illusory image of Gary Weber-as-master in my mind. Yet, Weber found himself changing in this regard and ulti-mately took on Ramana Maharshi. Personally, I like Ramana and have memorized his *Upadesa Saram* using the tools you'll learn in this book. But ultimately, Ramana doesn't resonate with me, probably because all our human gods inevitably have clay feet, and Weber seems to have done well to help ensure his students don't get stuck on him. By the same token, by engaging self-consciously with an idea of what his mental state and person are like, benefits have flowed.

Don't expect Poseidon, Popeye or the Pope to do the work for you, but please do explore mental frames and metaphors. I believe Ulfer's interpretation of Nietzsche is correct: we are compelled to symbolize and mythologize. Why not do it with eyes wide open and milk this characteristic of the human experience for all it is worth? So, for the record, here are some of the reasons "victory" and Poseidon as a metaphor for having a victorious mind resonated with me while writing this book:

- We punish ourselves by creating stormy seas of consciousness and doing nothing to stop these acts of self-torture.

- We can calm the seas of consciousness and memory just as Poseidon cre-ated calm seas for travelers.

- Poseidon also created islands; through practicing self-discovery we can uncover our true nature and create mindfulness and memory destina-tions that are stable even when the seas are stormy.

- Poseidon's triton may have its origins in the three-pronged fork carried by India's ancient Saivite sadhus, which may have symbolized the abil-ity to reduce suffering from the three human experiences of ignorance, desire and aversion (Dowman 3).

Could you also use victory and Poseidon to guide your personal progress? I don't expect it will be a fit, but certainly try the idea on for size if you find it appeal-ing. Even if Poseidon isn't right for you, the exercise of trying to use *something* like this can show you the power of adopting a mental metaphor to help create smoother sailing in your life.

Here are some alternative mental images. Perhaps you prefer the skies and wish to create a sense of "cruising altitude" as you transcend worldliness and soar above the clouds of brain fog and forgetfulness. If so, you might choose an eagle as your metaphor.

Over the years, I've had many students select the image of a gardener as they work their way from using ineffective mental metaphors to vibrant, powerful and effective mental images that serve them in substantial ways they can actually feel. One student started out thinking of his memory as a "graveyard" because that's where his "memories go to die." He's since upgraded to the garden image and is doing much better as a result.

Now, instead of just *thinking about* selecting a metaphor or guiding image, it's important to stop reading or listening and write down an image or description of your *current* mental state, and another for the mental state you would *like* to have. I'm confident you will experience victory faster and with greater impact if you complete this exercise (which I'll detail below). But first: please put aside all concern about the outcome. Many people who don't take action fail to do so because they want certainty in advance that these tactics are going to work. No such certainty is coming, so you may also need victory over the need to control outcomes. Taking action is the cure to this need because, as most of us know, it is movement that matters. Combining meditation with memory training is perhaps the most direct motion of them all, and it has been going on for thousands of years to maximize the mental freedom of dedicated practitioners.

But don't expect overnight results. In learning, one benefits when one gets a quick victory because these quick wins are thought to create dopamine spikes in the brain that ease the next step along the journey. It's nice when quick victories are available and hook people for life on building skills that will help them accomplish their goals. But there are simply no guarantees that all the dopamine spikes in the world at the beginning of a learning journey are going to lead you where you want to go. So here's the quick victory you can always be sure of, even if you don't feel it like a shot of cocaine: taking action despite not knowing the outcome of an action and cheerfully accepting whatever happens *is* victory.

Some things require marginal progress without instant reward. That's just the way it is. If you want to experience mental peace, you'll have to try a number of exercises and practice taking action as a good in and of itself. Action leads to "being in the zone" with limited or no I-oriented thoughts that create suffering. This state potentially allows us to escape the "doctor checking in" burden proposed by Shunryu Suzuki. To that end, don't overthink the exercises in this book. Just stop everything and start writing in your Memory Journal.

Exercise: Your mental metaphors

Write down your current and ideal mental metaphors. *Example summary*: My previous metaphor looked like a Francis Bacon painting and became more like a Poseidon. One of my students described his mind as a graveyard, but now uses a much more positive image of his mind as a garden.

Stop reading and complete this exercise now!

Have you done it? I sure hope so.

If not, just keep in mind that assembling with these processes is needed to experience any level of transformation. If this all sounds repetitive, relax. Please understand that each repetition is always slightly different. Stubborn minds need it more than others. Victorious minds seek difference in repetition for the new adventures it brings to the calm seas of a well-tended conscious experience. Besides, I wouldn't be writing this book if I hadn't heard the basic instructions repeatedly, and we all know the old Zig Ziglar line: "Motivation doesn't last. Well, neither does bathing—that's why we recommend it daily."

There's another aspect to repetition we need to keep in mind, and this explains the vast variety of techniques you'll encounter in this book. You might find yourself asking *which* techniques you should put into action, and the answer is two-fold.

First, you physically can't try all of them, so try as many of them as interest you. Second, come back at another time to the different techniques that didn't interest you. Often what doesn't pique our interest on Monday will feel gripping on Tuesday. As we'll see in the chapter on free will, much chance is involved in how we're feeling *when* we encounter great ideas. Many people dismiss genius ideas on the basis of bad mood. By revisiting the teaching we choose for ourselves frequently, we increase the chances that we take action on them. Keep exploring in the spirit of finding the differences through repetition. This point matters a great deal, because one of the misconceptions about both meditation and memory training that traps many people is that these practices involve just *one* kind of activity that benefits everyone in exactly the same way. Indeed, this assumption locked me in a holding pattern with meditation.

You don't have to look far for evidence of people treating meditation this way. In Peter Russell's bestselling *What Is TM?*, described as "The TM Book For Skeptics," he writes: "The practice of Transcendental Meditation is the same for everyone" (16). Therein lies the rub. Russell is wrong. We now know there is a range of preferences and great benefits to be had from rotating several practices. Likewise in memory training, we know that exercising multiple levels of memory by practicing a number of disciplines brings about the real benefits.

Moreover, we need variety for practical reasons. For example, I will suggest that you memorize a variety of chants or scriptures because the mind seems to "wear them out." It is entirely possible for me to chant 32 verses from the *Ribhu Gita* and think of other things at the same time because the *challenge* of reciting them has faded. It is almost certain you will experience the same outcome as the "training effect" makes the memory feats easier for you.

The good news is that there's a growth-oriented fix: by continually adding more seeds to the soil of your memory, you'll replenish the rewards and create "compound interest" that leads to new treasure. You'll also learn better observation skills as you proceed. As we'll discuss in Part II, growth comes from always monitoring and working within an understanding of the Challenge-Frustration Curve.

Dark nights of the soul and the paradise of now

After completing the rating and metaphor self-discovery exercises above (stop reading now and do them if you want to get the most out of this book!), you might be wondering what happened to these bizarre impulses to jump off bridges and all the rest of my misery? Good question. The answer is that they still arise from time to time, but I have a different response. In the past, I used pills—lithium, Lamictal, antidepressants, antipsychotics and the occasional dose of Ativan—amidst plentiful pints of Guinness, wine and, more often than was wise, I tossed in whiskey to manage, or mute, these impulses. Today, when these urges appear in my consciousness, they feel not only manageable, but resolvable. My attitude has shifted to confidence because I am no longer trying to fight the storm within: I realized, to take a cue from Sam Harris, I *am* the storm.

Even better, by learning to combine the memory and meditation tools discussed in this book, I discovered how to quickly navigate out of my own way. As a result, a lot more than just improved memory has entered my life. For example, I now spend hours on the side of extremely high cliffs shooting video courses in Spain. I wrote much of this book from the 15th-story lounge of my building (where I also swim in the rooftop pool).

On the other side of these problems, I sometimes remember my therapist in Saarbrücken—the one who offered to visit the bridge with me. Perhaps I was a fool not to take him up on his invitation to desensitize me in this way. But another of the

In Spain shooting The Habit Mastery Formula with Jimmy Naraine

issues we tackled was why I turned down an offer to have my Film Studies lectures filmed and released online. Ironically, at the same time I didn't want my teaching online, I used my basic HTML and website skills to create a site that shared the text versions of my teaching. But video was a no-go for reasons I believe relate to my reluctance to be around heights. The connection? I believe there was a relationship between these strange impulses and the "control freakism" I experienced over having my lectures filmed. Indeed, I even tried to be in control of the nature of our sessions. I remember lecturing him about how he allowed his patients to see each other in the hallway, horribly threatening the unconscious mind. I can laugh now, but I was very ill then and obsessed with controlling outcomes of uncontrollable aspects of reality.

In our final session, this therapist wished me well and expressed his belief that he would eventually be following my career online if I ever changed my mind. Indeed, I did end up posting videos online. Not one or two, but hundreds. These days, I am *fearless* about the video content I release and have minimal concern for the outcomes because they can't be controlled anyway. Frankly, if I could figure out a way to receive an email like this every day, I would:

> Anthony, Jim Gerwing, here. About 5 years ago, I began taking your online course and since signing up, I have taken a Latin course at the University of Alberta and scored above 90% (that is not common territory for me)! You have revived, and revived in me, the concept that where there is a will, there is a way. I then went into some memory competitions. I am now the 4 time, current, undefeated (and record holder)

of the Alberta memory championships. Even better; I just won the 2019 Canadian Memory Championships (AND the first ever pan-provincial championship). Thanks for your input.

How is it possible that a guy like me could help a stranger I've never met in person learn Latin with such ease and then become a memory champion? Well, this "three-pound brain," as Fred Davis often calls it, is unlikely to find a complete answer, but part of the mystery has to do with getting my ego out of the way and just letting myself *be part of the world*, not its scaredy-cat would-be master. This outcome is pretty much what my German therapist said he hoped for, but he knew enough to point the way and allow me to find it on my own. I help people like Mr. Gerwing by writing books, recording podcasts and holding marathon livestreams, and sharing all kinds of personal stories about my picaresque life and the lessons I've learned, all completely against the nature of a former me that "I" was—and fought hard to maintain despite the pain it was causing. The absence of the need to *be* the stories and let them teach everyone gives them something I could not ever create on my own. But we struggle to assemble when we think we are alone.

It's not just about memory competition, either. Far from it. Jeannie Koh wrote to say:

Magnetic Memory using Memory Palaces as taught by Anthony Metivier has been a delightful journey. After an initial couple of months of learning this approach, I have found memorising anything to be much less painful, and much more enduring over time. I learnt the ancient Koine Greek through brute force rote learning that took years of tears and pain. I now remember whole chunks of passages in this old language, and words of another language I'm learning with such ease that I often think it can't be this easy. The "work" has been to calm my anxieties and temptation to go down the brute force, and the effort to move towards creating memorable images which are tied to images and locations I already know.

I found it helpful to sign up for the private Facebook access and access to weekly Memory Dojo. Implementing the approaches takes a bit of guidance and Anthony is a very attentive, wise, and effective guide and teacher. So any personal guidance by him I found very helpful. I am very grateful to him.

I'm not sharing these stories to stroke what's left of my ego. I only get to do this work because I've had incredible teachers, both living and dead, and I've publicly put in tons of practice based on thousands of hours of research, writing and recorded documentation I never could have created without getting out of my own way. Many students have *assembled* not just with the incredibly important technicalities of the training, but also to the core message that underlies the real issue holding so many people back: Your ego is in the way of your efforts. Often, so is the teacher, which is why I myself strive to teach with abandonment so the students can truly learn.

The work itself, as Jeannie says, will calm you and help you stop trying to learn and remember information the hard way. There may well be a kind of Suzuki-esque Zen in learning through "brute force," but I've never found it. Rote learning bores me to pieces and feels like pounding a hammer against my brain. Even those who engage with "rote" do it in creative ways that more closely resemble memory techniques than the meaningless banality of raw repetition. Memory techniques are the closest thing to real magic I've ever experienced, but the mind works hard to trick us all into thinking this "mental martial art" is more difficult than other ways of learning.

The Magnetic Memory Method I developed and teach is not just a memorization tool; the combination of meditation, mindfulness, relaxation and different techniques is the key. It is "magnetic" because, as magnets attract valuable things, they also repel things that do not belong. When we focus our minds and memorize information that matters, we can push away the unhelpful thoughts and better focus on what we need to succeed. And this teaching is a "method" because I have no "system" to give you. Rather, once the ego is relaxed and ready to focus, you will learn to create your own systems based on the rules that govern human memory. They rule Jim Gerwing's brain, Jeannie's brain, my brain, and yours. Although it can appear that memory competitors are bending them when they break new records, I do not believe this is the case. Rather, I believe they are finding ways to assemble with them better than before.

To many people, "surrendering" to these rules in order to develop and maintain a practice feels more like "sacrifice." The question is: who exactly feels this sacrifice? It is the I-voice, the voice that has tricked you into thinking you are running the show. Of course, I recognize the very slim chance that this I will be the one who convinces you that there is no "I" in quite the way "you" think there is. But there's no doubt in my mind that the fusion of meditation and memory training devoted to dissolving I-oriented thought—practiced on a foundation of healthy diet and exercise—made so much peace and freedom possible for me that wouldn't have arrived any other way. All I know is that the surrender I suggest people make is not one of passivity, giving up or sacrifice. But it does require practice, and all the evidence in the world of neuroscience and ancient meditation approaches that involve directly or indirectly training memory suggest that what we're really doing is optimizing our brain states.

I don't know if everyone can feel like their heads are filled with luminous light. My academic training might have helped me get smarter, but I wasn't smart enough to have my brain scanned before starting this project so we could create an enrapturing "before and after" marketing campaign. And who cares about my brain anyway? I'm here to help you now, and to be clear, you'll still be that which we call human in the end, despite what many a guru may tell you. Certainly, I still experience stress and concern about different things. The rules of the world compel this body to participate in an economy and engage in all kinds of activity. But I also feel free of so much weight and released from the need to control any of it. Even if it's just a feeling of well-being, what other measure of life's value have we got other than how we feel—right now?

Discover the rules that govern all brains, use discipline to help you create consistency in the terrain of your own life and you will soar above the storm... by *becoming* the storm. Accepting that you are the storm is the first part of learning to harness the *existing* wind with your *existing* wings, and from there you can optimize the process as you go. The practices in this book are like the navigational tools that airplanes use to maintain cruising altitude during flight. Will you still hit turbulence? Absolutely. But skilled pilots know how to minimize the suffering of turbulence and don't rely entirely on themselves to do it. They have the best of all possible technologies both in their immediate vicinity and around the world via remote communications and radar. Cruising altitude is made possible only when the airplane assembles as a single unit with itself, the pilots, the ground traffic controllers and the sky itself.

A further point I hope to demonstrate in this book is this: *When we memorize information that enhances ourselves, we improve our ability to enhance, potentially, the entire population*. I'll explain why I think this is true in the next section. And remember: it's the ability to focus on the information that matters and repel the information that doesn't that makes it all *Magnetic*.

Part II

BECOME
THE STORM

2   MINDFULNESS, MEDITATION, AND MEMORY IMPROVEMENT

Why are mindfulness and meditation so important for memory improvement?

The answer: because there are few things more frustrating than not being able to focus on memory training because your concentration is shot. When you're trying to create your first Memory Palace Network or encode information (both topics we'll examine later), you don't get to experience *forgetting* important details if you can't actually concentrate long enough to remember them, much less develop a solid memorization practice. Your inability to remember something is related to your level of concentration at the time you sought to memorize it. Both meditation and mindfulness practices create concentration and "attentional control"—which is the key to memory recall.

What exactly is concentration, then? The simple answer: concentration is the ability to pay attention to just one thing or set of related things at a time. Concentration really comes into its own when you can extend the amount of time you apply your attention to just one thing. In other words, concentration improves with practice. Yet, when it comes to using memory techniques, you'll realize that there is never just one thing going on. You will multitask using these techniques, and in a very positive way. For this reason, we who use memory techniques need a special kind of concentration. The good news is that we can use memory training activities to establish and extend our concentration abilities, and vice versa.

Improving concentration and memory through meditation – a sketch of the research

Although meditation has existed for over 3,500 years, the scientific community has only been studying it for just over 50 (Thomas and Cohen, 2013). In one mind-defying example, Buddhist monks have been recorded controlling their body temperatures through a meditative practice called *g-tummo*. In controlled scientific tests, experienced monks were, within an hour, able to use their body heat to dry cold and moist sheets placed around their bodies. Some witnesses of similar experiments report seeing steam emerge from the sheets while they dried (Kozhevnikov et al. 2013). When they measured the body temperatures of the monks, the researchers found increases of as much as 17 degrees Celsius (63 Fahrenheit). How is this possible?

No one entirely understands the biological mechanisms behind meditation just yet. However, study after study demonstrates that meditation has far-reaching benefits—including for concentration and memory. Research has found that prior experience with mindfulness training improves attention-related behaviors both progressively and across a spectrum of "subcomponents of attention" (Jha et al. 2007).

Everyday people have also studied meditation and have discovered a lot about how it helps memory. For both scientists and laypeople, meditation has demonstrated impressive memory improvement and even fostered stunning feats of long-term retention and recall. Even Robert Wright and Daniel Ingram have remarked upon Gary Weber's memory based on Wright's personal observation of Weber in the university class setting. You can watch this discussion for yourself in a YouTube video called "The Path to Enlightenment" on the MeaningofLife.tv channel (published October 20, 2016).

When I suggest that you need to try different forms of meditation to progress, it is because each of us is different and while the subcomponents of attention are similar from person to person, they're arranged differently in each individual. From an evolutionary perspective, the scientific discovery of different kinds of attention possibly explains the emergence of technique-based philosophies like the eightfold path of Buddhism. Each of these *paths* involves mindfulness procedures that likely address different parts of the brain:

1. *Ditthi* or right understanding

2. *Sankappa* or right thought

3. *Vaca* or right speech

4. *Kammanta* or right action

5. *Ajiva* or right livelihood

6. *Vayama* or right effort

7. *Sati* or right mindfulness

8. *Samadhi* or right concentration

Indeed, "Siddhartha taught that right mindfulness (or attentiveness) is associated with the activities of the body (kaya), sensations or feelings (vedana), the activities of the mind (citta), ideas, thoughts, and conceptions (dhamma)" (Brooks). Throw in progressive muscle relaxation techniques and I'm confident you'll find that meditation is perhaps the *only* mental exercise with so much evidence of its ability to improve cognition and focus. You don't even have to be a monk or a scientist to start using this tool to better your own mind, body, and soul.

The easy way and the hard way to better concentration
As with many things, there's an easy way and a hard way. Real science doesn't skip over the hard way and investigates everything (and each of us must continually conduct real science in our own lives if we want to experience lasting change). Looking for links between meditation and cognition, researchers from the University of California, Davis, recruited 60 people for a study. Half were assigned to a meditation retreat to practice mindfulness meditation for an average of five hours a day for three months. These participants were committed! Not only did they volunteer three months of their time, but they also paid $5,300 to attend the retreat. The other 30 were used as a control group and placed on a waiting list. This was to rule out the passage of time as a factor in any differences between the groups.

At times throughout the experiment, both groups were asked to watch a series of lines flash on a screen. Participants were asked to click a mouse when they saw a line that was shorter than the others. This detail-oriented test forced participants to focus intently. Researchers found that those who meditated were significantly more likely to see increasingly small differences in the lines. In other words, the meditation group was better able to focus on small details through their improved concentration (Maclean et al. 2010).

As benefits to cognition had already been observed for longer-term meditators, some researchers were curious to see whether less effort could be effective (Zeidan et al. 2010). In a study conducted at the University of North Carolina, a group of 49 students volunteered for a meditation study. None of them had prior experience meditating. Twenty-four participants were randomly assigned to meditation, while 25 were assigned to listening to an audiobook. Each group performed their activity for 20 minutes, four times a week, for one week under laboratory supervision. At the end of the one-week experiment, the meditation group experienced significant improvements in concentration compared to their audiobook counterparts (Zeidan et al. 2010).

One thing this research suggests is that you don't have to wait months or years before the benefits of your practice kick in. So if you're worried about the time commitment involved in meditation, don't be. Within a week of consistent meditation, you can start to experience improved concentration. For example, you will likely start to notice that you are more generally aware of the world around you. Here's a detailed example: I remember one day in Berlin suddenly noticing a giant street sign that I'd surely seen hundreds of times before, but never *observed*. This sudden observation of the street sign was powerful for a few reasons.

1. It surprised me into a deeper level of observing my own process of observation (or previous lack of it). This meta-level experience of observation observing itself creates a lasting skill set that helps you better navigate the world. Sweet nothings you barely noticed before suddenly make a more powerful impact while, at the same time, statements that used to agitate you lose their sting.

2. I began to observe *exact* features of this ordinary street sign that make it, and the entire world, *extraordinary*. Its colors leapt out at me. I noticed scratches from stones tossed at it by passing traffic and the texture of the metal these marks exposed. The patterns of mud caked on its surface became fascinating and deeply satisfying—even more so than the best art in a major art gallery.

3. This "appearance" of something in the environment I failed to consciously notice before allowed me to create a new Magnetic Station—or location to encode information—I could use in a Memory Palace. More observation of the world leads to consciously creating new memory tools on a daily basis.

What's the benefit in this change in perspective? It's at least twofold. Such an enhanced level of observation improves the use of memory techniques, which rely heavily on accessing your past mental experiences of observing features in the world. The more present you are to them during the original experience, the stronger they remain when you draw upon them later. And secondly, some of this quasi-psychedelic fascination with previously banal objects in the world likely comes from how meditation increases certain chemicals in the brain. And who would complain about a heightened aesthetic experience of everyday life?

Do not underestimate the increased focus you will start to experience. It will lead to profound advances in how you use memory techniques while also positively impacting how you navigate life.

Will any of this really improve your memory?

Yes. The link between meditation and memory is even more direct: meditation has indeed been shown to improve memory as such, even without the use of memory techniques in the mix. Another research project used a randomized controlled test to study the effects of meditation on the working memory capacity in adolescents. Around 200 teenagers were recruited and assigned to either a mindfulness meditation practice or yoga, or were waitlisted as a control group. The groups meditated or practiced yoga once a day for 15–30 minutes and attended two formal teaching sessions twice a week. By the end of the study, teenagers participating in the meditation group had significantly better outcomes than their yoga counterparts, particularly in terms of their working memory capacity (Quach et al. 2015).

Meditation doesn't just improve memory for the young!

Yet another study looked at the effects of mindfulness training in adult students studying for the Graduate Record Examination (GRE) tests, which are a prerequisite for admission to many post-baccalaureate institutions in the USA. Sure enough, the meditating participants experienced less mind-wandering and an increase in working memory capacity. This result was achieved with only two weeks of meditating for 10 minutes per day (Mrazek et al. 2013).

Of course, it often feels as if there are as many ways to meditate as there are schools of Buddhism. Nonetheless, nearly all forms are flexible. They share in common these basics:

- You can meditate anywhere.

- You can meditate at any time.

- Mountains of scientific research demonstrate the validity of meditation for memory improvement.

- Thousands of years of meditation tradition have created many insights (even if some of these approaches lock people out of the goal due to dogmatism and self-imposed adherence to a single tradition).

- Certain meditation practices exercise your brain and memory while creating states of mindfulness. These are the practices we'll be learning in this book.

As your focus and concentration increases, the likelihood of short-term frustration with using the techniques will go down. In fact, you will develop a "scientific disinterest" in the outcomes as you run the experiments, finding yourself delighted with *whatever* might happen. Making "mistakes" will disappear as you learn to observe and improve upon any lapses in your memory.

The beauty of the Challenge-Frustration Curve

It is important to liberate yourself from frustration as you train you mind, because there is no progress without trial and error. In actuality, there is nothing with which to get angry, because, as students of our minds, we have only the tools of science to work with. What do I mean by "science"? Simply this: *Science is a tool that helps us produce evidence that validates or invalidates our claims about reality.*

In this book, the claim is that by following the exercises in Part III, you will improve your memory and experience a better mental state. Further, the more you practice, the more valuable this state will become for you and those around you. Only frustration can stand between you and your effective use of this tool.

When does frustration occur? The answer may surprise you, because it's usually not when things aren't going as expected. Rather, frustration takes place when people are caught up in the outcome. Instead of focusing on the process, they are attached to and trying to control a future that hasn't arrived yet.

The meditation approaches you're about to learn will help you free yourself from frustration by teaching you to ease back from it. However, in order to experience growth, you also must keep yourself challenged. When you don't have some kind of creative tension or obstacle to tackle, you will get bored and uninterested (not "scientifically *dis*interested"—which is more like being a curious and impartial observer). Finding this state of ongoing challenge without frustration can be difficult because it's not a fixed point. It's always moving along what I think of as the Challenge-Frustration Curve.[1]

Think of yourself as a surfer riding a very long wave. If the water isn't enough of a wave to actually "catch," then there's nothing to do, so you hop off your surfboard and find something else to occupy your time. But if the wave is too rough, it may toss you into the water so hard that you're discouraged from ever trying to surf again. You need a wave of rideable size. Next, to improve as a surfer, you need that wave to "test" you—you need it to keep changing in unexpected ways. This is the essence of the Challenge-Frustration Curve—finding that perfect point between challenge and frustration, and then finding it again and again, each time you practice.

Life is like this endlessly changing wave. Since memory training and meditation are practices that belong to life, you might think that keeping yourself engaged on the surfboard of these practices would happen on autopilot. Yet, unlike life, any ongoing training practice requires your consistent participation. You must keep getting your board into the water, keep predicting where the waves will be and keep paddling out to reach them. Next, you must stand up on the board and pivot it around to assemble with both the board and the wave. You must be as our modified Poseidon is to the ocean: its humble servant, and potentially, through care, its master. Do this and you're surfing in a beautiful performance as the world integrates with your body and a concentrated state of mind.

No one can do this for you. If you want to surf, it must be you on the board and in the water. Likewise with meditation and memory training. Even if assemblage acts of reading, listening, viewing and receiving coaching have a role to play, none of these can stand in for the actual activity. You and *only you* can perform the needed movements. At the end of the day, the *how* is quite simple:

1. Keep reading this book.

2. Find something you want to memorize.

3. Find a place to meditate.

4. Begin to memorize.

5. As the techniques get easier, find more challenging things to memorize.

The main mystery we must solve throughout this practice is why the ego gets in the way of your ability to enjoy the ride without worry, fear or concern for any outcome—especially considering that no one on the planet has any control over what will happen at the end of any given experiment.

There is a paradox here which I will attempt to resolve. Although you do not have control over the outcome of an experiment, by correctly running it you can possess the power to accurately *predict* its outcomes. Every time you meet a new person and correctly memorize their name using these techniques, you will feel a sense of accomplishment that comes from feeling like being in control of an outcome. This is not to be confused with *having* control over it.

It's too bad that I didn't know any of this sooner...

3 BREATHING, WALKING, REMEMBERING: AN INSTANT-ON MAGIC CARPET RIDE FOR YOUR MIND

I T'S A GOOD THING those hooligans broke my nose. Otherwise, I never would have discovered how obstructed my breathing was. I also never would have discovered Systema.

How this graduate student came to have blood pouring from his head in 2003 outside a pub in East York is a curious story. This area of Toronto was built to house soldiers returning home from WWII. I knew it like the back of my hand because I worked for Community Care East York, an organization that paired young people seeking work with seniors in the area. I did everything for them, from mowing their lawns to changing their light bulbs. I gained—later—countless Memory Palaces by remembering the homes I'd visited during these years and—at the time—a bit too much extra change I would burn on booze, partly for fun, but mostly to "manage" or, in truth, blunt my self-destructive impulses.

My friend Andrew and I used to hang out at a particular pub, where we often got a kick out of a janitor—always in uniform—who frequented this pub with his daughter and her friends. He was *unusually* friendly with his daughter. One evening I had a video camera with me and was playing around with it. A few beers in, the janitor seemed to think I was filming him groping his daughter (something police analysis of the footage did not confirm). In my memory, I did catch a snippet of fondling, but felt badly and turned the camera in another direction and then switched it off completely. Too late.

There was a tap on my shoulder. The instant I looked up, the janitor headbutted me. Across the table, Andrew—despite his martial arts training—completely froze. Blood gushing down my face, I headed blindly for the door. But before both of my feet touched the sidewalk, the daughter's boyfriend punched me so hard my nose nearly slid off my face. At the same instant, an ambulance happened to be driving past the pub. It squealed to a stop. I remember my assailants running off and getting into a car. I watched in silent shock as a paramedic wrote the license plate of their escape vehicle on the palm of his glove. They didn't get far. They spent the night in jail, and I spent the night in emergency.

The only interesting part of the criminal proceedings is the Memory Palaces I later built from one of Toronto's many police precincts and the main courthouse. I also wrote a victim impact statement that caused the attacker's counsel to advise that they plead guilty. "You don't want a guy who writes this well on the stand," she advised. (Her cheeks went bright red when she turned around and saw that I was in earshot.) Later, based on the strength of my writing in the statement, the crown lawyer asked me if I'd consider going to law school and joining the team. "That'll be the day," I replied in my best John Wayne accent.

It wasn't legal victory that held the silver lining for getting my face smashed in. It was my recovery. First, though, there was more torture. The first ear, nose and throat (ENT) specialist I saw advised me to press my nose back into place 30 to 50 times a day. I did this for a few weeks, spending hours in agony as each time my nose slid from center position back to its new station in the eastern region of my face. It felt like horses chained to the bridge of my nose were constantly tugging on it. The experience was hell with no end in sight. I was writing my first master's thesis at the time—without the aid of a single Memory Palace—and wound up defending it while high on drugs one of my students gave me. She suffered horrible menstrual pain and said that whatever she gave me was the *ne plus ultra* of painkillers. She wasn't kidding! I managed to pass the exam while speaking from a cloud in heaven.

One evening, some time later, I was drinking fine wine and smoking weed with a well-off friend in Richmond Hill. He mentioned that his brother had needed nose surgery and had it done by a University of Toronto professor who was considered a world expert in plastic surgery of the nose. The problem was that he didn't work on the public bill and focused only on private clients. "Just tell him my family sent you," Brennan advised. "Mention us by name."

At that time, self-care was not something I really wanted to add to my to-do list, but the chronic pain in the middle of my face was so ruinous to my concentration, I followed up the lead. It was probably the first time I'd seen social capital from name-dropping operate with such force: I laid out my situation exactly as Brennan advised and Dr. Krzysztof Conrad responded, "In your case, I'll make an exception. My secretary will set you up for next Tuesday." Having grown up in Canada, I know better than most of the world what the medical system is really like. If you cannot afford private, getting in line might be free thanks to the invisible way your taxes pay for the medical system. But "free" means being sent to the end of the line, a position that usually costs far more in terms of life-draining suffering than in currency you cannot take with you when you die. (I sometimes wonder what would have happened if I'd mentioned Brennan's family name *after* I told him how much the pain was distracting me from my studies and stealing from my quality of life instead of before. He probably would have thought I was just another snotty Liberal Arts student, and a graduate one at that.)

"Not only is your nose broken," Dr. Conrad told me after a full exam, "but you probably don't even know what a good night's sleep is like. You need septoplasty to clear up a serious blockage created by some unusually enlarged turbinates."

These were new words to me, but I wasn't going to say no to the offer. After having submitted to the public doctor's sadomasochistic nose-stabilizing exercise, I was ready to jump at *any* solution. That the solution came from one of the University of Toronto's most distinguished professors of plastic surgery at the time felt very reassuring. His list of credentials was long; among many other accomplishments, he was Founder and Chief Surgeon at the Nasal and Facial Cosmetic Surgery Institute in Toronto. He is also Founder and Director of the Facial Plastic Surgery Clinic at Mount Sinai Hospital, Department of Otolaryngology and Associate Professor at the University of Toronto. As if all that wasn't enough, he's also a founding member and past president of the Canadian Academy of Facial Plastic and Reconstructive Surgery, not to mention being a fellow of the American Academy of Facial Plastic and Reconstructive Surgery. In other words, I felt I was in good hands in a world where laurels and accolades might actually matter.

Although recovery from the surgery was tough, I was soon back at school teaching Film Studies tutorials and completing my own graduate courses. My black eyes and nasal drip seemed to bother me more than my colleagues and students. Then, one day on the way home from campus, I noticed a building on Coxwell Avenue with a red sign on it: "FightClub." The David Fincher film had been out for a while, and for obvious reasons, watching people punch each other for fun was not high on my list of pastimes. Yet the appearance of the training facility drew my attention. I made a silent vow that I would never again get blindsided as I had in the pub with Andrew. I also vowed I would never be like Andrew, who, albeit a trained martial artist, had been so drunk his skills didn't even show up enough to be useless.

A few weeks later, my face finally looking more like it belonged to Anthony Metivier than the swollen black body of an obese sewer rat, I opened the door and walked inside. It's a good thing Dr. Conrad made my breathing portals bigger so I could sleep better. I would sure need it after the rigorous training offered in the environment I was about to enter.

Emmanuel Manolakakis greeted me with what could only be called "disinterested interest." Except for picking my brother up from judo and watching a few of my grade-school friends compete in karate, I'd never set foot in a martial arts studio. I don't have any pictures of myself during my university years due to a 2013 purge of nearly all my belongings, but I imagine I looked as unathletic as I felt. I rode my bike everywhere and mowed lawns almost every day of the week, but poor eating and drinking habits kept my body rotund. My corporeal weaknesses screamed "wimp" loud and clear, but Emmanuel explained that everyone is a beginner in this class. *Every* class—no matter how experienced.

It turned out "FightClub" was just a name to spark interest. The real teaching Emmanuel offered me was grounded in the martial art Systema, which a man who would become a legendary figure, named Vladimir Vasiliev, had brought to Toronto from Russia. Always a reactionary to any form of authority and a chronic lone wolf, I loved the fact that Systema had no belts, ranks or competitions. New students dive into training with people who have been benefiting from Systema's unique approach to self-protection for years. Everyone instructs everyone else. I suggest people in the Magnetic Memory Method community operate this way too, based on the positive impact this decentralized learning approach has had on me.

Emmanuel and the other students quickly taught me the value of focused breathing: studying your breath, staying with your breath and coordinating your breath with your movements. Yet, Systema is not about memorizing the coordination or trying to play out an if-this-then-that pattern in a moment of conflict. Rather, the training teaches you to become deeply relaxed in situations of conflict. This dropping into relaxation starts to happen automatically as you learn how your body and the bodies of others react to implied and actual threats communicated to the brain.

As surprising as it may sound after having my nose smashed in, knowing how to willingly accept a punch became one of my favorite exercises. As you learn in Systema, a relaxed body can emulate water and pull what seems like a successfully landed blow into a swirling vortex that reveals weaknesses in the opponent's stance. You "receive" the opponent's forward motion in order to "take" even more motion. Then you put them on the floor. It's almost like folding paper.

I accelerated my training by buying a slim volume by Vladimir Vasiliev called *The Russian System Guidebook* and all of the DVDs Emmanuel had available. Although I never wound up training with Vasiliev in person, his teaching via writing and video has been essential for my learning. As with memory technqiues and the enlightenment tradition you'll discover later in this book, you really can learn from the master without him being anywhere in sight. Systema also introduced me to Scott Sonnen, who taught kettlebells and club bells. I used these to develop greater strength and stamina in addition to the breath-intuition development exercises of Systema. Later, this form of study would assemble with practice in Systema schools in Vancouver and Berlin, compounding in value the more study and practice combined to make the teaching matter.

Following the advice in Vasiliev's guidebook, I started studying breathing in a more intense way. This was before I kept the rigorous, daily meditation practice I follow today. I also followed up with Vasiliev's recommendations that Systema students douse themselves in cold water after waking up and before bed. His book includes reasons for practicing cold water exposure that likely aren't grounded in testable and falsifiable science, having something to do with positive and negative polarities that will reverse through your body to cleanse out any infections. But I set my skepticism aside and did it. I still do. The practice feels so refreshing, I've never since stopped using cold water exposure for any length of time. It was, however, the breathing exercises that struck me as the most valuable, even if it would be many years before Wim Hof came to my attention and I began following his suggestion of deliberately combining breath training with cold water exposure.

Another Systema teaching—knowing how not to project nervousness and essentially erase it through breathing in coordination with movement and deep muscle relaxation—has come in handy many times. And not just during the stresses of sitting for my PhD defense. There were field exams I had to sit for, and worse events too. Some time later, while writing my dissertation, I was living in Washington Heights, a district north of Harlem in New York City. I was walking south, down to the 170s from the corner of 187th and Cabrini, where I stopped to use a bank machine. On my way out, a man stood in front of me with something resembling a gun in his pocket. Exactly as it happens in the movies, he gestured in quick spurts of energy, so that my eyes dropped and looked at his pocket.

"Give me your wallet and all your money," he demanded.

My Systema training kicked in. Instead of having my shoulders shoot up with anxious tension, as I had seen Emmanuel observe most of his new students doing (including me during my first lessons), my mind automatically followed the training I'd received. Without willing it, my shoulders dropped and my mind and body synced with my breath. In a way that still completely bewilders me, a smile came across my face. I don't know what I looked like, but my expression unnerved the mugger. It created the stress in him that should have been in my body.

As I continued to breathe and smile (perhaps an early version of the Buddha Smile yet to come?), I was in some kind of instinctual holding pattern. I don't want false memory syndrome to creep into the story and make it more dramatic than it was, but then, that's the point. The drama was *entirely in the mugger's head* and I could see it in his body as my peripheral vision monitored the object in his pocket he said was a gun. For all I know, he could just have been pointing his finger through the cloth, but my mind didn't get in the way by making a decision and panicking. After what seemed like an eternity, the mugger said, "Wipe that fucking smile off your face or I'll shoot you."

At this point, my smile grew wider and I started to laugh. An instant later, it felt right to move. I took one step forward into his space and angled to the left with the second and third steps. I didn't break his gaze and watched as his eyes and entire head tracked me as I moved past him. Then, still operating completely on autopilot, I started to run and found myself in a cleaning supplies store filled with mops and buckets. Blackberries were all the rage at the time, and I soon had my wife, Ingrid, on this strange new mobile phone with a typewriter on its face and got her to call the police. The rest of the scenario is a blur, but I recall speaking with the cops about how these situations are handled and probably took a taxi back to our apartment in Washington Heights. I remember writing a story about the event that the entire family shared via email and after that, it faded into yet another crazy, but all too common, New York adventure.

When I wound up in Vancouver, I gave JP Gagliano's Systema class in the Commercial-Broadway district a chance.[2] JP had been to Russia to study Systema directly with its masters and had trained extensively with Vladimir Vasiliev himself. Shortly after I started training with JP, *Let Every Breath: Secrets of the Russian Breath Masters* appeared. Written by Vasiliev with Scott Meredith, the book is a masterclass on different breathing methods. Although it tells some stories about Vasiliev that sound too good to be true, one breathing exercise in particular has helped me train my mind and body to great effect when it comes to being able to focus on using memory techniques.

Exercise: Pendulum Breathing and Progressive Muscle Relaxation

In the breathing exercise called Pendulum Breathing, the idea is that you "swing" the breath. If you've ever really watched a pendulum, then you know there is an interesting moment at the end of each swing where the pendulum seems to hang for an instant and then move up a little bit further before falling back the other way. It does this back and forth. Pendulum Breathing mimics this motion. To start, fill your lungs normally and then pause slightly. Instead of exhaling, breathe in a little bit more. Let the breath out naturally and pause again. Instead of inhaling, exhale out a little bit more. By circulating your breath in this way, you are "swinging" the air like a pendulum.

Try it now.

I have found Pendulum Breathing very useful for calming and focusing my mind before studying and memorizing information. This practice reduces stress overall and comes in handy many times throughout the day. If nothing else, implement Pendulum Breathing in your memory work before, during and after you sit down to use Memory Palaces. This method of breathing makes Memory Palace creation and the generation of images and associations so much easier because you are putting yourself in a kind of oxygenated dream state. Combine pendulum breathing with Progressive Muscle Relaxation for maximum effect.

Here's a quick guide to Progressive Muscle Relaxation, a practice that's calming and rewarding. We often performed this work at the beginning and end of a Systema class, and it is useful anywhere. For example, I used Pendulum Breathing and Progressive Muscle Relaxation in combination while waiting to be called in for my dissertation defense. As with the MA examination I undertook while on borrowed painkillers for a broken nose, I was deeply relaxed. But during the dissertation defence, the medicine was all natural.

To get started, sit on a chair or lie down on a bed or the floor. As you "swing" your breath, on the inhale, flex, and on the exhale, release:

1. Point your toes upward and hold—then release.

2. Point your toes towards the wall and hold—then release.

3. Flex your calves. Keep releasing after every flexion.

4. Flex your thighs.

5. Flex your buttocks.

6. Flex your stomach muscles, lower back muscles, chest and shoulders (all core muscles).

7. Flex your hands, forearms and upper arms.

8. Flex your neck, your cheeks and the muscles surrounding your eyes.

You can try different patterns as you breathe, hold and release. Usually I inhale as I'm flexing. Then I hold the flex as I'm holding the breath and complete by releasing with the exhale. You can also inhale, hold, exhale, release and explore other possible patterns.

One of the key benefits of this exercise is a heightened perception of the many layers of your experience, through the linking of movement and the manipulation of your muscles with the manipulation of your breath. You start to notice how your body and breathing are objects appearing in your awareness. It might take some practice to make using these techniques a habit, but once you've reached the other side, there's potentially no turning back. I don't know if I'll do this forever, but nearly two decades in, these exercises continue to provide the reward of relaxation and focus.

Although it may seem difficult to concentrate on *both* your breathing *and* doing other things (such as imaginative Memory Palace creation and memory encoding), it really isn't that tough. In some ways, it's like being a drummer who is creating three or four different patterns, one for each limb. With practice, the ability will come to you. It is incredibly relaxing, so consistency pays off. If you do it often enough and happen to encounter a mugger, the ability to instantly drop into deep relaxation might just save your life as it (perhaps) did mine. On that day, I "remembered" my Systema training, which was just as valuable as how I was able to remember advanced research facts during my exams. This instant turning to the training undoubtedly comes from how developed neuronal connections and procedural memory operate together to create performance. When thought is out of the way, the moves seem to take care of themselves.

Hopefully, you won't ever be mugged, but most of us will undergo stress-inducing exams and job interviews during our lives. These techniques will help you perform in many such situations. And if you've ever had issues with anxiety that have impeded your success, Pendulum Breathing and Progressive Muscle Relaxation might be just the ticket you need. I know this anecdotally because having my nostrils widened so I could breathe better at night had been the least of my oxygen problems for many years due to extreme, self-induced anxiousness.

"Suffocating" on a blue moon in the desert

> *"You don't have to take LSD. Just listen to Ministry."*
> — Jørn Stubberud

Breathing had been an issue for me since age 14 when an LSD experience went awry. This is what happened.

It was fall in Kamloops, British Columbia, Canada. I was in Grade 9. A friend arranged to get me a "double-dipped" dose of Blue Moon acid. In other words, it was twice the amount I was used to consuming, and since the names people came up with for the "lots" of acid they produced often informed the nature of the adventure you were about to take (frame effect), I knew I was in for quite a ride.

In fact, my friend told me the dose was sourced through some bikers and was the best he'd ever had. Since I took my friend for a bit of a guru in matters ranging from how to get away with spray painting walls to the correct way to inhale nitrous oxide from whipped cream canisters, and bikers had legendary status in our minds, I figured this stuff *must* be good.

And it was! He gave me the small tab wrapped in tin foil at noon and I dropped it under my tongue while standing in the church parking lot in front of our high school. I next remember watching Smurfs on the chalkboard in my Graphic Arts classroom and having to leave early due to the overwhelming, albeit positively amusing, intensity of this display. On previous trips, I had always preferred being outside, and this time was no different. Tripping in school, or inside the mall or a restaurant was a recipe for disaster, and adults were often on the lookout for kids behaving strangely in these public places. Adults, back then, were the enemy.

So I ditched class and walked towards my father's home. Mount Peter and Mount Paul in Kamloops swam in the distance as I walked. Kamloops is semi-arid and its desert topography of sandy mountains spotted with sagebrush lends itself to a special kind of hallucination. Right before my eyes, these structures fused together into one giant being, not unlike the old man wizard with his lamp and cowl on the Led Zeppelin albums. Then the twin mountains *were* that druid and Moses at the same time as something in the back of my mind kept telling me a new Bible was being written on the other side in a thousand languages at once.

I'm not sure what I was thinking when I dosed that afternoon because I was supposed to perform that evening with my band, "The Unholy Silence," at St Anne's Academy. I'd worked for months with Manuel, considered the most talented guitarist in Kamloops, so I could perform the complex riffs of our songs on my bass. If I had planned to play the gig on acid, the Blue Moon melting my face as I sat on my dad's bed staring into the mirror had other plans. My face dissolved and rebuilt itself until I looked like a portrait of Jim Morrison painted by Francis Bacon, and then my dad was home asking me about the gig. A star burst warmly from his head as he spoke. I mumbled something about how I didn't need a ride to the concert and he disappeared. After some time in my own room watching my Iron Maiden posters swing at me with flags and axes, I headed out in the complete opposite direction of the concert.

An eternal bus ride later, I found myself at the Westsyde home of my friend, Rain. My other pals Scott and Doug were there too. Stretched out along the North Thompson River, the Westsyde district ends with a shopping center and massive parking lot where kids skateboarded at all hours of the day and night. In Rain's house around the corner, these kids were up to no good when they introduced a Coke can with holes poked into it as a makeshift pipe. I don't know if I was hallucinating or they were really talking about a new drug called "Shrine," but given the severe way my sense of reality would soon be distorted, it was probably marijuana sprayed with PCP or DMT. Whatever it was, my foolish brain estimated that its psyche could handle it because the LSD seemed to have faded.

How many times I inhaled from the makeshift pipe is not clear to me. But I recall a reckless longing for something other than the world driving my deep toking as my friends waited for their turn. I don't remember passing either the Coke can or the lighter to anyone else. Suddenly, the entire universe went black, all of it expanded to the ends of infinity until it snapped back into a microscopic space of crystal-clear clarity. It was massive and tiny at the same time, everywhere and nowhere. Imagine your conscious mind and body as an elastic band being pulled by an invisible force, almost to the breaking point, before snapping back into place. That is what my time in the nothing felt like.

I don't know if I heard it in that room or somewhere else, but the phrase, "watch out for that rollercoaster acid, man," lives somewhere in my past. On rollercoaster acid, you might feel like the trip is over, but in fact, you haven't yet reached the highest peak. It is possible that this happened to me. Rollercoaster or not, whatever remained of the LSD in my system fused with the new drugs and laid the foundation for years of anxiety to come, all of it focused on my chest in ways that interrupted my breathing worse than the minor problem of having closed nostrils.

When I could see again, a giant sword made of *both* fire *and* ice was in my mouth. In order to breathe, I had to take the entire blade into my lungs and force it out again. My friends were laughing at my distress, each of them distorted and indistinguishable from insects. Doug was particularly difficult to watch. Wrapped in a green and red knitted blanket, he seemed like a giant laughing worm, a nightmare version of the caterpillar in *Alice's Adventures in Wonderland*, which is *already* nightmarish enough.

I appealed to Scott, the friend I knew the best. It took a lot to persuade him into believing that I couldn't breathe. The lighting, the music, the laughing—it was all overwhelming and added to the weight of the sword in my mouth and lungs. When he and I finally got outside, I kept repeating, "I can't breathe... I can't breathe." With each step, I felt horrible sensations of doom as I fell off the surface of the world and slammed back onto it again. A spot of light started ringing beside my ear before flying off into the distance, strangely growing louder the farther away it traveled. Because this sonic beacon was physically connected to me, my relationship to the sound grew stronger the more it orbited the universe. It was night by now and the same sky that had given me so much pleasure to stare into during previous acid- and weed-stoked adventures was now a hostile enemy.

My heart pounded as Scott tried to calm me down. We went behind an elementary school where X-rays were hanging in the windows. This started the music from *The Mind is a Terrible Thing to Taste* running in my mind. An album by the band Ministry, it begins with strange nail gun and drill sounds and the voice of the brutal Sergeant Hartman from *Full Metal Jacket* urging you to "Get up! Get on your feet!" I had the feeling that the entire album was playing in my mind, each individual second of each song blaring in unison at the same time, its repetitions grinding into the very core of my being.

After a trip to the grocery store for some menthol candies I thought might help me calm down, I spat them on the ground and caved in.

"I have to go to the hospital," I told Scott.

He tried to take me to the bus, but a guy standing there freaked me out when he asked me to light a firecracker because the last one had blown his hand off, the same hand he was using to hand me the red M-80. It made no sense and I couldn't handle the mind-warping challenge of reconciling the contradictions piling into my experience with fractal intensity. I asked Scott to go with me to the home of the Arthurs who lived nearby, people from my mom's church, and one of many *ersatz* families I stayed with when life at one of my parent's homes descended into yet another swirl of chaos.

"You're on your own, man," Scott whispered. "I can't get in trouble for this."

Scott waited for my blessing, which never came, then was gone.

I found the family's home on my own and the eldest son took me into his care. I remember sitting on the stairs, struggling to breathe.

"Are you sure you want me to call your dad?" he asked a thousand times. I didn't want him to at all, and yet I insisted upon it. With Sergeant Hartman, mechanical drilling and the ringing of a mystical beacon circling the universe terrorizing my mind along with a zillion other things, what else could I do?

When Mr. Arthur came home, my dad was already en route. Mr. Arthur lectured about sending me down to Nicaragua on one of the church missions. If I really wanted to put myself through hell, he suggested, being a missionary down there was a finer way to do it. My dad eventually arrived and packed me in the car for a ride to the emergency room. I don't remember much about his attitude during that car ride. All I know is the celestial radio knob in my mind started turning until the dial landed on Ozzy Osbourne's "Suicide Solution." Lying on a gurney in the emergency room, I heard the first two lines play over and over again:

Wine is fine but whiskey's quicker
Suicide is slow with liquor

Those two lines became an earworm that would barely pause for many years to come. It's little wonder I wound up living them.

I saw many horrible things over the next 14 hours. My heart stopped and I flew up far above the planet and saw reality for what it probably really is: a mass of competing energies intertwined with such complexity that one thing can't see that it is the same thing as the other. Back on planet Earth, monkeys descended from the ceiling. They positioned a giant stone clock face on my chest, upon which they danced and laughed. Worse, they sang endlessly, even bringing in giant speakers to make sure the message sank in loud and clear:

Wine is fine but whiskey's quicker
Suicide is slow with liquor

The monkeys attached electrodes all over my body, shocked my heart back into action and forced me to drink a strange pink potion. My dad excused himself every 10 minutes to smoke cigarettes outside.

I made it through the night as the drugs wore off, leaving psychosis in their wake. Back home, I was so abused by the imagery and sensations I had experienced, I couldn't tolerate my bedroom and its dozens of heavy metal and horror movie posters. The minute I built up the courage to enter my room again, I tore down the entire collection I'd assembled for the love of heavy metal. During the year following this event, I often ran out of school with the same Ozzy Osbourne song running through my head, a terrifying inability to breathe ripping at my lungs. I sat for many hours in the church beside the high school staring at a cross covered in snakes, earworms coiling in my mind. I had already befriended Dan, the church's youth pastor, and been blazed out of my skull on many drugs under his care in the past. He hadn't known about that (or never said so if he did), but because the secretary of the church was the matriarch of the home I'd landed in during the worst hours of my mental blitzkrieg, everyone knew why I was skipping school.

Dan the Pastor Man took me under his wing and suggested I read *The Teachings of Don Juan: A Yaqui Way of Knowledge* along with another book called *The Bondage Breaker* by Neil T. Anderson. Even at age 14, I was skeptical of the idea that demons had somehow crept into my "soul" and would require prayer if I was ever going to break their chains. *The Teachings of Don Juan* intrigued me much more. I understand now why Dan gave it to me. Although many people have discredited the book's claims to cultural anthropology, it still offers great insight into how the author (or a fictional character invented by the author) survived horrible psychological turmoil caused by the decision to imbibe certain chemicals and transformed it into positive, healing experiences. Reading this book didn't fix my breathing, but I no longer felt so alone in my terror.

Even better, reading Castaneda gave me a taste for more sophisticated literature at a very young age. After returning Dan's copy, I found it again in the public library and used bookstores and consulted these copies like a Bible, flipping pages for snippets of wisdom. Unlike the Piers Anthony fantasy and sci-fi books I had been reading at the time, which were always surrounded by more fantasy and sci-fi authors, Castaneda would be embedded in fields populated by Albert Camus, Franz Kafka, Hermann Hesse and Thomas Mann. Among these writers were even more colorful characters like William S. Burroughs and L. Ron Hubbard, who had once been joined at the hip on the quest for enduring self-revelation.

But none of these authors talked about anxiety so bad that you feel like you can't breathe. I suffered in despair and the issue was clearly behind why I skipped school as much as I could get away with throughout the rest of high school. The constant anxiety also provided a good excuse to feed my preference for reading the books that interested me in the library shelves, not those pushed on us by the school. I felt even freer from the anxiety during the time I dropped out of school completely.

During my self-elected leave of absence, I wandered the hills and listened to CBC radio on a giant yellow Walkman until I either lost signal or ran out of battery. I learned more about being a contributing citizen of planet Earth from Peter Gzowski and his guests on Morning Side than from any of my high school teachers. They were great promoters too. I often followed up with the books mentioned at the library or Bookingham Palace, where I eventually worked. No one ever asked why I wasn't at school, not even at the grocery store, where I nourished myself on apple strudel and chocolate milk by the gallon. No doubt the temporary relief of these "meals" only added to my mental distress after the sugar high-induced focus stopped distracting my attention from my mental landscape.

The anxiety persisted throughout my first two years of university when I would visit doctors in various states of panic, convinced I was having a heart attack. I was taught techniques to combat hyperventilating, even though it was clear to me that this wasn't the problem. It was either the lingering effects of a sword built from ice and fire... or I was in bondage to demons as Dan had suspected. The latter was impossible though. The long trail of books Dan had initiated showed me, through the twisted lenses of madmen like L. Ron Hubbard, just how insane a belief in demon control is.

All of my anxiety hit the ceiling when I moved to Toronto to complete my full first year at York University for a B.A. in English Literature. I had already been in the city briefly but never started my studies, partly due to anxiety issues. Yet, after having lived in Toronto and experienced by contrast how lacking in metropolitan sophistication British Columbia was when it came to film festivals, museums, art galleries and creative people fanatical about having all of these options at their door, I had to return. At the time, the Internet was little more than an email address and a way to read people's opinions, so if you wanted a piece of the action, you really needed to *be* there—even if it stretched your personal comfort and caused the odd anxiety attack.

Over time, the attacks became less and less frequent until one spring day in 1999, when I started writing a very long poem. It was called "Judas and His Goats." The sprawling piece was partly fashioned after T.S. Eliot's *The Wasteland* and heavily influenced by the voices of Ezra Pound and HD (Hilda Doolittle). It is almost as if I had put all three of them in a blender—or *assembled* their influence—to help tell the story of a budding scholar trapped in the body of a poet. Convinced of the genius of this writing, I started using email to send the emerging passages to every address I had—including my poor professors. I wasn't sleeping at all while working on the poem and probably told everyone about this too. What I thought was a sign of inspiration, they considered madness.

To be fair, it was. My schedule ran something like this:

- 6:30 a.m.—Get up and bus the 30-something kilometres from Brampton to the York University campus. This would require 2 or 3 buses (depending on timing) and could take more than 90 minutes.

- Morning to early afternoon—Attend courses and read or write in the library on a laptop the size of a suitcase.

- Afternoon—Bus back to Brampton.

- 3:30 p.m. to midnight—Work at Para Paints filling paint orders and packing them into trucks for delivery across North America, all the while writing my poem and outlining essays.

- Midnight to late—Wilson, the Para Paints foreman, would usually lure me into doing overtime.

- 3 or 4:00 a.m.—Return home, type up my handwriting, email it out and lie on my bed—my mind completely on fire.

In this hectic time, the ideas came fast and hard. I could barely keep up with them, and yet I felt on top of the world. Feelings of anxiety and trouble breathing had completely disappeared from my life. At school, I remember asking my friends if they thought I was on drugs and then explaining at length how I hadn't taken any. They assured me that I seemed very much like myself, and that even these requests to monitor my state were in keeping with my normal antics.

During a meeting, one of my professors told me a story about a journalist who went full-blown manic while reporting in the Middle East and wondered if I wasn't experiencing something similar. I rejected this possibility even though I remember well knowing that something was wrong—just not necessarily with me. But at one point, the good feelings started to sour. I thought a fellow student was conspiring to persecute me. I recall something in my mind telling me this paranoia wasn't right, but my friends kept reassuring me that things were fine. I kept writing my poem, and announced a great reading of the completed draft at the end of the following week.

By now, the poem had been completed. The opening stanza, a love song to the Imagist poet Hilda Doolitttle, ran like this:

reading all these men
upsets me
i'm getting to h.d.
in a moment
she is on my shelf
burning with want to be open

Burning with want for readers, I had copies for the 16 attendees I'd gathered for my performance. These were printed, stapled and stacked in my backpack—the same backpack that would stink of McDonald's and taunt me with yet other possible "suicide solution" a few months later.

But at that point, I had no plans to do anything other than read my poem in the classroom I had booked and then find a way to sleep. I'd gotten the keys to a professor's office and figured I would hibernate on the floor in undisturbed silence for at least two weeks, surrounded by precious books while she was off at a conference. The lightning of the same creative force that had so clearly struck the many poets I was studying would have passed, and a long doze would restore life to normal. I was sure of it and planned a trip to Paris on the phone with my friend

Jennifer, mapping out a life where I would write in a cold apartment, make capitalism die with the power of the word and live happily ever after wrapped in scarves and typing on an Underwood through fingerless gloves. She would play her guitar and record albums everyone would love.

Well, I *have* since written books while enjoying much nicer conditions in Paris, and Jennifer did eventually record albums many have loved, but it didn't come about in quite the way I'd planned that day. One afternoon, shortly before the reading, a chance encounter threw a wrench into the gears of my great plans. The teaching assistant of one of the professors to whom I'd been emailing my poem approached me after a lecture. I listened to him, still with tears in my eyes from the beauty of John Keats's "Ode to a Nightingale," which we'd just been discussing, as he explained that although my poetry was good, it was also strangely sexual and violent. He proposed that I talk about it with some people he knew at a place called the Clarke Institute.

The Clarke Institute is a psychiatric hospital at the corner of College and Spadina. At the time, I knew it well for two reasons. I'd read and loved the novel *Headhunter* by Timothy Findley in which the setting of the Parkin Psychiatric Institute was based on the Clarke. And my friend Brent's wife was doing residence work related to her University of Toronto degree at the hospital, so I thought at the very least it was a chance to say hello. It was a "hello" that would last three months, and soon all the anxiety I thought I'd left behind would come slamming back down onto my chest harder than a stone clock face covered in dancing monkeys.

Exactly what transpired in the Clarke Institute is best summed up as a kid resisting taking lithium until the medical system tired him out. I've written about the full adventure in a book called *Mother Love* and won't repeat it all here, but there is a part of the experience I've never told that relates to breathing.

Bad diet, bad sleep and intense poetry on a collision course

T.S. Eliot begins *The Wasteland* with a sardonic reference to *The Canterbury Tales*. Whereas Chaucer's poem begins with "When in April the sweet showers fall," Eliot's poem begins: "April is the cruellest month." On April 20th, locked up in the hospital after completing my poem, it certainly was that for me.

Although I do not think the diagnosis of bipolar disorder is without its merits and don't want to lead others astray in how I share my experience, it seems obvious now that poor diet, time management and sleep habits on a collision course with a simple burst of poetic inspiration were the true culprits for my condition. I feel that I probably would have done just fine sleeping on the floor of the professor's office after reading my poem had I not crossed paths with the teaching assistant who persuaded me to share my seemingly brilliant "Judas and His Goats" with medical professionals instead of my peers.

I do, however, understand their concern, because the most stressful episode I experienced while in hospital occurred in the dayroom of the Clarke one afternoon while tragedy spilled out from the television. I seemed to be the only person horrified to be watching footage from the Columbine High School massacre. I ran to the nursing station and seriously questioned the wisdom of allowing news like this to play in the hospital environment. I was told that they saw my point but thought the disturbing news oozing from the television set was fine. The other patients were either nodding off in their seats, or watching the footage through the smoking room glass where I had recently seen a patient try to butt out a cigarette using her left eye as an ashtray.

Blaring Columbine was not fine for me and caused even more anxiety as my mind extended and played out the footage. When I look back at "Judas and His Goats," I see it does contain some violence—and fantasies of control over an uncontrollable world. The more I study the mind and read from people like Jordan Peterson, who talks about his own experience of violence in *Maps of Meaning*, I think it's possible that the lung-constricting stress I experienced from watching the news reports stemmed not so much from the news and feeling threatened on its own. It's possible that the anxiety also came from contending with my own capacity to *be* a threat. This is a lesson that I would eventually have to wrestle with in even deeper ways when confronted later by the seemingly radical psychotherapy of Dr. Robert Langs in New York.

But the poem also has many moments of beauty, and any fan of modernist literature or philosophy will pick up many amusing references and allusions. The grotesque passages and blunt sexuality clearly bear the mark of William S. Burroughs and J.G. Ballard, whom I had recently read in anticipation of Canadian filmmaker David Cronenberg's version of Ballard's notorious novel, *Crash*. The fact that I wrote it in April and that so many suicides and other tragedies happen during this "cruellest month," as Eliot put it, opened my eyes wide to the suffering of others subject to similar states of mind, and they have been open ever since.

Indeed, while teaching at Rutgers University in New Jersey during the last stretch of my PhD years, I used the empathy earned during my hard passage through the spring of 1999 to counsel deeply disturbed students following the Virginia Tech shootings of April 16, 2007. The reaction of one student in particular who reached out to me led me to contact the Rutgers English department, much as I imagine the teaching assistant once expressed concern about me. The English department assured me I did the right thing, and as far as I know, this student managed to overcome his stress and complete his year without further incident.

But I wouldn't have been so calm or learned to help others if it hadn't been for Georgina Cannon. During a hypnosis training I completed under her tutelage, my anxiety struggles and the clamp they could put on my breathing came out. During one exercise, Georgina had participants place one another in a state of relaxation, which we then deepened through verbal suggestion and by eliciting a number of images through visualization. At one point, Georgina got involved in my induction while I was describing a black snake I envisioned coiled around my heart and lungs.

I remember the look of concern in her eyes when we discussed this outcome of the exercise after I woke up from the trance. I can't explain how or why, but my investigation into breathing to help remove whatever this black snake symbolized is connected to her in some way. I still don't think my experiences with drugs at age 14 opened any portals to demons or black snakes, but it is clear that the mind conceptualizes pain and suffering in images and stories—in symbolization.

The more you know about how your mind might be doing similar things to you, the more tenderly you might solve your issues by exploring your breath. Here is yet another technique that has helped me find the calm needed not only for success with memory techniques, but daily life.

Exercise: Psychic Alternate Nostril Breathing

No, Psychic Alternate Nostril Breathing is not about mind-reading your nose. It's a form of breathing exercise I learned while studying hypnosis with Georgina Cannon in Toronto. In her classes, the goal was actually to spot and *eliminate* mind-reading. By "mind-reading," hypnotists mean the way so many of us presuppose we know what others are doing and thinking. Doing so can harm our own progress and *create* the same problems we're trying to avoid. Being in control of your breath helps you stop making decisions based on the cognitive biases that lead you to believe you know what others think.

I hadn't expected such lessons to come out of learning hypnosis, but the instincts that led me to Cannon's training paid off. After finally deciding to write my dissertation about friendship at around the time I was learning hypnosis, I was reading up on how friends shape each other and soon came across the matter of persuasion. As a long-time amateur magician, I remembered a quote from the Amazing Kreskin that "hypnosis is nothing more than the acceptance of a suggestion." Since friends make suggestions that are accepted all the time, before I knew it, I was deep into the fascinating realms of therapeutic hypnosis and something called neuro-linguistic programming (NLP).[3]

As I've pointed out, the peace of mind and freedom from anxiety I've built to last through practice comes from the compound value of working with many techniques progressively over the years. Among them all, I've found Psychic Alternate Nostril Breathing to be one of the best for rapidly relieving anxiety and developing your focus on the present moment. It's a fantastic distraction from anything that causes panic or even makes you nervous. If I feel unsettled before giving a memory demonstration in the community for any reason, this is my go-to exercise. I often go to it even when I am feeling on top of the world.

Again, it's got the word "psychic" in it, but this has nothing to do with mind-reading. The exercise is called *psychic* because of how you use your mind to pretend that you're closing off your nostrils without actually blocking them off with your hands.

Of course, you can perform manual alternate nostril breathing simply by reaching up and closing off one nostril with a finger or thumb as you breathe in. (It's a great place to start if your focus isn't ready yet for extended concentration, or you are in a mood of distraction.) Then, before exhaling, you close the other nostril off and exhale out through the newly opened nostril. After that, you continue circulating back and forth. Try it now and journal about the experience.

If you want the benefits of both the breath control exercise and more focus and concentration, you'll want to practice closing your nostrils purely as something you're thinking about in your mind. In addition to practicing concentration and focus, the process teaches you a lot about how mental focus can create physical experiences of awareness purely by how you choose to link thinking with breath. This was also the finding of Ramana Maharshi in the *Upadesa Saram*, transliterated and translated by Gary Weber in *Happiness Beyond Thought*:

Vaayu rodhanaal liyate manaH
Breathing by restraining is absorbed (by the) mind

Jaala pakshivad rodha saadhanam
In a net like a bird for controlling a means (i.e., breathing this way is a means of controlling the mind)

As Gary Weber translates these lines: *Control the breath and you control the mind, like throwing a net over a wild parrot.*

In whatever way you perform alternate nostril breathing, it is the alternating that matters as much as the breathing. It gives your mind and memory a point of focus. If you wander from your practice, remind yourself to come back to the breath and don't judge yourself for getting distracted. It is truly that simple.

Psychic Alternate Nostril Breathing can be performed during a sitting meditation, or anywhere you desire focus and relaxation. You can enjoy the focus and relaxation it brings for long periods of time while talking, writing or reading. I regularly practice this form of breathing while waiting for my turn on the stage to give a presentation, and this simple process banished all but the healthiest of stresses while defending my dissertation. With just a small amount of training, my once-shattered nostrils, perched in front of an anxious, medicated brain, had become portals of rapid relaxation and focus. The peace this technique brings keeps getting better and better, the more I practice. I predict the same results will happen for you over the years to come.

Exercise: Combining Psychic Alternate Nostril Breathing with other practices

As you've likely already realized, you can combine the patterns of Pendulum Breathing with the patterns of Psychic Alternate Nostril Breathing. It doesn't particularly matter which side you start on, but to give you an example pattern, you could:

> Right nostril inhale—stop—inhale again
> Left nostril exhale—stop—exhale again
> Left nostril inhale—stop—inhale again
> Right nostril exhale—stop—exhale again

Again, you're not trying to actually open and close your nostrils with your mind. Rather, you're focusing on the action *as if* you could and benefitting from increased concentration skill as a result. You're focusing on your breath, which deepens and extends the flow of oxygen, and you're essentially meditating.

In Systema, you also learn to link your breath with your gait. Once again, you can link their practices with Psychic Alternate Nostril Breathing. The way I've practiced one possible assemblage of these practices while wandering neighborhoods around the world involves setting up a progressive challenge that absorbs the mind in focusing on the procedures.

For the first cycle, inhale on your first step and exhale on your second. You can alternate your nostrils or breathe through both nostrils without the additional mental exercise. I do not believe it matters whether you inhale and exhale through your nostrils exclusively or also use your mouth, though I encourage you to experiment with both approaches, or decide based on pollution levels in your area. Observe the results and make changes as you see fit.

1 step = 1 inhale
1 step = 1 exhale
Repeat 5×

When you've done this five times, inhale over two steps and exhale over two steps. Then increase the number of steps you take while inhaling.

2 steps = 1 inhale
2 steps = 1 exhale
Repeat 5×

3 steps = 1 inhale
3 steps = 1 exhale
Repeat 5×

4 steps = 1 inhale
4 steps = 1 exhale
Repeat 5×

5 steps = 1 inhale
5 steps = 1 exhale
Repeat 5×

See if you can repeat the process until you complete 10 steps across a single inhale and 10 steps across a single exhale. When you can do this, you can then reverse the process by moving back down the number of steps from 10 to 1.

For another variation, you can include breath holding. As with all these exercises, please consult a doctor before putting any of them into action, especially anything that involves holding your breath. To include breath holding while walking and alternating the breath between your nostrils, the process is simple:

1 step = 1 inhale
1 step = 1 step of holding oxygen in your lungs
1 step = 1 exhale
Repeat 5×

2 steps = 1 inhale
2 steps = 2 steps of holding oxygen in your lungs
2 steps = 1 exhale
Repeat 5×

3 steps = 1 inhale
3 steps = 3 steps of holding oxygen in your lungs
3 steps = 1 exhale
Repeat 5×

Add steps until you get to 10 (or as high as you can go) and scale down as desired.

As an alternative, you can forgo paying attention to the number of steps and count instead. I will sometimes inhale to a count of 4, hold for a count of 4 and then exhale for a count of 4. It's helpful to involve your hands to keep track of the count. Press thumb and pointer together for one, thumb and middle finger together for two, and so forth. Or, you can replace numbers with "Sa Ta Na Ma," "Ah Me To Foa" (we'll talk about these strategies for meditation later), or just make up your own syllables. I have found that adding some kind of mental activity based in numbers, sounded syllables or Sanskrit while breath-walking is useful for creating physical and mental peace.

Whatever you use, focus your mind on the experience of consciousness. Do this by concentrating on the breath and the deliberate choice of select mental content rather than random thoughts coming and going on their own whim. We'll devote a lot of time later to different kinds of mental content you can choose from, along with detailed mnemonic examples. With consistent practice, you'll develop a "muscle" for noticing exactly when random thoughts are taking over. You'll develop a rapid, if not instant, means of labelling these thoughts and choosing to replace with a focus on the breath and non-intrusive mental content, such as counting or syllables that bring you back to the present moment.

How to get started?

Pick your favorite walk. If you don't have one, open up Google Maps or just get outside and start walking. Parks are great because you can walk in a circle, uninterrupted by traffic stops as you practice. Because they are based on simple numerical systems, the breathing patterns I've shared are not difficult to memorize. But if you're concerned about forgetting them, there's no shame in bringing your copy of this book or jotting them down on paper (you'll learn how to memorize instructions with numbers in them later). Once outside, take your first step and inhale.

These walking and breathing processes can make you feel quite heady, so please check with a medical professional before diving in and using any of them. When you have memorized some of the texts suggested by Gary Weber (as I've been doing and will share with you later), you can mentally recite these self-inquiry passages while managing your breath in these suggested ways. Although you are deliberately creating a self-interfering system by asking your mind to juggle multiple levels of mental and physical behavior, it is *precisely* attempting the challenge that creates so many benefits for both your body and mind. You will simultaneously exercise for physical fitness, focus, concentration, better memory and mental peace all while enjoying a stroll through your neighborhood or local park.

Remember, these practices offer themselves to many scenarios, not just walking or sitting meditation. You can practice them while listening to others and not have them create a distraction. In fact, quite the opposite will occur. You'll feel more focused and connected to the content that is coming into your consciousness thanks to the clarity created by consistent attention to your breath and the content of your mind.

Rituals for overcoming resistance: Taking cold showers in winter... in Berlin

I was intrigued but also cautious when I began Wim Hof's course based around breathing techniques and cold therapy. I'd been dousing myself with buckets of freezing cold water for years based on the lessons of Systema, so I was anything but a cold-water virgin when I went into the techniques of this charismatic Dutchman who had suddenly burst onto the scene with the eponymous "Wim Hof Method." However, Wim Hof offers a significantly different take on what to do with one's breathing before, during and after taking cold showers. That's why, in October 2015, as Berlin descended into an especially chilly winter, I started on a new level of adventure.

Hof, who is often referred to as the "Iceman," has found fame for regularly exposing himself to extreme cold in both natural and scientific laboratories. He attributes his ability to withstand the cold not only to cold exposure as a practice, but also to how he uses his breath. He performs athletic feats of yoga by standing on his hands on snow-draped rocks high up in the mountains while simultaneously talking about how his breathing techniques can help you beat everything from arthritis to grief and depression.

Obviously, I was intrigued.

The core of the Wim Hof Method involves controlling the breath in three ways:

1. First, you engage in 30 cycles of rigorous inhalation that completely fills the lungs with a much less active process of exhalation. There isn't a focus on emptying your lungs. Instead, you fill yourself up with as much oxygen as possible.

2. Following 30 inhalations, you inhale with one last massive effort and then release this breath as completely as possible. Then, with emptied lungs, you don't breathe for as long as possible.

3. When you can last no longer, you inhale as completely as possible and hold your breath *in* for as long as you can before letting it go. Repeat the process as desired.

Theoretically, if you complete this breathing exercise before hopping into a cold shower, freezing lake or tub filled with ice, you'll automatically cope with the cold better and benefit more from the exposure. One can spend hours reading all kinds of scientific articles explaining why this is the case, or listen to Hof explain it on podcasts. He is open about not understanding all of the scientific terminology himself, but many of his fans share and discuss the scientific data that directly relate to his project, or independently verify it.

Whether or not the evidence validates or discredits the claims people make about the Wim Hof Method, the benefit in my mind has little to do with activating the vagus nerve or "cleansing the system," as Vasiliev discusses in *The Russian System Guidebook*. In my experience, the breathing and cold exposure create a means for acquiring discipline and consistency when it comes to getting started with difficult tasks. No matter how routine certain activities become in our lives, the mind always seems to resist. Getting up early, drafting book chapters, exercising, going to work... We throw up barriers between ourselves and the things most likely to get us the results want.

These resistances are paradoxical. You'd think the things we do repeatedly would get easier with time. Yet, for some reason, the level of difficulty in getting started always seems to be about the same. No matter how many books and blog posts I write, for example, getting started poses the same old challenges. It's like being the Tin Man in *The Wizard of Oz* mashed up with *Groundhog Day*. No matter how well Dorothy oiled up your hinges the day before, somehow you wake up just as frozen the next day. Getting started remains *getting started*.

The good news is that a more effective oil for the gears of getting started (again and again) is available in abundance. When you consistently practice rituals that place your body and mind in a state that helps you overcome the default settings of the mind related to work, daily tasks do seem to get easier. This happens in my experience because getting into the cold shower is *always* more difficult than anything else I have on my plate. Once I've tackled what is literally the iciest task of them all, the proverbial ice is broken and the procedures I use to tackle other challenges flow. It all comes down to something rare and special: mental toughness. It seems that the mind power needed to goad a naked body into ice-cold water is a transferable skill that directly helps making clothed bodies get other things—from meditating to language learning—done.

And not just done, but done consistently and quickly, because it becomes ritualistic and biologically mechanical. Through breathing and submitting to the cold, you're rigging your brain to *perceive* the tasks at hand from a completely different neurochemical standpoint.

As an additional step, Hof suggests using his breath withholding patterns while in the shower. Obviously, doing so comes at some risk, so I have only done this when I am in showers with a solid handrail and while someone is home with me and aware of the practice. In my view, it is not wise to practice any kind of breath withholding whatsoever in a tub or a lake and certainly not without an observer trained in effective resuscitation. Do not take risks, especially if you want a brain capable of remembering information.

I mention these caveats because some people like to take these techniques into risky territory. The same Wim Hof enthusiasts who share and discuss the scientific articles are sometimes the ones who take these practices too far. *Carpe diem*, but always *caveat emptor*.

The "pain" of our labors is an illusion created in the mind

Some of the posts about cold exposure in Wim Hof's Facebook group are quite over-the-top. I wasn't interested in entering the wilderness in search of extreme cold, like some of its members. For me, wintry showers were enough. I found the cold not only caused what I assume were changes to my brain, but also provided a metaphor and a psychological frame.

The value of the frame is self-evident when you think the home cold shower process through. The actual temperatures many of those using Wim Hof's teaching to self-administer cold exposure therapy are probably not nearly as cold as we think. Although I never measured the temperature of the water in my shower, I doubt it was lower than 15 degrees Celsius (59 Fahrenheit) even on the coldest day in Berlin. But it sure *felt* cold! The mind helps, and if you explore how its tricks are done, you can fight back without fighting.

For example, more exposure to cold showers has *never* made getting into them a shred easier. But therein I have found the mindset benefits. The more aware I became of how my mind created more cold than my shower could produce, the more I came to appreciate so many of life's seemingly intolerable metaphorical temperatures. Isn't it nice to know that a daily reminder of how your mind creates illusions is waiting for you in your washroom? It is, and just wait until you start using that same room as a Memory Palace to deploy the tools of self-inquiry covered later in this book.

Exercises: An infinite array of breathing patterns

When you put these breathing practices to work for yourself, either in a park or seated on the floor before submitting to a cold spray of water, you'll discover countless ways to inhale, exhale and withhold your breath. You can also mix and match the patterns with various memory exercises. I do, and the effect is powerful.

One pleasant breathing pattern involves inhaling to a count of 5, holding your breath for a count of 7 and exhaling to a count of 8. Why these numbers? I'm not entirely sure, but I came across them, enjoyed the process and used the pattern for months before moving on to another pattern. You can also combine breath withholding with Kirtan Kriya or other mantra meditation, which I'll describe in Part III. Variety appears to be necessary for humans, so whenever you feel bored, change the numbers to recalibrate your focus and keep the exercises fresh. Remember to keep seeking the sweet spot on the Challenge-Frustration Curve.

Ultimately, my feeling is that long-form chanting of texts like the *Ribhu Gita*, which I'll walk you through later in this book, create a "close enough" effect to the breathing patterns and breath withholding. You've probably heard of the well-documented phenomenon of runner's high; well, "singer's high" is not far behind. This is according to the research of Gunter Kreutz, a German professor of *Systematische Musikwissenschaften* (the systematic science of music). Kreutz found singing increases the presence of helpful chemicals while reducing the damage of bad ones in the body. Singing can also help with verbal memory, particularly in young students. I mention Kreutz's research (which includes many co-authors and parallel studies) to underscore what I hope to make clear in this book: better memory, focus and concentration that leads to a more positive and enjoyable mental state *combines* a number of physical and mental activities, learned by assembling them through practice. Although we know that the brain is physical and thoughts can cause structural changes, it is also known that including the diaphragm and lungs in a variety of ways maximizes the outcomes of these practices.

You can readily squeeze a variety of breathing and mental meditation practices into the first 10–15 minutes of your day. Do them with consistency and a long-game mindset. There might be no such thing as a perpetual motion machine, but putting all of these experiments to work in the laboratory of your life in a consistent manner might just be the next best thing.

4 YOU THINK WHAT YOU EAT

IN THIS CHAPTER, WE'LL explore another, more comprehensive form of biohacking than controlled breathing or cold-water exposure. Have you considered how much your diet—the foods and drinks you bring into your body several times a day—affects your mental state? Two experiences taught me just how much a proper diet contributes to memory and peace of mind, and caused me to reflect on the role of food in my mental life more generally. The first was a year-long false alarm with gout. The second was the day in Cairo when a camel nearly broke my back.

We'll get to those stories soon, but to understand what the stories really mean we first must answer the question: how specifically does diet relate to memory? For one thing, if pain stands between you and *paying attention*, focusing on the information you want to memorize can be uphill battle. As it turns out, food causes so much of our pain. This fact means there are many, readily available solutions. Of course, the exact solutions depend entirely on your current diet and your chemical makeup. If you suffer from brain fog, short attention span or inexplicable physical pain that disrupts your focus, your eating habits are one of the first places to search for clues. If you're anything like I was, completing an elimination diet might be what sets you free from suffering faster than developing a meditation and memory practice. Throw in a rotation-diet lifestyle for good measure and your entire relationship to food will be optimized for mental clarity.

Please note that you really do need to start with yourself. This is important because you cannot model the dietary approaches I'm about to share with you in any exact way. The benefits will come from understanding the strategy behind my decisions and then testing the effects of different foods on your own body by progressively removing and adding them. As you'll learn, I sought guidance, and I recommend you do the same. Hopefully, you will choose to take action before pain and suffering rubs your nose in the raw reality of physical misery. Unfortunately, self-imposed misery through poor diet is exactly what I have been through. Much of the concentration, memory and depression issues stem from features of my dietary upbringing long before my own poor choices of adulthood. It all came to a head in April 2013, during a break from touring with my band, The Outside, when my ankle exploded with crippling pain.

Food had been an issue for most of my life. To help you understand why, I'll describe a bit of my childhood. My earliest memories of eating as a miserable activity involve food served by Mrs. Lang, my childhood babysitter. Mrs. Lang was an overweight armchair evangelist. Her husband, Henry, was similar, but less enthusiastic about the endless hours of Bernice Gerrard and *100 Huntley Street* playing every morning on their television. While endless hymns and testimonies rolled out of the screen, my brother and I would try to sleep on their couch after our mother dropped us off on her way to work at Royal Inland Hospital. Depending on my mother's shift, we'd arrive at the Langs' at 5 a.m. or 5 p.m.: just in time for a miserable breakfast or unpalatable dinner.

Not *every* aspect of their dinners was awful. They sometimes included peaches, pears or cherries from their own trees, but it was breakfast I dreaded most. The Langs bought dozens of loaves of the cheapest bread possible and froze them. Slices from these icy bricks went straight into a horizontal toaster and came out soggy. Butter came from similarly aged and poorly frozen loaves. After cramming freezer-burned toast into my reluctant mouth, stomach pain from the melange of soggy bread and sour butter haunted me throughout the school day. Lunch was even more diabolical when all I had to eat were peanut butter sandwiches made using the same bread-like substance. Peanut butter came in tins back then, and you could taste metal in every bite.

Then there were the lunches from home during the trailer park years. Memory is unreliable, but I don't think I'm exaggerating when I recall having nothing more than an apple to go with whole wheat crackers and slimy slices of bulk cheese. More often than not, the cheese came from poorly refrigerated blocks purchased in bulk from Costco. I remember carving off patches of white-green fungus that had grown on it through long storage. I'm sure spores from those lunches live in my gut to this day.

Needless to say, I coveted the expertly wrapped lunches of my friends almost as much as I did their apparently stable family lives. I remember receiving donations of fruit wraps, sometimes half a sandwich. I traded Wayne Gretzky hockey cards for juice boxes. Many of the items I bartered weren't ideal for the health of a growing youngster, but fruit wraps and cookies felt better than starving after tossing the putrid food I'd been given into the large yellow dumpster by the school's bike racks.

Other times, I used my best persuasion skills to elicit invitations to eat lunch at the homes of friends who lived close enough to the school to walk there and back within the hour. Sometimes I would wait in the garage and accept an apple or orange stolen from the family fruit bowl when I had tapped out the welcome of someone's parents. (Many of these homes have become Memory Palaces I still employ for learning projects.) Others suffered home lives just as difficult as mine, if not more so. These friends were as embarrassed by the glimpses of madness I saw in their lives, as I was every time they witnessed the loose threads of mine.

The chaos at home led to destructive behaviors at school, or so I assumed until I began to understand the role of diet in the workings of the mind. In retrospect, I'm confident most of my behavioural issues in school stemmed from these misadventures with food. I could never sit still or think clearly during class, that is, unless I was doing my own thing—drawing stickmen battles or reading Roald Dahl or Hardy Boys novels tucked inside my textbooks. I fearlessly instigated fights, sang during class for no reason and even swore at teachers. At one point, I was sent to the hospital for my behaviour because they didn't know what else to do with me.

Placing me in a room on the pediatric floor with someone my age who was practically dying from pneumonia seemed to be the best answer my teachers, parents and social workers could conceive. Ignoring the school work I'd taken with me, I watched Eddie Murphy's *Raw* on the hospital television and a 1980s VCR the size of a small fridge. The other boy and I memorized Murphy's crude routines for endless, self-amusing hours of recitation later. I recall pretending to be Murphy while a nurse pounded this poor kid's back to help him empty his lungs. Murphy's expletives and off-color scenarios seemed to lighten the mood as his hacking kept death at bay.

Since my mom worked in the hospital, she visited me during her lunch hours, crackers and cheese in hand. This rancid food had suddenly become appealing in my new world of even grosser hospital food. Beyond amateur comedy and hanging out with mom, I filled the emptiness of my incarceration with roaming the hospital corridors. I listened to music on a Walkman loaned to me by a friend as I paced. It came loaded with one Iron Maiden cassette, the lyrics of which I committed to memory; oddly enough, this would be the origin of what would become a deep love of poetry. Or maybe it wasn't odd at all—the final song on "Powerslave" is a 13:45-minutes-long adaptation of Coleridge's "Rime of the Ancient Mariner" and the mood of singer Bruce Dickinson's interpretation described my situation all too well:

Day after day, day after day
We stuck nor breath nor motion
As idle as a painted ship upon a painted ocean
Water, water everywhere and
All the boards did shrink
Water, water everywhere nor any drop to drink.

There may have been an abundance of water for me in the hospital, but the nurses and the candy stripers in their infinite wisdom gave me Canada Dry Ginger Ale every time I asked.

When I finally returned to school, it was not to the normal stream but a special class for other bad actors. Social misfits before being corralled into the "special needs" category, we became even weirder when they taught us to type and program using BASIC (Beginner's All-purpose Symbolic Instruction Code). My writing career budded in this room. Left mostly to my own devices, I wrote bizarre stories and saved them to enormous floppy disks. One of my tales won a short story contest, the award for which included meeting a famous Canadian author at Caribou College (now Thompson Rivers University) in Kamloops and then having lunch at a nearby McDonald's.

I ran on fumes most of the time. The only reprieve during elementary school was that toxic fast-food prize I won and Hot Dog Day. A few times each year from first through seventh grade, we took order forms for hot dogs and chocolate milk home and begged our parents for the needed funds. I did everything in my power to get at least three of them in my belly each time. I used to dream about when the next Hot Dog Day would come around.

By the time I was in grade 7, my father's alcoholism had plummeted to one of its most destructive lows while my mother's addiction to religion made her evermore hectoring and obstinate. Caught between them were my brother and me: two young children in a house of strife. I remember shuttling between wild drunken parties, deranged religious babysitters and foster care homes. Much of my childhood aside from this is lost to blocked memories. I do know at least one exorcism was performed on me by the pastor of my mom's church. My refusal to agree that the Beastie Boy's album *Licensed to Ill* really meant "License to Kill" and allow them to destroy my precious escape-music on the basis of such an obvious and ignorant misinterpretation was itself interpreted as demonic possession. My struggle in the lap of the pastor and attempts to convince him of the hip grammar of 1986 as he screamed at evil spirits was like being Winston Smith during the miserable duress of Room 101 before O'Brien breaks him into admitting that $2+2=5$ to appease Big Brother. When they couldn't break me, they sent me away.

Plunked into a foster home, I struggled to tolerate yet crueller ways of being, stripped of escapist fantasy to make space for spectacular flights of faith. The wicked mother confiscated my Piers Anthony books because they featured demons on their covers. I cried over the loss at their dinner table, while secretly relieved by the presence of a solid meal before me. But having a fully rounded lunch bag for the following school day did not stop me from attempting to flee or punch the kid beside me when forced to attend their hysteria-driven church, which was even more poisonous than my mother's.

To say that my early education was irreparably damaged by these trials would be false. Battling the beliefs of people who could strive to know better undoubtedly helped me achieve the academic rank of professor in later years. Paradoxically, my parents are both amazing people despite the personal and parenting flaws. They brought chaos upon themselves and their children because they came from it. I've come to see more blessings than curses in the turmoil, even if I have suffered many repercussions in adult life. It is well established that children of alcoholics often grow up to experience chronic pain and mental illness. Less well known are the detrimental effects of destructively religious upbringings, as discussed by people like Darrel Ray in books like *The God Virus: How Religion Infects Our Lives and Culture*. But I find myself strangely grateful for the deranged experiences of watching people speaking in tongues and slain by the sword too. As intellectually intolerable as church was, something halfway nourishing often came along for the weekly ride through lunacy during post-congregation potluck.

This was my domestic background when, as a 12-year-old, I had the chance to study at the Summer School of Music and take a course with Canadian brass trombone legend Rob McLeod. I'd recently landed back at my dad's place after a stint in a foster home. I loathed his new girlfriend. Worse than her constant sniffing from allergies was the scented cloud around her from the constant aromatherapy or ointment applications. I often left the house without eating breakfast just to avoid *smelling* her, let alone seeing her. To eat even the tastiest Cheerios or Shreddies with those scents in the air was to invite unpleasant sensations in the palate. One day, I was so famished I could barely hold my trombone. I broke into tears when Rob asked me if I'd eaten anything. During the break he took me to the school canteen and ordered me whatever I wanted.

Guess what I ordered? Hot dogs and a can of coke. They didn't have chocolate milk, but I knew from other malnourishment experiences just what a dose of sugar like that can do. I remember feeling like I'd been rocketed straight up to heaven when these substances entered my system. Perhaps the bliss is still with me, waging a Holy War from up in my brain against the cheese spore monsters still at play in my gut.

There were many other scenes of dietary trouble. All through high school I would collapse regularly on the couch with searing gut pain. Later, an appendix removal operation led to speculations about Crohn's disease that I had to ignore after their nightmare explorations convinced me that a lifetime of suffering was better than *ever* submitting to a colonoscopy again. I suffered throughout university, and no wonder: as soon as I was able to feed myself, I didn't have the remotest clue about nutrition, let alone a sense of rhythm. For a few years, I lived largely on pizza, ice cream and Guinness.

In other words, the food difficulties that came crashing down on my ankle in 2013 all have a long history. The ankle incident occurred when the fairly successful heavy metal band I was in, The Outside, was taking a mid-tour break. I was back in Berlin, working at my desk one afternoon. I had just happily closed my laptop and was leaving the room. I had recently memorized the lyrics to Marlene Dietrich's song "Wenn Ich Mir Was Wünschen Dürfte" and was singing them with abandon. But I'd hardly got through the first line when I felt a crack in my right ankle. It felt like I'd broken it. I must have gone into shock. Instead of going to the hospital, I had the brilliant idea of taking the S-Bahn (Berlin's suburban passenger rail system) to the home of Sarah, my new girlfriend, for yet another delightful evening in the chemical bath of a brain in love. I'd met Sarah at her birthday party at the famous Jägerklause beer garden. A nurse with an infectiously mysterious smile forever tipped in the direction of irony, she was surprised that I wanted her number when we found ourselves camped together the next morning in my apartment. She was perhaps more surprised that we wound up spending hardly more than a few days apart for the next several years.

Once at her apartment with my "cracked" ankle, I talked with her and decided to go to the doctor the next day. Yet, all during the night, I crawled back and forth to the washroom and, by 3 a.m., I was in severe distress and burning with fever. Sarah called for the "Hausartzt." The doctor came to her apartment and pronounced me ill with gout. He lectured me on my drinking and eating habits, stuck me with a syringe filled with cortisol, and then left. The next morning Sarah secured a pair of crutches for me and I would use these off and on for the next two months. At one point, I even pushed myself around in a wheelchair. It's not as fun as it looks.

After hearing my story and seeing some blood test results, my own doctor agreed with the house-call doctor's lecture. I was referred to a rheumatoid specialist to confirm it was gout. Before I left his office, he gave me a prescription for allopurinol to lower the extremely high levels of uric acid in my blood. I made an appointment with the rheumatoid specialist and immediately reduced my drinking (though not my habit of washing pills down with beer when I did drink) and started making changes to my diet. As for The Outside, I managed to finish the tour and play a few more local shows.

Curiously, I kept experiencing shocks in my hands when I carried equipment. The pain was so bad on the final show, that I vomited into my mouth on the stage. A younger version of myself would have thought that it was "so punk rock!" to end my musical career like that, but in addition to leaving the stage ashamed, for the first time ever, I did not give my habitual post-show card magic performance. The pain was stealing yet another of my many passions, and although music can be forgiving in the ears of a headbanging room full of drunks, sleight-of-hand audiences watch you like a hawk. My days of performing anything fun or interesting for anyone seemed over.

By now, I was spending half my time on the crutches or using a medical cane. Having done intense research into gout, I was eating the best possible diet I could. For many people, these foods would have helped, but in my case, the pain kept getting worse and worse. Plus, I was packing on weight, which is totally absurd when you're rarely eating anything other than Mediterranean salads and vegetarian chili. But Sarah and I did a lot of traveling and couldn't seem to stop drinking ourselves into epic stupors that led to deep domestic unrest. Inebriated, I would skip the recommended food choices for days and nothing got better.

In Málaga, Spain, I discovered a cane in an antique shop that looked far more interesting than the medical one I'd been using. It was black with a silver tip. Walking around the shop with this dashing accoutrement in my hand made me feel like Salvador Dalí. It didn't entirely suit my heavy-metal-cum-stoner-rock vibe at the time, but it wasn't out of place either. I put it back in the rack. As I told Sarah, upgrading my "handicap jewelry" would be like marrying the disease for life. I wanted to live! Instead, I focused on a better mental image of health and kept the cheap medical cane. I knew I would return it to the pharmacy the instant the pain went away.

My dietary compliance started to improve, even if the foods were, unbeknownst to me, far from right. I also finally cut out drinking altogether after a drunken row with Sarah. Her drinking did not stop. Although she tried following my lead, it was not in her to do so at the time. This lifestyle imbalance between us led to more conflict. I emailed my friend Haydee Windey (whom you'll hear about later), seeking commiseration, sympathy or wisdom, and she replied by asking a question: "Why do you keep trying to symbolically heal your father's alcoholism?"

This question cut through the misery of my love life so thoroughly that only my poor health and the absence of free will can explain why my brain could not get me out of the situation the very next day.

When I finally saw the rheumatoid specialist, he said he could find no evidence of gout. I went back to my doctor's office. In this consultation, he noticed the redness in my cheeks. A few questions later and he delivered his strong suspicion that what I really had was psoriatic arthritis. Great. Another disease. Even better, the hallmarks of this hard-to-spell condition are nasty oozing skin and, often, gradual deformities to the hands and feet. But I'm grateful he mentioned it because this time, we found a clue that would lead to impactful change. I just had to make a detour that nearly broke the camel's back first.

The great Cairo fiasco

The collision of my new dietary issues with Sarah's disinterest in giving up booze led us to part ways. It was a relief to finally act on the truth Haydee's question had revealed to me, a truth that had been staring me in the face since she asked me that question. But I had a hard time believing I could actually go on without alcohol, especially since it played such a prominent role in my social life, love life and self-medication program.

With Olly at the British Council in Cairo

At this time, a contact I met and corresponded with often, Olly Richards, let me know in certain terms that if I wanted a comfortable place to stay in Cairo, the time was nigh. He was leaving his job with the British Council to focus 100-percent on his online language learning business, *iwillteachyoualanguage.com*.

My first impression of modern Cairo was of a labyrinth—raised motorways, insane traffic and ancient backstreets and, over it all, howling prayers and baking dusty sunlight. In this setting, Olly introduced me to a driver named Hanni. I soon hired him to take me all over the city. First stop, bed, so I could sleep off the travel fatigue.

That night, terror struck. I awoke to the sound of an explosion. With no context for what it might be—perhaps a backfire, fireworks or an industrial mishap—I put myself back to sleep with a round of Savasana yoga. I should have taken the explosion as a sign of the trouble to come. The next morning, we found out the nearby Italian Embassy had been bombed. The British Consulate warned everyone not to leave Cairo. On that cheery note, Olly left me in the hands of Hanni.

Hanni waiting for coffee and koshary

Visiting the pyramids is an obvious must when in Cairo. Hanni told me he could arrange a special camel ride. But first he introduced me to *koshary*, the rice-lentil-pasta dish at his favorite restaurant. Later, we landed in a strange perfume shop where the business of a camel-back pyramid tour could be arranged. After paying a price that marked my gullibility and general lack of concern for fairness while travelling, I climbed on the back of an ill-tempered camel. It hefted me seven feet off the ground and, swaying with the animal's undulating strides, I entered the ghetto of corridors that leads visitors into the desert. For some reason, access to the Sphinx was closed, so I saw it only for a few seconds through a portal to the right. One of my guides rode a horse while the other tugged on the camel's rope.

Too stunned by the mass of humanity crammed into the pathways to even try and make Memory Palaces from the journey, I settled in to studying the paranoia preventing me from enjoying the ride. The entire time, I was wondering when we would be entering the a portal like the one I had seen when we passed by the Sphinx. We seemed to be getting deeper into the kind of poverty-stricken area where naïve tourists like me wind up getting stabbed to death in cul-de-sacs. Then, after a few more twists and turns, the desert opened before us. To my right, a long wire fence separated the dunes from the flat field where the pyramids stood in the distance. We passed countless other tourists on camels with their guides. All was well... until we started making our way back.

The guide with sufficient enough English to speak with me had started calling me "Canada Dry": "You want to take the horse back, Canada Dry?"

Everything in my gut told me to say yes. Yet, something else in me reasoned that I would probably never ride a camel in Egypt again, so I hopped back up in the ornery beast's saddle. I was hardly one minute back on his humps when I heard, "You want to go fast, Canada Dry?" In slow motion my eyes went wide and my head swivelled to yell a huge "No!" It was too late. The guide's whip had come down hard on the camel's rump. It violently bucked and I fell *hard* on my hip on the ground. Lying in the dust, I had to verbally fight the guides not to try to move me. I was sure I'd broken my back and thanked my lucky stars when I saw the massive stone next to my head. I'd landed hard, I recognized, but it could have been a lot harder.

When I finally felt ready to stand, I still had to fend off the guide who was trying to get behind me and crack my spine back into place. It was my hip more than anything that had been harmed, but I did not want to be moved with any help outside my own agency. Strangely, the shock to my system created a vast inner stillness of gratitude as I finally started hobbling back in the direction of the ghetto. I was limping badly but knew I would survive. The sun was descending rapidly, so I decided to get on the horse, and we rode back as slowly as I had strength to insist on. Most of my verbal resources went into demanding that the guides not beat or starve the camel against a tirade of threats. When they finally got me back to the perfume shop, I told them sternly that it was the guide's fault, not the camel's and (strangely enough) gave in to their requests for a tip.

After Hanni apologized profusely about the guides he'd arranged for me and got me back to Olly's, I settled in for a two-week eternity of lying on my back to heal. There would be no healing though. The shock to my system sent the psoriatic arthritis into overdrive. This is the part of the story where only the phrase "hit rock bottom" is apt.

I'll spare you the gory details and just say that the psoriasis skin wounds that opened on my back led to my throwing away most of my clothes and Olly's bedding before I left for the airport and headed back to Berlin. Olly took me to a pharmacy for an ointment that helped somewhat. This wasn't saying much, as this felt like the worst physical situation my body had ever suffered. Although I did manage to get out and see more of Cairo—and even Memphis—at great risk and despite strict orders not to leave the city (a thrilling tale for another time), I spent most of my remaining Cairo days researching my condition and making my course *How to*

Learn and Memorize Hiragana and Katakana in 1.5 Hours or Less, a challenge Olly and I came up with to help occupy my mind. I got it done, but as often happens, a new pathway soon revealed itself.

Eating in mind

Lying on my back in Cairo, I continued researching health options online. At the time, I belonged to a business mastermind group called Next Level Marketing run by a fellow memory improvement trainer named Ryan Levesque. One member, Cliff Wilde, a health coach, posted a compelling dietary note in our online discussion group. Thanks to timing, I just happened to see it in the waterfall of ideas that constantly poured into the forum threads. One thing led to another and I found myself on a call with Cliff. A charismatic British fellow with some obvious experience, Cliff explained the brain-gut connection and I rapidly committed new terms like "autoimmune protocol" and "elimination diet" to memory. Although I was not sure I could take on some of the mindset recommendations he suggested in addition to the practical mechanics we would apply to my diet, I took everything under consideration and said I'd get back to him about his offer to walk me through a six-month program with his wife and partner Marta. Although Cliff used a lot of medical and scientific terms, I was able to capture enough to perform some follow-up research. Everything soon snapped into place with the idea of n=1, another term I would soon pick up from a "super-learner" named Jonathan Levi in Tel Aviv.

Jonathan and I shot a course together called *Branding You*, dedicated to helping people like ourselves write books, create video courses and broadcast our messages around the world by creating multi-media "ecosystems." We'd met after I found his Super Learner course and invited him on the Magnetic Memory Method Podcast. At the time, he'd yet to publish a book or start a podcast, so I shared some of my battle stories from making these complex matters work on the Internet. Assuming my memory is correct, about six months passed before I heard from him again. He'd basically followed the formula I'd shared (and assembled with by learning from others before me) and came back with a hit podcast and book of his own. I'm not sure who proposed it first, but we both knew we had to help others follow in our footsteps, and thus, *Branding You* was born and soon my inflamed, boozing body and moody brain found itself shuttling across the world again in yet another plane.

When Jonathan saw me limping and suffering from visible reactions after eating the otherwise *amazing* food in Tel Aviv, he "sped read" through articles online hunting for solutions. It was not ideal for shooting our video course that my skin would sometimes turn red and veins start popping out of my hands like a scene out of *The Exorcist*, but Jonathan's research concerns were for the long haul. I told him about Cliff's ideas and offer, and Jonathan used his speed demon research skills using a vast library of keyboard shortcuts he'd memorized as fast as I could mention "leaky gut" or "rotation diet."

To this day, almost every time we meet, online or in person, Jonathan and I mastermind on some aspect of health and it's a blessing every time. We've hit the gym in Tel Aviv and Berlin, helped each other steer clear of bread in restaurants and even vowed to abolish alcohol from our lives together. To my knowledge, he's stuck with it and I only fell off the horse once, showing up to a memory competition jet lagged, hung over and burning with pain in every joint. I memorized well enough to demonstrate that afternoon just how profoundly these techniques work even under the worst of physical conditions, but I wish I'd shown up in better shape all the same.

That hangover came from Thanksgiving celebrations in Vancouver during the Fall of 2015. With two bottles of wine in my system after months of sobriety, I bid my friends adieu at 5 a.m. and stumbled toward my Air Canada seat en route to Toronto. I was hoping to sleep but soon found myself in slurred conversation with the woman beside me. It was hardly a minute before she told me she was bipolar, to which I responded, "Me too!" We shared war stories for the next four hours and I didn't catch a wink.

In Toronto, excitement got the better of me. The memory competition was nagging me and I knew I needed to get some sleep. My joints were on fire and sobriety still felt a million miles away. "To hell with it," I reasoned, dragging one of my uncles out to watch a ball game in a Cuban bar with a friend somewhere on Queen Street. It was 3 a.m. before I got my uncle home, and whatever sleep I received between 4 and 7 a.m. hardly deserves the name. Soon, I was traveling to the Ontario Science Centre. I had my drugs to stave off any mood swings my poor sleep and drinking mishap might create, but the real reason I wasn't overly worried is because I had no intention to compete. I was just popping in to report on the event as a memory blogger and vlogger.

The Canadian Memory Tournament was hosted by Farrow Brain Games. Dave Farrow won a Guinness World Record for the most decks of playing cards memorized in a single sighting in 1996. He broke his own record in 2007 to reclaim it after someone else broke it in 2002. I introduced myself to Dave when I arrived and felt he was a bit suspicious of me. Hoping any hint of alcohol had dissipated, I told him straight that I was just super enthusiastic about the techniques and wanted to observe. He said I should compete, and after he repeated the suggestion a while later, I said I'd only be willing to throw down the gloves if the prize money went to charity. He agreed, and said if I won, he'd double it. If he won, the prize would go to his charity.

Dave and I discussed the details of the competition shortly thereafter on my podcast, but what I remember most was nearly blowing the first card. If memory serves, it was the 6 of Clubs, but I almost said Queen of Clubs, which was a few cards down. It might have been the other way or around. For this particular competition, we both memorized the same assortment of cards from a sheet of paper. We had two minutes to memorize as many as we could, and then two minutes for recall, collecting points for each correct card we named. We took turns, which meant that you must mentally verify that your opponent's cards are correct before naming yours. It was nerve wracking, not only because I felt like hell, but people were watching, many with cameras, and a digital clock was spinning down with rapid intensity.

Dave has an infectious smile and grinned at me before naming his card after mine. "I thought you might have already lost there," he said. "Close," I said with a nervous laugh, "but no cigar." The next time I hesitated, Dave was ready to pounce. "Can I steal your point?" "I haven't gotten it wrong yet," I countered. He leaned back and smiled again, and we continued, with me matching him card for card until I ran out. True to his Guinness Record, Dave memorized twice as many cards as I had, but I was proud of myself. Despite two hesitations and one near miscall, I had been 100-percent accurate and memorized half as much, all without having practiced cards for months and feeling like I'd swallowed five miles of barbed wire.

I wasn't prepared for what happened next. I'd felt that Dave had been suspicious of my presence when I first arrived, but now he seemed open. I'd proved myself as someone who really knew the techniques. We sat and I shared my process and why I thought I'd been a bit slow and almost blown the first card. He discussed how he encodes up to six cards at a time. It was such an honor not only that gave me this insight, but that he stopped with *what* he does without explaining *how*. This gift sparked my imagination and I've explored and used a similar practice ever since. I now encode typically three cards at a time, still half as much as Dave, though sometimes I'll go as high as five.

This one return to the bottle and nearly disastrous cameo at a memory competition aside, I got myself back to Germany in one piece and confessed my "sins" to the world via the Magnetic Memory Method Podcast. If Jonathan disapproved of my lapse, he didn't show it and our health and business masterminding carried on. Jonathan's steady devotion to optimizing health, down to the granular details shared in his course, "Become a SuperHuman: Naturally & Safely Boost Testosterone" continued to inspire me. I was skeptical of Cliff's claims, but Jonathan had rapidly produced and analyzed research studies that substantiated the process and suggested I think about the project as a case study where the number of subjects in the experiment was one (i.e., n=1). During breaks between polishing our video scripts, Jonathan helped me analyze everything from kombucha to fecal implants, the latter option finally convincing me to follow Cliff's plan before seeking a healthy donor to put anything *into* my gut when all I wanted was to get the monsters *out*.

It was good to have Jonathan's help fact-checking this brave new world of bio-hacking as we worked toward getting my body back in shape. After Cliff described how he would analyze my fluids, I pointed out that we had better start after I got back from London. In addition to shooting *Branding You* with Jonathan, I was booked for video delivery training sessions in the U.K. so I could improve my camera presence. Despite my condition, I was determined not to miss any of them.

"If you want to get this problem sorted," Cliff said, "it doesn't matter where in the world you are. You just get us the samples and we'll get them into the labs."

After laying out approximately 10 grand for Cliff's guidance out of my misery, so it went. Back in Berlin, assisted by a friend visiting from Vancouver, I found a private lab that could draw my blood. Throughout my friend's visit, he watched as my condition grew worse. Often within minutes of eating at a restaurant, my cheeks would develop sores and the pain in my joints put me squarely back into the seat of a taxi and on my way home.

Later, in London, I delivered yet more fluids with instructions for sending them by courier to Poland, followed by more blood going to Arizona. True to Cliff's word, I received supplements at my hotels in both London and Manchester. As hokey as it sounded to me then and still sounds now, the supplements had an *immediately* noticeable effect. Of course, the drastic improvements made me think about the placebo effect, but as recent researchers like Ted Kaptchuk have suggested, I could also have a lot of COMT in me.

What's COMT? It's an enzyme that Kaptchuk thinks might explain why some people respond better to healers and medications than others. His work also "suggests that placebo and drugs do not involve separate processes, one psychological and the other physical, that add up to the overall effectiveness of the treatment; rather, they may both operate on the same biochemical pathway—the one governed in part by the COMT gene."

Either way, after a few days of supplements and small dietary changes, I felt on top of the world. My energy had shot through the roof and I told Cliff I was concerned because I suddenly felt aggressive. He speculated that my body probably had not been receiving the amount of nutrients I was now giving it for a very long time. By changing the acid levels in my stomach and clearing out some creatures tests had revealed in my gut, I was suddenly being fed after a long period of starvation (so to speak).

Cliff's program also included some reading, largely for shifting my mindset. I suffered through what I felt were clearly bogus books but did begin the habit of meditating on my gratitude after eating. This practice wasn't spelled out in any of the books in particular, but it emerged from my existing gratitude and meditation practices and was based on the general perception that my thoughts about food somehow contributed to their physical integration into the body. I still feel this practice works at some level, and even if it's self-delusion, I find it worthwhile to feel grateful for the nourishment my body receives. Nonetheless, all the gratitude in the world does not negate the effects of foods that don't gel with my system.

After Cliff received and analyzed the full results of my fluids, I received a new meal plan. I started it as quickly as possible and saw even greater results. Although the suggested elimination diet will likely seem extreme to many people, when you experience the levels of suffering I was in, it's all just crazy enough to make sense. Since I've always had an "in for a penny, in for a pound" personality, I dove straight in.

The report I received and the plan I worked from came in the form of a LEAP ImmunoCalm report (LEAP stands for Lifestyle Eating And Performance). I still have the documents and carry the card I received with its summary in my wallet. The foods in red were thought to be very bad and the foods in yellow to be treated with caution. Except on rare occasions and usually by accident when it happens, I haven't eaten any of these foods since.

PATIENT:
ANTHONY METIVIER
PHYSICIAN:
C. Wilde
TEST PROFILE:
MRT Test ML150
TEST DATE:
09/23/2015

ALMOND	PAPRIKA
CANTALOUPE	SWT. POTATO
CATFISH	WATERMELON
GOAT'S MILK	
ASPARAGUS	OLIVE
AVOCADO	RASPBERRY
BANANA	S.M.B.SULFITE
CABBAGE	STRING BEAN
CASHEW	SUNFLOWER
CAULIFLOWER	TUNA
CLAM	TURMERIC
EGGPLANT	WALNUT
FD&C RED #3	POTATO
GR. PEPPER	ZUCCHINI
HOPS	

I've also been almost entirely pain free and enjoy much clearer skin on my face and scalp.

This card has been tremendously useful when travelling, and restaurant staff marvel at my "magic list" of forbidden ingredients before running it back to the chef. But the LEAP report is not meant to be a magic bullet. Rather, it helps you decide which foods are the most likely sources of your suffering, brain fog and other issues (which may include strange behaviors and thoughts that impede your progress with memory techniques). You receive the ImmunoCalm report first, then, using a rotation principle, you drill deeper by progressively removing and adding foods and keeping a food diary to help make sense of the data.

I persisted for six months with Cliff's help. Today, I still eat much the same diet I discovered through this process. My wife, April, helps manage it by creating meal plans that follow the principle and removing foods when my food journaling and other observations tell me something has to go. Most recently, we completely removed chicken because I kept feeling "apocalyptic" for about half an hour after eating it.

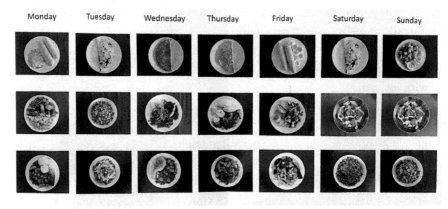

April helps me carefully test and retest meal plans like this. She's a chef and an artist!

"Apocalyptic" is a word I heard Jordan Peterson use in discussing the repercussions of his own diet. It's an apt term. Depending on the food, I will feel like yelling, physically lashing out or jumping off the balcony—perhaps even with my smartphone livestreaming the journey on YouTube. I've burned up hours of my life in suicidal ideation—for instance, thinking about the exact methods for contriving a noose from a backpack strap and a door handle, among many other gruesome endings.

In *Night Falls Fast: Understanding Suicide*, Kay Redfield Jameson suggests that a vast number of suicides occur on a whim. I cannot help but wonder if it's not so much a snap decision but rather a history of food-induced melancholia meeting a particularly "rajasic" food. I first encountered this word in Gary Weber's *Happiness Beyond Thought*, in which he discusses eating according to Ayurvedic principles. He recommends keeping a food journal and suggests that mental peace can be assisted by seeking out "sattvic" foods. Whereas *rajasic* foods are said to create a lot of energy at the expense of peace of mind, *sattvic* foods calm the mind. Then there are *tamasic* foods that leave you feeling dull and possibly moody.

Even though the eating life cannot be simplified so easily for all people, if you put some thought into these categories and test the side effects of what you eat accordingly, you will almost certainly be rewarded. This is the logic behind n=1 elimination diet and the rotation diet. "N=1" is one of those scientific terms transplanted from one science into another that essentially has come to mean: "There is only one test subject in this study: you." And that is the basis upon which I proceeded, and I think we all must proceed. Memory training and meditation are much the same.

Operating on this basis is important because the foods that caused *me* to suffer excruciating suicidal impulses despite generally appreciating my life might be peace-inducing for *you*. It doesn't matter what anyone else's list of "sattvic" foods says because the raw apples that have been one of the worst culprits for me could be completely fine for the vast majority of test subjects in all kinds of studies. The key is to practice these diets over the long term as the only subject in your own carefully designed and tracked dietary experiments in order to observe meaningful patterns. By proceeding carefully and keeping records, I was able to discover compromises; for instance, I found that sometimes preparation matters—it turns out that baked apples are fine for me.

After discovering the logic of n=1 and no longer allowing doctors to make recommendations based on where I generally fit in age and weight demographics based on millions of strangers, I made a bold leap. Having spent over 15 years on either lithium or Lamictal (with the odd dose of Ativan to take the edge off an apocalyptic fit that arrived without rhyme or reason), I decided to take the most fulfilling risk of my life. Knowing what I now knew, I slowly started eliminating Lamictal from my diet. As I insist you do, if you want to follow a similar path, I enlisted the help of my physician and informed my inner circle of the decision. In my case, I also let my YouTube and podcast audiences know and asked if they would keep an eye on me, in case I suddenly announced I was writing another epic poem or otherwise acting strangely. Not everyone has such an audience to whom they can appeal, but I was pleasantly surprised to receive ample support and gratitude for being brave enough to share my story.

It's possible that it's not bravery at all, but rather a combination of proper eating, sleep and meditation healing my brain to the point that, for the first time in my life, confidence is coming from being fully human. It's possible that my control freak ego was finally dissolving and assembling with the world.

Whereas I spent years relying on rock-solid memory techniques to lend me confidence, I now have these *plus* improved health for stability and courage. I've been free of all drugs for several years and work daily to maintain that status. As of writing this book, I feel like a completely revived personality, minus remnant childhood behavioral issues and food freakouts. When I listen to my old podcasts and videos, I hear a zombie slurring through a swamp of impoverished brain chemistry, straight-jacketed by pills. Now, I hear someone *alive*.

The freedom to feel fully alive comes at the cost of maintaining discipline over my diet. I even pay attention to the effects of mixing foods and, although my particularity might seem to be just another form of control-freakism to an outsider, we all know that most of what people eat today has no place in a human diet. People take greater care with the food they offer their pets. When I keep my carrots separated from the peas on the plate and eat them individually, it is not a sacrifice, but an act of surrender to "rules" I've discovered through practice. As my mentor Tony Buzan once told me over dinner in the UK, "the rules will set you free." It's just that most of the time, you've got to find them and then stick with them long enough to see which ones to value, noting that even then, not all rules will be needed forever.

Putting it all together in one diet

It should be no surprise that diet affects mental well-being. Here are some suggested steps you can take to start making change in your life:

1. **Do a full analysis of your current diet.** Be brutally honest and use your Memory Journal to chart out everything you're eating. Some items will obviously not be conducive to a healthy lifestyle. I suggest not judging them or even removing them right away. Just let yourself become aware of the status quo.

2. **Create an action plan and commit to it.** There are different ways to proceed and different ways to make the commitment. But we know that these steps matter in experiencing transformation. Allow the plan and your commitment to emerge in stages. As I hope to have shown in this chapter, my

own transformation occurred not only through consistently taking action but also by letting observation guide future actions—my journey will end only when the time to stop eating arrives. We truly are built of the food we eat. So long as our bodies need nourishing, we must monitor our progress on a continuum with no end game in mind. The rules that govern human bodies and how your body interprets them are also subject to change as you age or even live in different places. For example, after moving to Australia, a style of plaque I'd never seen before started building castles around my dental implant. The best my dentist can tell is that Australia has changed the nature of my saliva in combination with possible differences in the mineral makeup of regional food and water.

3. **Get expert advice.** If you can take the results with a grain of salt and not expect a magic bullet, I believe the LEAP blood analysis is worth every penny. Look into the science behind it and learn more about what n=1 experimentation means in the context of elimination and rotation dieting. Your body really does interpret the rules that govern all bodies on the planet, and the differences matter. You just need to get more involved in the experiments that help you read the data and create better maps for exploring what to fix and how. Prioritize making the changes that seem most likely to help, even if your favorite foods are involved. It might be difficult to believe now, but a lot of what you think you like to eat will become unpalatable once cellular regeneration has disentangled you from it.

4. **Although you can add or increase** the amount of blueberries, salmon, walnuts and green tea in your diet, n=1 is about finding and following the evidence of what is placing barriers between you and the mental clarity needed to learn faster and with greater retention using memory techniques. This approach is also not about developing beliefs. When you follow the evidence and keep re-testing it in the true spirit of scientific analysis, you don't need belief. Evidence is far more satisfying than faith in matters of dietary and mental improvement.

5. **Be thankful for your journey.** Make food part of your gratitude journaling and meditations. I include food and water almost every day in my handwritten list of 10 things I'm grateful for. I meditate after meals more often than not and let myself mingle quietly with the new inhabitants of my body. You wouldn't invite a new friend into your home without some small talk and a

quick tour, would you? Why do we do it with the food we introduce into our bodies? Welcome it in and show it around.

6. **Be present for your diet.** Be *all in* with the processes you create for life. Once you've felt the benefits of testing and retesting your diet, you likely won't want to go back. Yet, because constant change is a reality, it's important not to become dogmatic or fanatical about even the most stabilizing dietary patterns you land upon. Chicken didn't bother me for a long time, then suddenly it did. This is likely due to the accumulation of chemical markers in the body. Maybe I'll bring chicken back in the future and it will be fine for a time. Who knows what will have to disappear from my plate next in order to buy back more peace of mind? Who cares? Mental peace is worth the price.

What matters is consistency with the circular testing and observation process. If you fall down at any point, the depth of your commitment and consistency of practice will make it easier to get back on the horse. Meditation will help you stick with your plans too, just as a better memory will help you keep the particulars of your diet in mind. But there's another path to mental peace through memory I want to share before teaching the Memory Palace. It involves a simple morning memory exercise anyone can complete.

5 VICTORIOUS DREAMING: HOW TO REMEMBER YOUR DREAMS AND MILK THEM OF GENUINE MEANING

"We are what we are because we have been what we have been."
— Sigmund Freud

"Fled is that music:—Do I wake or sleep?"
— John Keats, "Ode to a Nightingale"

WHEN I WALKED INTO Dr. Langs' Manhattan office in 2006, I was hoping to find an alternative to lithium so I could lose weight. Instead, I wound up gaining victory over an aspect of my mind, and this victory has gone on to help many others since.

I'd recently moved to New York to live with my first wife, Ingrid, who was shuttling between apartments in Brooklyn and Washington Heights. We spent hours going back and forth on the A-train as she worked to sell off her Brooklyn property. Since we'd both been labelled as manic depressives, we constantly talked about dealing with the condition all hours of the day and night. The American medical system was completely new to me and I had a hard time understanding a number of concepts, but she helped me wade through the massive book of doctors our insurance provider gave me to choose from. It took me longer to even vaguely understand why I needed to bring doctors a "co-pay" cheque at every visit, but, supported by my wife's exhaustive willingness to explain the workings of insurance, I got there.

Since I had recently added Wellbutrin to my diet of lithium and Risperdal at the suggestion of a Toronto psychiatrist, I needed to have this cocktail monitored. I knew I wanted the drugs in my system only for as long as absolutely necessary. I was using memory techniques to prepare for my PhD field exams, but it was clear to me that as sharp as these tools were, the drugs were as much a barrier to focus as the manic depression itself. One of the downsides of lithium is that it can easily reach toxic levels in your blood when anything changes, ranging from diet and hydration to regional elevation and temperature. During the hottest months in Toronto, I used to sweat the stuff out of my body to dangerously low levels that left me feeling ill and in need of temporary dosage increases. It was so impractical to have these constant sea changes while trying to study for exams and research my dissertation.

After Googling a few doctors from the giant book, I landed on Dr. Robert Langs, who caught my interest when I saw he'd written 44 books on dreaming. I made the call. I remember him sounding suspicious on the phone, but when I named the insurance company and my dual-path goal of keeping my psychiatric cocktail monitored and hopefully making some changes in the near future, he suggested a time the following Tuesday morning at 10 a.m. I remember the time well because I would visit Dr. Langs week after week at exactly this time for many months to come.

Located on 72nd Street, Dr. Langs' building stood a few blocks west of the well-known Dakota apartment building. I marvelled at this novel setup for a few reasons. As a film buff and budding film studies scholar who had never in a million years dreamed of living in New York, it was neat to make the connection of the building with *Rosemary's Baby*, which used it as a location. Of course, the murder of John Lennon practically outside the Dakota's front door is the stuff of legend.

Although I'd seen a number of celebrities on the streets of Toronto from time to time, in New York it took a while to acclimate to the novelty of looking someone famous in the eye almost every day. It didn't help that Ingrid's Brooklyn apartment was in DUMBO (short for Down Under the Manhattan Bridge Overpass) which was home to a vast number of celebrities and "important" creative personalities, from artists to television executives. We spent hours in the lobby gossiping with the doorman and listening to banal stories about such people. They seemed interesting and exciting to me at the time. When I was really attentive and actually made eye contact with any of them, they just seemed like anybody else on the way to work or the gym or to catch a bite to eat. Human... all too human.

Dr. Langs' office was on the second floor just above a violin repair shop. If everything in New York feels like you're in a movie, it's because watching hundreds of hours of movies deposits its scenes deep in your episodic memory. Still, I had never seen anything quite like the way Dr. Langs divided his waiting room and consultation room.

While waiting, I had nothing to do but look at one abstract picture on the wall. There were no magazines to leaf through or fellow patients to ogle. Then, although the door leading into his consultation room did not open, I heard it open. And *then* it opened. There were two doors, which created the ghostly sound effect. After reading many books by Dr. Langs, I finally discovered that he was trying to create death anxiety with his arrangement of the two doors. I didn't know this at the time, and throughout my months of sessions, the architectural quirk remained as much of an enigma as Langs' approach to dream-based psychotherapy.

On that first day, however, I just wanted to have a professional look at my blood and manage the pills I was taking to help the corporations pour their psychotropic sewage into my system. At least, that was the way I felt at the time.

Dr. Langs was in his 70s—a gaunt though animated man. Thinking back, his baldness, deceptively sleepy eyes and rolling drawl remind me of acclaimed actor Jeffrey Tambor. But Dr. Langs didn't speak much. He was a sharp listener, and the few words he did speak rang like one of Nietzsche's tuning forks. After he heard my story of hospitalization and finally giving in to a life on lithium, he ignored the body weight issue and said he could help monitor my meds and then took the conversation on a detour.

"Do you ever remember your dreams?" he asked.

Indeed I did. I explained how I'd kept a dream journal off and on, and that I'd studied Freud and Lacan and even sat in seminars with Slavoj Zizek at the European Graduate School. I had already taught film studies for a full year as well. Even my early dissertation scribblings on friendship spoke of how the cinematic dreams we share on our screens tell a very different unconscious story about our closest contacts than the conscious ways we describe these relationships.

Langs told me he had a spot available every week. He advised that I no longer keep a dream journal, but simply come and tell him whatever I remembered over the week. In a few spare, yet seductive sentences, he promised I would discover the process as we went along and how useful it would be. Always a goal-oriented person with a special strain of stubbornness coursing through my veins, I told him that would be fine, so long as we were also exploring a replacement for lithium. He nodded in a non-committal way that seemed to say, "Let's wait and see what your dreams tell us."

Overall, my initial consultation was such an odd experience that I started ordering some of Dr. Langs' many books as soon as I got home. Although I'd dismissed much of Freud, I also remembered Foucault's lesson in "What Is an Author?": the value a historical figure brings is not always in their ideas, but in the discussion that their ideas makes possible. The books arrived and my sessions with Dr. Langs continued. As I read his works over the weeks to come, it was clear that Langs was extracting *only* the ideas from Freud that supported his own ideas, but also drawing from multiple studies. He seemed to reject Freud's notion that dreams directly connect with conscious content or reveal anything about wish fulfillment desires or sexuality. I saw his name cited alongside figures I recognized like Philip Zimbardo, and knowing the treasure that lies beyond opinion in the quest for truth from data, I felt that working with him was real science.

Lending to this feeling of practicing something above and beyond shoe-gazing into your own past was Langs' theory of dreams: he thought dreams allow us to learn better ways of living by discovering uncomfortable truths about our communication styles. In the psychoanalytic setting, a rigorously introduced "death anxiety" would amplify and accelerate the patient's perception of their mental content due to the extreme, but controlled, pressure. Primarily a Darwinist, Langs suggested that death anxiety evolved alongside language to deal with environmental threats: "Evolution deals with survival under changing, life-threatening environmental conditions and thus with adapting to endangering physical and psychological realities. Humans have a unique conscious awareness of the existence of some aspects of this struggle because they alone have an explicit awareness of death" ('Unconscious Death Anxiety and the Two Modes of Psychotherapy,' 792).

Furthermore, by creating an internal narrative filled with rules negotiated through words, the "unconscious mind universally advocates the use of an ideal, archetypal, secured, inherently enhancing set of rules, frames, and boundaries" (815). The double doors seem to be part of encouraging the mind of the patient to feel safe because care is taken to ensure their privacy while at the same time communicating outside of language that they are "trapped" behind more than one door. Dr. Langs believed that the unconscious mind craves rules and structures and feels violated in their absence, even if the conscious mind appreciates special exceptions—and although we feel consciously pleased when we get to be the exception to the rule, he theorized that we feel unconsciously violated due to the costs of exceptionality. For example, if a patient brought in a cheque with a mistake in the fee, even if it deviated only by a couple of pennies, the conscious mind might appreciate the doctor waiving the mistake as nothing. The unconscious mind would track the doctor's offering an exception to the rule as a violation of a practically sacred structure or "frame." This sense of violation would then emerge in how the patient verbally related stories about their dreams and life to the analyst. Then, something I witnessed myself doing as I learned to *hear* my unconscious speak, patients make references to what they're really thinking about violations to rules and frames.

Theoretically, by learning to listen to yourself "encoding" your unconscious perceptions of violations in the stories of your dreams and your own analysis of them, you could learn to perceive how others do this as well. For this reason, Dr. Langs seems to have left behind any notion that dreams meant anything and focused instead on how they could serve as tools for *revealing* meaning. During my time in his office, he never interpreted any of my dreams, but would only ask me to interpret them myself. Then, at key points, he would ask the most puzzling question: "What does this have to do with me?"

Even though his books revealed why he was asking this question, it was still unsettling, because as I learned to apply his technique to my everyday life, I could no longer be certain whether I was commenting on him and others in encoded terms or not. It was the expectation effect turned up to 10 as I realized I did seem to be encoding my perceptions about him in how I was relating the stories of my dreams and exploring their implications. If I fell silent, his only other statement was, "Whatever comes to mind."

French psychiatrist Jacques Lacan said of psychoanalysis that there were too many possible words and grammatical combinations of those for any patient to ever adequately create a portrait of the truth in words. For me, more than feeling the pressure of "too many words," I felt embarrassed by the thoughts and ideas that came to mind. Often, I couldn't bring myself to speak them aloud, which added to my distress. This effect is called "resistance" in the psychoanalytic literature. Since part of the game of psychoanalysis is to consciously recognize your resistances, it's gruelling to confront how fickle and feeble you can be as you wrestle to get yourself to share things that should have no consequence to the stranger you're paying for this privilege. But, having looked these thoughts squarely in the face, you really can be free of them. Or, if not free, you at least know that you're keeping your mouth shut for reasons that are more animal than human.

For example, the mental content that came to my mind while talking to Dr. Langs tended to be about base impulses and desires that have no place in normal conversation. I remember at one point, I told him a dream that involved me reading books I shouldn't have been. As I recounted the dream in detail, I became slowly aware that I was unconsciously encoding an admission that I was reading his books. Yet, I couldn't get myself to just come out and say it. It was a bizarre internal confrontation because why on earth would I care if some old man knew I was reading his books? Yet, I felt this childlike embarrassment over something that was likely very obvious to him, but only became obvious to me throughout the course of therapy. Rather than feel disappointed when I could not verbally express the ugly truths as all kinds of fantasies flooded my mind, I usually left his office feeling elucidated. I seemed to know more about myself and how my mind works, or *fails* to work, under pressures in his office that metaphorically reflect pressures presented in daily life.

I heard other people differently as well, and was often able to avoid conflict when someone would tell me a story that previously would have triggered a fight. One day in Saarbrücken, Ingrid came home from the grocery store and, to the casual observer, I might have appeared to be whiling away yet another fruitless afternoon on the couch watching a movie in our home theater. In reality, I was watching a movie for the fifth time to prepare for my film studies lecture later in the week. I didn't jump up to help her as I normally did because I was deep in mental processing. The virtue of my reason for being so focused on this movie aside, Ingrid, burdened by heavy bags of groceries, launched into a story that went something like this: "You should have seen what happened at the grocery store. There was a guy there with his daughter. It took forever at the checkout because he was letting his poor little girl put all the groceries on the conveyor belt while he was flipping through some kind of entertainment magazine..."

According to Dr. Langs' theory, this story did not emerge from my wife's mind merely because it was something that happened to her. No, she was telling me in unconscious terms from her mind to mine, that I was like the man at the grocery store. As a symbolic analogy to the man letting his "little girl" place all the groceries from the cart on the conveyor belt, I was allowing Ingrid to struggle with the groceries. The fact that it was entirely a coincidence that this man was reading an entertainment magazine in no way hides the parallel fact that in my wife's mind I was sitting around with the cinematic equivalent. Even if her conscious mind knew I was hard at work, for all intents and purposes, I know just how often a film professor appears to be engaged in a lot more fun than labor, especially when there are groceries to be put away.

Of all the dozens of stories she could have chosen to share about her day, her brain picked that one. Top of mind because it had happened to her so recently? Mere coincidence? Try listening to people in this way yourself and decide. According to the model described by Dr. Langs in more than 40 books, my wife's unconscious mind selected this story to help her deal with anxiety created by my lack of attention to her burden. Had it been untrained, this theory states, my own mind would have felt preyed upon because she was interrupting my work and "should" have recognized that I wasn't ignoring her at all. Whether or not Dr. Langs is perfectly right on these matters, I have found time and again that trying to hear what is *really* being said in situations like this has saved me hours of arguing. Prior to my sessions with him, I likely would only have heard Ingrid's story as an interruption of my focus and balked. I'm certain we would have squabbled over it, and then it would have come up later at the bar, and possibly again several times more. Yet, because I at least attempted to use his model, I simply paused the movie, apologized for not helping, got busy with her in the kitchen and asked more about her day.

It's important to realize that Langs thinks suffering comes not just from feeling preyed upon at the unconscious level; he also thinks that we feel guilty for being preyed upon and we feel guilty for how we react to the "predators." We spend tremendous energy both monitoring and fending off the perceived offenses and consciously and unconsciously feeling badly about our reactions. Since becoming aware of this model, it's been my experience over many years that much mental energy has been saved by perceiving and responding better to many issues; what previously would have escalated into histrionics is rationally drained of steam before the engines of conflict even get started.

True, Ingrid and I still divorced in the end, but it was in a mature manner aided by the lessons learned from Dr. Langs' approach to using dreams to understand one's communication style. And true, I would go through several more troubled romances before finally finding a soulmate, April, with whom I have a relationship that I'm confident will stand the test of time. That is thanks to knowing more about my communication style. When I tell her stories, I try to think about what I might be *really* saying, and have become a clearer and more direct communicator as a result. Plus, knowing more about the role of food and rest, I've attained even more clarity and mental peace. And what a soulmate! She tells me she rarely has thoughts about anything, and I don't think it's delayed aging or skin cream that accounts for the lack of wrinkles on her face. For whatever reason, she seems to have been *born* with a Victorious Mind. I doubt I would have even perceived that if I hadn't done so much towards establishing my own, let alone been attractive to her without working on my own mental peace.

In total, Langs suggests there are three major guilt-related sources of death anxiety. These are:

1. Predatory anxiety (from the feeling of being preyed upon by others).

2. Predator anxiety (from the feeling of having preyed on others).

3. Existential anxiety (from random or unpredictable elements of reality, such as storms and car crashes.

According to Langs, the unconscious mind eradicates our recognition of the fact that we threaten and attack others all the time while filtering out conscious recognition of being preyed upon. It is extremely difficult to admit this, and if you're struggling to see the logic behind this, Langs went so far as to suggest this may be because your unconscious mind is blocking your ability to recognize it as a fact. Predatory anxiety occurs when we feel that we have been preyed upon in some manner. This could have to do with competition at work, insults received or seemingly petty things like being cut off in traffic or having someone steal our place in line at the grocery store. The idea that the unconscious mind serves as a kind of filter is a core premise Dr. Langs unfolds most completely in his book, *Death Anxiety and Clinical Practice*. It's not light reading, but still recommended.

Trust me: I realize how bonkers some of these "theories" sound. I probably haven't done them justice, and reading Langs' critics is as fun as thinking through his own arguments if you're even remotely interested in the history of psychotherapy and philosophy. Yet, at least one other independent psychologist has devoted volumes to this topic. *Deep Listening: Hidden Meanings in Everyday Conversation* and *Between the Lines: Unconscious Meaning in Everyday Conversation* by Robert Haskell read like carbon copies of Langs' core ideas. Apparently they never met and I recall reading from Langs' website (sadly defunct since his demise) his interest and excitement when he discovered this body of work. I can hear some of his critics downplaying the connection and using it to make arguments about poor research. Such is the world.

I've also applied much of what Langs learned to how movies help us communicate about our anxieties. *The Theme of Cultural Adaptation in American History, Literature, and Film: Cases When the Discourse Changed* includes a chapter in which I apply these theories, and many film scholars "psychoanalyze" what movies are "really" saying to great effect. Movies are just assemblages made by people, so you might consider "unconsciously" or "listening deeply" to what they're trying to tell you as you might also listen differently to a spouse or friend—or your resistances when it comes to any kind of self-development training that requires consistent practice.

This point is important because if there's one wish I've heard from students more than anything else, it's that they want to download knowledge directly into their heads. People constantly refer to *The Matrix*—a film series whose scripts are vastly more sophisticated than the crowd-pleasing karate kicks and explosions suggest. There's a scene in the movie when Neo, a computer hacker who realizes that reality is an illusion created by computers, finds himself freed by a group of rebels who need his help. But first, he needs to know how to fight inside the realm of illusion. Using a metallic spike inserted into a brain portal, they download vast libraries of martial arts knowledge into his mind.

When Neo says "I know kung fu" in one of cinema's most iconic scenes, Morpheus challenges Neo: "show me." After they spar, Morpheus gives Neo another test and more training, followed by another test and yet more training. Soon enough, the tests are coming at Neo from the cowardly Cypher on his own team, the enemy agents and their strongest representative, Agent Smith. The movie ends by showing how Neo's graduation is nothing other than an opportunity to go back into The Matrix to rescue more people. And what happens after that? Two sequels filled with more training, more tests and increasingly difficult rescues.

Most people stop at the fantasy of having knowledge instantaneously arrive without effort. But that's not what the movie is really saying. It's a hero myth like *Star Wars* and a thousand other tales that is trying to communicate that in order to make anything happen, you must "do or do not, there is no try." A lot of this wisdom leads to people confusing activity with accomplishment, such as when they create Jedi cults. Worse, other people dress in black like rebels from *The Matrix* and shoot up high schools. But it's clear to me that we humans are constantly trying to tell each other how to behave better in the world. Sometimes we're whining like babies, other times, we've hidden critical messages in mire, which people like Sam Harris in his book, *Lying*, try to help us avoid.

All I can say is this: the more I explored my dreams and the daily content that my unconscious mind has denied my conscious mind, the more I learned about the human experience of having a mind. Like everything in this book, testing is key and remembering your dreams and analyzing the communication in your everyday life as part of using the other techniques in this book may really help you reduce (or even remove) anxieties from your life. The therapeutic and reading experiences described in this chapter certainly have provided tools and relate strongly to memory and meditation, and my apologetic runs: *carpe diem*, but also *caveat emptor*.

Can Dr. Langs' theories help you?

There are at least two ways you can use Dr. Langs' ideas in improving your memory by combining them with meditation:

1. Remembering your dreams is a creative memory exercise that both improves recall and gives you greater access to memory tools such as Memory Palaces, Magnetic Imagery and Magnetic Bridging Figures (we'll get to these in Part III).

2. Second, interpreting your dreams in a way similar to what Dr. Langs suggested is a means of using these images and narratives as a catalyst for exploration to arrive at *insight* for the future rather than meaning about the past. As far as I can tell, the countless guides that gather archetypes and possible interpretations of what it means to drown, kiss or set things on fire in a dream amount to little more than pablum.

Singh Harvinder
July 29, 2019

Hello Dr.Anthony and all MMM members, It is immense pleasure to announce that I have successful completed 2nd Session of teaching French Class to a NGO.
Thanks you Dr. Anthony for the Language learning tips and tricks. I am using in all the way in other subjects like English Language for ielts exa TEF exam, ISO 27001 cert in my professional front and my day to day li Thanks and Regards
Harvinder Singh

Harvinder Singh's Facebook post about MMM.
Imagine learning and then teaching a language so fast!

If you're willing to eschew even the slightest thought that dreams encode anything "meaningful" and are prepared to use them simply as objects for reflection without expecting any particular outcome, you stand to be richly rewarded. It is a form of self-inquiry related the kinds of questions Gary Weber proposes in *Evolving Beyond Thought*, such as "how do my thoughts behave?" and "are they useful?" The only difference in this case is you're asking, "How do my dreams behave?" And then you make them useful within the rules or bounds of reality so that they can set you free—especially from the seductions of dream analysis woo-woo.

The form of dream recall and interpretation I'm proposing is a two-tier psychoanalysis of your most intimate self. During the process, which Langs describes in detail in *Decoding Your Dreams*, you act as both the analyst and the patient, ideally on paper (remember that Memory Journal). Through diligent inquiry, your dreams provide the means of revealing more to you about your mental content and the true role it plays in causing the highs and lows in your life. You then simply ask, as Langs asked me over dozens of hours in his office, "whatever comes to mind?" and push to find what ideas might arise. At the same time, you will discover mountains of mental imagery and scenarios that will complement your memory improvement activities.

For example, Harvinder Singh, one of the most active participants in my Dream Recall Intensive sessions, has recovered 85 Memory Palaces just from keeping track of his dreams. He has also shared many drawings of strange images that have been useful in helping him learn and memorize both French and English vocabulary. The best part is that he uses his memory skills to give back to his community. In the years since I've known him, he's learned French well enough to teach it and does so for an NGO while completing certifications that will take his career higher.

Whether you are using this exercise to psychoanalyze yourself or discover more mental tools for your memory projects, the self-inquiry process is the same. The free association—"whatever comes to mind"—that I learned from Dr. Langs can be used when looking at a dream you've recorded. You can simply ask, "what potential Memory Palaces come to mind?" Take note of the ideas that arise, jot them down and start drawing your Memory Palaces. You'll be astonished by how many locations you will remember simply from engaging in this simple process.

When it comes to dream recall for pure self-analysis purposes, you will likely find the same distribution. Over the course of a month, all your dreams will fascinate you and all of them will contribute to the practice. But only a tight percentage of them will lead to epic, "Aha!" moments. None of the others will be a waste, and you never know when in the future they will transform into having more value for self-analysis or use in your memory practice. A case in point in my own experience involves a dream with pyramids from 2004 finally coming into play after I visited Egypt in 2013 and saw a few pyramids with my own eyes. If I hadn't been practicing dream recall with a dream journal, the pleasure and use of making deeper connections would not have been possible.

What should you do if you cannot remember any dreams at all? Follow these steps anyway and then write something to the effect of, "No dreams remembered." Followed consistently, this simple step can serve as the catalyst for starting to remember dreams.

How to begin capturing and analyzing your dreams

The actual process of remembering your dreams is quite simple. It begins with preparation:

Journals

I suggest you consider using two journals. The first will live beside your bed. I find a hard-cover journal with A4-sized paper works best as it is highly visible on my bedside table. The second, you will carry with you throughout the day to capture any new details that arise, and accordingly it should be smaller. Both journal and notebook can be either lined or unlined. I prefer unlined as it makes it easier to sketch the imagery and Memory Palaces I recover from my dreams.

Depending on your personal preferences, you can either shop at a dollar store for your dream journal or buy a luxury journal with creamy paper, a leather cover, etc. Such private decisions really matter. If you want to invite general affluence into your life (along with intense, detailed and accurate dream recall) you can likely accelerate this by approaching the practice in a spirit of abundance. In other words, please consider not skimping on your dream-recording tools. This is especially so since you'll likely want to hold onto them for years. Possibly, you'll even bequeath them to a family member or to a dream society for cherishing and analysis. In short, respect the fact that your recorded dreams will become a library archive of all your writings.

Writing implements

Buy a pen or pencil that you deliberately intend to use solely for recording your dreams. Avoid the temptation to use it for anything else—even if this means having another pen on your nightside table (the same single-purpose ethos goes for your dream journal). Exclusivity is essential. The more you preserve your pen or pencil for this task and this task alone, the more your mind appreciates your dream tools and the more powerful they become as you deepen your dream practice.

Once again, put some thought into the writing utensils you choose. Do you prefer a merely functional pen that you use for "dream recall from the trenches," or would your mind prefer a bit of luxury to signal to yourself the care and importance you place on your dreams? I've heard of someone who purchased a $1,000 pen from a pen specialist in Yorkville, Toronto. I myself have been more personal and modest. For years, I recorded my dreams with the pen my aunt and uncle gave me when I earned my PhD. Using this gift exclusively for dreaming assigned importance to the instrument. The effect of this symbolism yielded dividends because the pen started appearing in my dreams.

Resources

Acquire some books on dream recall, dream science or dreaming in general. Place these where you will regularly see them. It doesn't matter if you agree with their contents or not. It doesn't even matter if you learn anything from them. So long as they have the word "dream" in the title and genuinely discuss dreaming, they will likely help trigger more dream recall. Having such books on Kindle will also help, but will in no way have the same potential effects offered by physical books you constantly bump into.

When you buy your dream books, it's best to have them in several locations: by your bed, on the coffee table, on a bookshelf, on top of your fridge, in the bathroom, on your desk at work, in the glove compartment of your car, in your backpack, etc. The more you run into books about dreaming throughout the day, the more you will be stimulated to repeat your conscious intention to recall your dreams.

After preparation are the action steps you can take tonight:

1. **Make a conscious decision.** Deliberately decide to record your dreams by consciously telling yourself that this is your intention. It's as simple as

mentally declaring, "I will record my dreams." Get in the habit of saying this at least once before going to sleep. You can compound the effect by saying it several times throughout the day. I also recommend that you deliberately decide that you will record your dreams for at least a year. One thing which some people find useful is to write out a contract with themselves to help ensure their success. While I have not done this with dream journaling, I have done it for other projects. It certainly helps "seal the deal." Either way, I would predict that after two or three nights of actively telling yourself that you will remember your dreams, you'll already feel the impact on dream recall. Such quick victories will likely be all the impetus you'll need to keep going.

2. **Give a chronology.** Record the date for the following morning at the top of each page in your dream journal. If you plan to write in the dark, it is best to always start on a fresh page so that you're sure you know where to start writing.

3. **Prime yourself.** Leave the dream journal lying open so it is ready to be written in.

4. **Ease into sleep.** Practice some form of relaxation as you settle into sleep. I recommend Pendulum Breathing combined with Progressive Muscle Relaxation. (There's detailed training on pendulum breathing in Chapter 3, Breathing, Walking, Remembering.)

A lot of people ask me about alcohol because I speak openly about my years as a lush and my newfound joys in sobriety. In my experience, extreme drinking reduced dream recall, but not predictably. I did not think at the time to track amounts in my dream journals, and it wouldn't really matter if I had. If you use alcohol, you can find out what impact it may have using the power of journaling.

As your dream recall deepens, you'll likely notice yourself slipping into dreams even before you fall asleep. Is this because you're already dreaming or because you're suddenly noticing the extent to which you continually fall into fantasy throughout the day, including during the moments before you drift into sleep? I'll let you decide as you experience this transformation. Although you may not be able to exercise any conscious control over these transitional dreams, it is an amazing feeling and an excellent sign that more dream recall and potentially lucid dreaming is nigh.

Here are the action steps for whenever you awaken with a dream-ripe mind ready for harvest:

1. **Write your dreams in as linear a format as possible.** When you become skilled using Memory Palaces, you also have the option of memorizing some of the core scenarios, figures and ideas that emerge using the corners of your bedroom or another room. This, of course, takes practice. Note that the goal with memorizing dreams directly into Memory Palaces is not to replace the writing component. Rather, I started doing this so I could sleep more and still recall multiple dreams from throughout the night. It's still important to write out the dreams later—the results are better and the flow of dream recall is maintained.

2. **Don't dither at first.** Don't worry about any details or sequences you miss in recording your dreams. Just jot down the notes fast. You can add fuller descriptions later.

3. **Take a little time later.** Stay in bed or at least in the bedroom for a while after awakening and journaling to see if any more dreams come to you. Or you can take your dream journal with you, but take care to return it immediately upon finishing any additional writing. Far better is to use your supplementary dream notebook for recording additional dream sequences and fragments that come to you. These can be compiled later.

4. **Immediately list any potential Memory Palaces you can recover that you haven't thought about before.** As an example of this, I had a dream that involved my friend Clayton. I suddenly remembered that he had lived in two different houses during elementary school. One of them I'd never used. I allowed my mind to wander over that second home, drew it out, and *bang presto*, another Memory Palace was added to my ever-growing network.

5. **Note future avenues.** Write down any personal associations that come to mind that you may want to finesse or work with further in your dream analysis.

Tips on performing dream analysis

Ideally, you will carry out your dream analysis in a quiet setting using your dream journal. Although Dr. Langs discouraged the writing of dreams for the purposes of his in-person psychoanalytic process, we're not doing that. For our purposes, writing down your dreams strengthens your memory muscles. It's a form of self-testing. With practice using a Memory Palace, you can soon memorize the narratives and images without writing down your dreams. Even then, I strongly advise that you write them down as you retrieve them from the Memory Palaces. You can also meditate upon the meaning of your dreams throughout the day if it does not distract you from your other activities. Is there a best time of day for dream analysis? Langs thought it was at night, but *best* is a perilous term. *Experiment.*

Read through the descriptions of your dreams from the previous morning and week. If you are using advanced dream memorization, reviewing your dreams presents the opportunity to wander your Memory Palaces as well (and you should follow this form of recall with reading through your record of the dreams). The more you create feedback loops in this manner, the more intensely you'll dream, the more dreams you'll recall in a complete manner (with the occasional dream fragment) and the more dreams you'll have to interpret.

So, seated on the floor in a meditation pose or in a comfortable position on the bed (does it really matter?), step inside the emotional landscapes and atmospheres of your dreams. Allow your mind to reflect on the events of the previous week. Do not judge the associations that come to mind. Simply allow them to present themselves.

As you begin to receive a pool of associations, explore which dream elements naturally connect with your daytime experiences. You might find that, no matter how interesting and even pleasant your dreams may be, your conscious mind will associate them with moments of either making decisions or of anxiety, stress, trouble and, especially, guilt.

The more you practice this form of self-inquiry (and I'll detail more direct forms in the chapters to come), the greater resources you'll have for dispelling such experiences. I have found it useful to consider all my dreams in relation to the three anxieties: predatory, predator and existential. Although confronting your own mind may be uncomfortable at times, developing an advanced awareness of the animal part of your brain will improve your overall life and grant you deep insight into the true intentions behind the behaviors of others, and more importantly, your own actions. You will have new interpretive tools for navigating the waters of waking life. These tools will ideally produce self-knowledge, elucidation and states of relaxation. You just need to be willing to look at this material for catalysts to honest interpretation of your current life. Forgo the fanciful. If you entertain all kinds of wild ideas and woo-woo, that's fine, but be prepared to pay the price. I predict that if you're willing to apply your dreams to more practical matters, you'll be rewarded in far more substantial ways. I know how tough this can be and have spent hours in resistance in front of perfect strangers, such as Dr. Langs and other therapists (and I have been experiencing an increasingly Victorious Mind over this resistance). You might spend hours resisting yourself, but I'm confident that with practice, real insights will emerge, especially when you keep asking the basic self-inquiry question at the core of this book:

"To whom exactly are these dreams and interpretations occurring?"

As you allow your mind to wander and associate, don't force the outcomes or judge the mental content that you actively make appear in consciousness. Just allow your mind to go wherever it wants and observe. As in other forms of meditation, you may find yourself fantasizing about the future or about an alternative version of your past based on a "what if I had done X instead of Y?" model.

You may also find yourself experiencing a pleasant, imaginative story or slipping into a dream. As meditation expert Shinzen Young urges in *The Science of Enlightenment*, it is just as important to subject the good to dispassionate inquiry as it is the bad. Simply allow your mind to follow these avenues and wait for daytime associations with your dreams to occur naturally. With practice, they will come with greater ease, frequency and depth of meaning. As with dream recall, dream interpretation is a cumulative process that will only significantly blossom if you develop daily practice.

Be willing to accept that, at the end of the day, these are *just* dreams. It is unlikely that many of them bear much meaning or deep importance. You need to acknowledge the role of self-invention and the expectation effect as you draw out stones from the streams of imagery. Weigh them in your hands and examine their dimensions with the tools of self-inquiry by simply asking, once again: "To whom exactly is any of this happening?"

Seek the source of the self in your field of awareness using this form of mental content. Sometimes you'll find that some elements are truly notable and worth placing in one of your Memory Palaces for repeated consideration. Just be sure to approach all of your dream interpretation activities in a spirit of scientific play. Validity in your efforts will emerge quickly through honesty and openness of spirit, especially when you surrender all of it to self-inquiry and always ask to whom the dream is really occurring. Are the dreams and your analysis of them happening to you as your ego or to the witness of your ego—which some people call "pure consciousness"? If you cannot tell the difference, keep asking these questions and let dream recall be part of how you refine these questions over time.

On my own journey through working with dreams, Dr. Langs did ultimately help me get off lithium and onto Lamictal, which did not help me lose weight due to excessive drinking. Several years later, I finally said goodbye to all psychotherapeutic medicines after removing all booze. As I continue to seek growth, I expect my life to continue improving that much more without pills. Dream recall practice also plays a less central role now. About once a year, I go on a dream excursion and spend a month with interested Magnetic Memory Method students in a Dream Recall Intensive—of which you've already heard, in my note about Harvinder and his 85 dream-based Memory Palaces. For me, this is about the right amount of dedicated dream recall at this point in my life. I hope you'll find ways to make deep transformation using dreams as a tool for yourself too, if only for a time.

A Memory Journal decorated by Pai

Before n=1 food experiments and after

Even as a kid I was clobbered by depression and
lived by the bad policy anger explored
by my first band

Hard at work on *Branding You* with Jonathan Levi.
Little did I know I would be soon working
to get rid of my "self"

Josef Johansson used inspiration from *The Matrix* to personalize his memory journal

With Tony Buzan, the original Warrior of the Mind

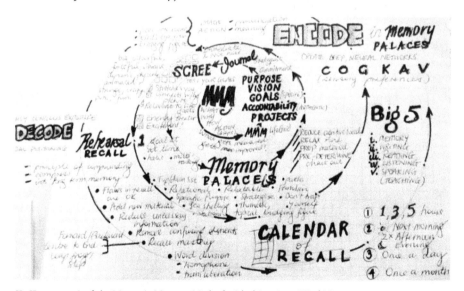

Ke Ko summarized the Magnetic Memory Method with this unique Mind Map

William Gordon, who designed the map in this book shares my love of heavy metal and sums up the goal best: *Remember in Peace*

I wore my Systema shirt on tour all over Europe but would need to get a lot more systematic yet to shake my mental issues for good

Bender helped me learned words like *Bereich* in German quickly. During dark days of no focus I drew what I needed in my Memory Palaces rather than abandon the practice

Michael Swain
February 18 at 5:07 PM · 🏷 Add Topics

It's Sunday night here, and I've come up with an intense goal:

1000 Japanese vocab words. One Week. This week.

Parameters:... See More

👍😊😮 8   3 Comments Seen by 49

👍 Like   💬 Comment

Michael Swain used Memory Palaces based on video games to rapidly learn Japanese. Now he has created the Kanji Project to help others

Part III

CALM

THE STORM

6 HOW RULES HELP ELIMINATE THE TYRANNY OF FREE WILL

"We live in what we are doing, we do not control what has been done, but are rather controlled by our past works which we have forgotten. This is because we dwell in the action and its fruits instead of living in the soul and viewing the stream of action from behind it."
— Sri Aurobindo

I'VE DISMISSED SHOE-GAZING PHILOSOPHIZING a lot so far in this book, and hopefully you've received it with the humor I intend. All joking aside, I have benefited from beard-stroking and chin-scratching my way through one topic in particular: free will. It's worth the time to convince you that free will is a barrier because this book is about how a "control freak" let go and found great relief. Paradoxically, the memory techniques that helped break through some of the final holds of the problem *seem* to involve enormous efforts in controlling mental imagery. But that assessment couldn't be further from the truth. As you'll learn, memory techniques work best for learning faster and memorizing large volumes of text when you set control aside and work with the information that is *already* in your mind—information that found its way in there due to random chance as we bounce upon the worlds of our families, schools, professions and pop culture. When you relax and do the exercises so you can *let* association happen *without* control, well... perhaps this book should have been called *Happiness Beyond Control*, because that's exactly what you'll get.

Here's what this chapter is not: It's not about the neuroscience of free will, which some people have told me was debunked in a recent Atlantic article. Chances are that if you think *any* real science gets meaningfully punctured on the pages of an online news magazine, you don't have the free will you think you do. That kind of response to journalism is evidence of a will-less reaction to a catalyst, not a wilful *slowing down to reflect* and consider this new thought in the broader field outside of online "journalism." When asked, all of the people who told me about this article admitted they had not read the scientific research discussed in Bahar Gholipour's "A Famous Argument Against Free Will Has Been Debunked." Pressed further to explain why they didn't dig further rather than taking this piece of journalism at its words, these people simply did not know.

As far as I'm concerned, the neuroscience has not only *not* been debunked (certainly not on the strength of Gholipour's reporting); neuroscience is far from the crux of the argument, one that has been going on for thousands of years. Frankly, if people had any free will in the matter, they probably would have stopped griping about it long ago. But they can't, so they don't, and it's a matter of how the rules that govern reality force us to select from a limited amount of options in the field. We seemingly have to talk about something until we die, and death anxiety, as we saw in the chapter on dreams, may be the true source of why the issue carries on. And perhaps, as discussed in the previous chapter, death anxiety is so strong, some brains literally filter the obvious pressures of having no free will out of mind. As André Gide put it, "Everything has been said before, but since nobody listens we have to keep going back and beginning all over again."

No matter where you fall in the free will debate (did you "choose" your position?), thinking the issues through, even if the process gets repetitive, will reward you when it comes to self-development because the topic can emancipate you from any guilt you harbour about the past in ways psychoanalysis and dream therapy might not. Even if I can't be 100% conclusive, surrendering to the rules that govern good research and debate on a topic like free will has certainly helped me craft a better path forward without thinking I have something that apparently does not exist. It's clear to me now that a huge part of the harm OCD I suffered for years stemmed from a mental image of being in control, or its concomitant perception that I had "free will." This feeling is almost certainly an illusion, and yet, like the illusions performed by magicians, it can still influence your life, even if what we see play out on the stages of life is not real. Separating the control you have from the control you don't can be incredibly healing and support great accomplishments in your life.

What is free will? Nothing. Like Santa Claus and the Tooth Fairy who still owes me $20, it simply can't be shown to exist. Yet, like those fantasy figures and many others, all of whom show up against our will, the concept of free will plays a role in our lives. Many people believe they are in control of their lives. They feel certain that, if you gave them access to a time machine, they could go back and do things differently. Others claim that the rules governing the universe are so full and complete that even if time machines were possible, these rules would ensure that everything would play out in exactly the same way. But like neuroscience and its findings, time travel is irrelevant to the discussion because, even if you could build the machine, pay the energy bills and survive the trip, you would physiologically not be the "you" visiting "yourself" in the past. You would be a separate version of "you," one equally constrained to act under certain conditions—the conditions we're going to ferret out in this chapter and turn into tools of progress. Chances are, right now you have a mental image of these conditions, or rules, that do not serve you. Learn the real rules in charge of the game and those rules will set you free, if you can get yourself to surrender. Much of what we've already discussed in terms of mental metaphors, breathing and diet should help towards the end of being free from free will.

Will, willpower, free will and how teachers and students assemble to create change

Teachers and their teachings, if they are any good, act as catalysts that help you become your own guru. Using your Memory Journal, analyze your own history of experiences in classrooms. When has a teacher really "taught" you anything? If you think about it, you'll likely discover that the best lessons came when you were influenced or prompted to discover something—whether you wanted to or not.

Let's say a teacher holds out a lantern for you. For this light to be of enduring use, you must take it into your hands and walk into the unknown. No number of stories or instructions from the teacher will get you anywhere. In fact, too much talking about the lantern and its fire can impede your ability to do anything. It might be a fun activity, but when you need to see the world illuminated, looking at the lantern and hearing about it will never become accomplishment. Only taking it into your own hands and moving it around to see and explore the territory will make anything of interest happen. This distinction matters because the word "guru," at its core, simply means "to banish the darkness." And that sounds about right when it comes to the process of being a self-directed learner: be your own guru.

Ultimately, none of us "chooses" our teachers. In the great pinball machine of life, all the more random and chaotic since the dawn of the Internet, we are mathematically bumping into more and more gurus than ever before. Ben Fishel randomly drops Gary Weber's name and then off I go into the realm of reducing, if not eliminating, thought. If I had free will, I would have "willed" Ben into making the recommendation decades earlier. I certainly begged the heavens for reprieve many times before—the heavens, unfortunately, told me it was a-okay by them and everyone else in the world to snuff it. But thanks to *acts of will*, I have developed the wherewithal to experiment with even those things that raise my skeptical hackles, which is what scientific living is all about.

Before introducing some techniques in detail, I think it will be helpful to establish a frame of mind around the subject of will—including "free" will, will-power and how these differ from acts of will in a world where nothing is "free." Gaining some clarity around these concepts may help you take the lantern, and select rather than choose from the abundance of lanterns out there so they can help *you* illuminate what you can and cannot control as you map the dark territories yet hidden from you. For those suffering the need to be in control, whether you agree with these assessments or not, thinking the issue through should be freeing. And it seems that both scientists and spiritual people have been on the same page about these matters. As Ramana said in his great *Upadesa Saram* (*Essence of Instruction*) and as was echoed by Stephen Hawking in *Brief Answers to Big Questions*:

"None of us controls the laws of physics. So why do we worry about them?"

At least, that's how I interpret:

kartur aajnaya praapyate phalam
of essential reality by the laws obtained result

karma kim param karma taj jadam
action is it limitless action that is inert

kriti mahodadau patana karanam
of action vast ocean fall cause for

phalam ashashvatam gati nirodhakam
result limited liberation obstruction

In other words, our experience is governed by the laws or rules that govern the universe. Our efforts come from and return to a vast ocean that cannot be fought against. And yet, strangely, so many of us expend ourselves in the attempt while denying the existence of these rules. We want to be the exception to them, and this desire for exceptionality is the source of so much suffering.

Some people think scientists like Stephen Hawking have just turned science into another form of faith. For example, he writes, sounding a bit like Ramana in his many dialogues:

When people ask me if a God created the universe, I tell them that the question itself makes no sense. Time didn't exist before the Big Bang so there is no time for God to make the universe in. It's like asking for directions to the edge of the Earth—the Earth is a sphere that doesn't have an edge, so looking for it is a futile exercise.

Do I have faith? We are each free to believe what we want, and it's my view that the simplest explanation is that there is no God. No one created the universe and no one directs our fate. This leads me to a profound realisation: there is probably no heaven and afterlife either. I think belief in an afterlife is just wishful thinking. There is no reliable evidence for it, and it flies in the face of everything we know in science. I think that when we die we return to dust. But there's a sense in which we live on, in our influence, and in our genes that we pass on to our children. We have this one life to appreciate the grand design of the universe, and for that I am extremely grateful.

There is no need to have faith in the observable rules that at least *seem* to return us to dust. What most people call "faith" is actually an attempt to control the conversation and make *their* faith appear to be the correct one. Both Ramana and Hawking *surrender* to the awe of what is—with no need to add a second thing that no one can prove exists. Although Ramana did use the word "god," it was to sweep it out from under his interlocutor's feet as part of the teaching process. Likewise Hawking might use the term "grand design," but these are words. A Victorious Mind has no need for a grand designer, and can't demonstrate there is one. Thus far, we have exposed only the existence of some of the "laws" governing things. If there is a secret to peace, it is finding contentment with that.

You might need to work at freeing yourself from these habits of mind, of course, so let's get started with the big picture first, followed by the exact tools I've used personally. Don't worry: none of these tools is the product of a single mad scientist working in isolation. I picked up all of them from the best teachers on the planet and, if I improved them, it's because I modified them based on my personal consumption preferences and existing competence. I expect you will do the same. This is why the context of the stories matters. I want you to be able to hit the ground running with more detail to work with than I had. Maybe the woo-woo I had to strip from them to be useful to me will actually not be woo-woo to someone else. *Caveat emptor*, dear reader. Let the games begin.

First, for the purposes of establishing your Victorious Mind, I want to focus on why the notion of free will creates suffering. Once we have this knowledge in hand, we can use memory training and meditation to reveal the illusion of free will and remove the pain it creates.[4] Why am I scapegoating free will as the horrible monster keeping so many of us down? It's because, even if you're not consciously thinking about it, this "bug" infects many minds, constantly convincing people like me and you that you:

- Are a person capable of making choices in the present moment.

- Are a person capable of making choices in the future.

- Are a person who could have made choices differently in the past.

All of these options are impossible for a number of reasons. Your own analysis of experience will validate this claim. For example, choice is an illusion because we never actually make choices. What we call "choice" is actually *selection*. You can call it choice if you want, but free will is the fantasy that you have control or agency over what you do. I ask you, how is it possible to have control or agency over the choices you make in the supermarket when, in reality, you only have a limited set of products from which you can select? Unless you are a marketing and product manager involved in deciding which products to feature on which shelves and at which prices, you're selecting what you will buy from an existing range of options decided by someone else, not choosing at all in the sense of free will.

"But wait!" you're thinking, "I could easily choose to go to another grocery store altogether!"

Sure, if you want to choose a less than vigorous meaning of the word "choice." In reality, you are *selecting* from a number of possible grocery store destinations that have appeared in your reality. It's not choice, but limited options within a frame. To expand the frame does not give you more choices. It only gives you more to select from, which creates the kind of decision anxiety responsible for holding people in stasis. Worse, they may go into analysis paralysis, which keeps the mind busy and much of that activity creates the illusion of accomplishment, when nothing has in fact been done.

The whole point of this chapter is not really to argue about whether free will exists or not, but rather to help you see that it isn't necessary for progress. We progress by positioning ourselves to harness the flow of the "laws" or "rules" governing reality—both inside and outside of our heads. It's just a shame that so many egos are using so much brain power to get in the way of flow. Believe me, my ego gets away with this nonsense too! The question is... why? And how to stop it?

Part of the *why* is that we *feel* we have free will mainly because of reflexive self-monitoring. The ability to observe ourselves and think about how we might act differently in the future is very real. The more educated we become through repeated exposure to good ideas, the more encouraged we are to make positive changes, and thus the more likely we are to actually implement the changes to beneficial effect. Then there is the opposite effect: the more negative material we expose ourselves to, including negative messages inside of our own minds, the more we can hold ourselves back despite our best intentions. As you'll see and have already encountered in the form of the Challenge-Frustration Curve, we also need reflexive self-monitoring to optimize and maximize the outcomes of the changes we make so that we experience maximum growth. And for that we need the right kinds of fertilizer and fuel.

Now to the question of how to stop all of the ego-interference in our progress. In all of this work of making positive changes, we are tapping into our capacity to engage in "acts of will," even if we can't quite muster our willpower. What's the difference between will and willpower? (Remember the anxiety mentioned by Lacan: too many words! Don't let the cascade of words get you down. More terms are coming, always more terms, as long as there are people to use them... but you have the mental resilience to keep up with it!) As Benjamin Hardy demonstrates in *Willpower Doesn't Work*, the sense of will we experience is densely tied to memory and how our memory helps us make new skills easier to use until they feel like second nature through overtraining and "outsourcing" various aspects of willpower to our existing environments (171). Remember those cold showers I take? Whereas the first times may have been driven by much willpower, now I've outsourced some of the "power" part of will to habit, routine, and my close awareness of the benefits that daily cold shock brings me. My procedural memory has taken over and free will is irrelevant, all based on a chance encounter back when I started with Systema and later, by the same luck had the technique reinforced by Wim Hof.

"Willpower" is only a part of making change and establishing habits in a world that is constantly distracting us from our intentions. It's because of this world that our will isn't free. We must overcome the illusion of free will to accomplish goals, to feel spiritually at peace and experience the highest levels of memory. When we can release ourselves from this illusion and harness more of our will, we can work on crafting meaningful "habit stacks" that help us navigate life's storms with greater consistency and ease. Even better, we can stop mentally punishing ourselves if we fail, because we can look with more clarity at the laws underlying the situations and spare the energy previously used for self-flagellation to make corrections instead.

If you base your goals for change and better habits on existing competence, you are more likely to achieve them. This is one of the core messages of Jordan Peterson's *Maps of Meaning*. In this book, he dives into much of the memory science available at the time he was writing to show how we can deal with uncertainty and the unknown by using the light of our existing skills to move into the future. It's just a matter of having good information in your memory and good interpretations of that information to draw upon. Don't make the mistake of pigeonholing this notion into utilitarianism or psychology or post-modernism or some other buzzword of the day. We're talking about the quality of your memory at its core.

Sadly, as Peterson has gone to great pains to point out, we've *forgotten* much of the collective wisdom that equipped earlier versions of humanity with various levels of competence. When we are versed in mythological narrative, we can know both intuitively and practically how to act in the world based on wisdom in narratives like those offered by Shakespeare. In fact, in one of the most stunning passages of *Maps of Meaning*, Peterson demonstrates how Freud's competence in understanding the psyche was not so much learned as discovered, because "much of the information derived from a story is actually already contained in episodic memory. In a sense, it could be said that the words of the story merely act as a retrieval cue for information already in the mnestic system (of the listener)" (75).[5]

Stories contain many solutions and cues. If you take the wisdom from an instructional book with stories (perhaps like this one) and bring some of it into your life through practice, you will likely get results if you base those practice-actions on skills you already have. These skills exist in a number of memory levels, and don't need to be made from scratch. When I pick up a book like *Happiness Beyond Thought* and read about stretching, for example, I'm readily able to build new competence because what I'm really doing is refining an *existing* level of competence. When I read Giordano Bruno's *Thirty Seals* and discover new ways to use memory techniques, I don't start from zero. I *assemble* new knowledge from Bruno based on the knowledge already there by consciously seeking to snap them together like mental Legos.

By consciously seeking out what already exists in the mind and being prepared to fuse it with new things through self-conscious elaboration or weaving—*assemblage*—learning might not go faster, but it's easier and much more fun. It doesn't need to go faster anyhow. We've all heard we live in a culture obsessed with speed and efficiency, but you don't have to jump on this train. The attachment learners have to quick absorption of information does not usually serve them and the speed may actually hinder absorption. What does it matter if you're going a million miles an hour if you're headed in the wrong direction? In other words, get started based on your existing competence as much as possible. Each person will need to do some analysis to figure that out or work with a coach who can help you find an appropriate port of entry.

As I work on my goals for change, I rely on a stack of habits; each one in itself helps me in my progress, and the repetition of the stack brings compound value. My habit stack in the morning involves:

- Stretching

- 3–5 types of meditation

- 2 types of journaling

- Fitness

- Memorization and Recall Rehearsal (You'll learn about this soon.)

Where one of these activities begins and ends is not always clear, but so long as I complete these activities before the computer goes on, the entire day goes much better than those mornings when I don't. Perform these habits and I approach the day centered, focused and filled with energy. Once put into place and reinforced by a holding pattern of powerful repetition, such rituals take on a life of their own and reveal much wisdom.

Free yourself from the illusions of time and free will

Given the simplicity of such habits and the well-known nature of what they are and how to do them, why do so few people succeed in sticking with them? I believe that clinging on to the notion of free will is at the core of the problem. Why? Because when I tried to be in control of things without rules, I failed and suffered as a result. But by surrendering to the logic of putting structure around events and sticking with it, many great things have happened as a result.

Another part of the difficulty is that we cling to illusions of time. When we dwell on the past, we're caught up in the illusion that we can possibly do something about it now, but the past is over—so let it go. When we fret and fantasize about the future, we're also catching ourselves up in illusions of prediction or expectation, because the future is not ours to dictate. If we can release that worry over what we cannot control in any of the illusions of time we experience, much mental space will open up for an even more rewarding memory improvement as meditation practice.

What is not an illusion is the present moment.

Since the universe is governed by laws outside of our control—that is, not by our free will—and one of the most easily examined for the purpose of disillusionment is time, let's perform a quick study of this problem in the past, present and future.

The Past

It's pretty simple to establish why free will cannot exist in the past. The past is over, and no one has access to it. Even the finest historian must agree that presenting information they've found from historical evidence always comes with interpretation. In fact, you cannot be a very good historian without permitting yourself to interpret. Even further, historian Niall Ferguson makes the case in *Virtual History* that we need to interpret not only what we think the evidence tells us probably happened, but also the "counterfactuals"—or the things that might have happened had certain conditions been different.[6]

Likewise, no matter what might have been different or how I interpret the effects of my past actions, I cannot travel into the past and counsel my younger self not to gobble down so many psychedelic substances that were probably laced with rat poison. Nor can I make one more attempt to save a failed relationship that I think of from time to time, even if I can "time travel" through the brain chemicals of my memory to relive some of the great love I enjoyed while on one of our wild adventures. That kind of fantasy aside, there's simply nothing we can do to change the past in any way that lends credence to the notion of free will. So let's move on.

The Present

We experience a legitimate sense of "will" in the present. The more educated we are about how this feature works in the absence of free will, the more successfully we can make it work. One of the key barriers to our progress is fantasizing about versions of the present that aren't currently happening. For example, you might be at work, but wishing you were at the beach. Or, you might be at the beach, but wishing it was sunny instead of raining. A massive amount of mental energy goes into such projections—and that's all assuming you're not so bombarded with thoughts about past and future that you're barely aware of alternative-present ideation.

Worse, wishing the present was different is like breathing and blinking. Just as you can select the option to blink or breathe by exercising your will, you can switch fantasizing on any time. It's often quite useful to do so. For example, I started writing this chapter in the park. A heavy wind arose and it started to rain. I started wishing it was sunny. I then imagined what it would be like sitting in a cafe instead.

I found another place to sit between the park and the cafe and even as I settled in, the thought of a steaming cup of coffee beside me instead of my crinkled plastic water bottle popped into my mind more frequently than I liked.

In the first case, I actively used my ability to envision an alternative version of the present by imagining myself in a cafe. It was like choosing to blink. But the thoughts of coffee? They arose automatically and outside of my will, just as blinking will happen automatically without consulting my will.

Are the thoughts of coffee that arise annoying to the point of suffering? At the moment, as I write in a cafe—no. But in my past, before serious dividends from meditation kicked in, any number of impulses prevented me from completing any serious, concentrated efforts. I still wrote a lot, but was extremely finicky about the precise conditions. As I mentioned, the window had to be boarded shut just to stop me from thinking about jumping to my death while trying to concentrate on writing my film studies lectures and dissertation. In that case, the disjunction between the "alternative present" I kept imagining and the present reality was extraordinarily painful. In terms of interruptive power, thinking about having coffee by my side is just as disruptive. The point here is to reach a level of acceptance about the things we can't control, rather than suffer because we can't control them and believe we should be able to.

The Future

I've framed my recurring thoughts about coffee as I type as an alternate-present issue. Such thoughts are also future oriented. If they don't already involve images of moving myself to the cafe, standing in line, receiving the product and imbibing it, they soon will. These are relatively trivial matters. The suffering is minimal. What about when you're writing a book and thoughts about its success continue to arise? These thoughts involve everything from how to get it edited, who will do the cover and how the coming reviews will impact its success. The entrepreneur comes in and keeps reconfiguring the book's place on the ascension ladder and the future debt to be paid in terms of creating marketing videos and writing email campaigns and possibly tossing coins into a variety of paid advertising engines is never far from awareness. All that's on top of thinking about how previous books in my catalog have played out. And coffee keeps coming to mind again and again.

Yet I'm firmly focused on what I'm writing now and feeling this humming sense of bliss of everything being completely right with the universe as it is right now. I can focus on all of these "what-ifs" without forming any serious attachment to them and just let them be. Due to the nature of reality, no amount of thinking things through now actually lets me control what will happen in the future.

This book will be released into environments in which no one else has any free will about what will happen either, so there's simply no sense in worrying about it or attaching myself to the thoughts.

Free yourself from thoughts, too

Whether you're writing a book, desperately trying to sleep, trying to memorize information or pestered by recurring desires for some object in the world, the trick is to step back from the flow of these thoughts and realize something important: these thoughts *are you* when you're assembled with them to a point of saturation that nothing else exists in your experience. Yet, they are *not you* in the same way clouds are not the sky and, like clouds, they will pass.

As Adi Shankaracharya writes in the *Atma Bodha*, "The Self seems limited because of ignorance. Destroy ignorance and the limitless Self is revealed, like the sun when clouds pass away" (13). Think of the self as what your consciousness would be like without thoughts about yourself. As Sam Harris helps listeners experience with his Waking Up app and Greg Goode explores in the exercises included in *The Direct Path*, it is really thought above all that makes you feel limited, when your experience of what is has no limits. How could it? It just is what it is. "Ignorance," then, is failing to see this. It is the state of being in the darkness without a lantern, and the darkness is all the thought that makes it darker yet, as the febrile mind tries desperately to make sense of the suffering and control its way out of the abyss.

This model suggests that what you *really* are is experience itself witnessing the constantly changing weather patterns. Left to your own devices, you will limit your perspective to the point of just being the small boat rocking on the wild ocean as these thoughts push at you, making it impossible to set a course, let alone stick to it. When you realize that what you really are is the boat, the ocean and the wind all at once (metaphorically speaking), you stand a chance of filling your sails with the best possible wind, even if bizarre little thoughts keep lapping at both stern and aft. Keep practicing, and the sound of those thoughts will go down. You will see them as ignorant little clouds that will pass and, with practice, will reveal that the calm sun of your consciousness behind them never flagged for a second. It just seemed that way due to ignorance.

I believe based on my own practice that the most direct way to experience freedom from recurring, intrusive thoughts is to do the practices that create distance between yourself and the thoughts, and then let them be. More and more, the Sanskrit verses I've memorized remind me of the impermanence of these thoughts. A self-inquiry question you'll learn later helps me test the usefulness of these thoughts in a way that rapidly dissolves them. Word for word, the question Gary Weber provides is: "How do my thoughts behave? Are they useful?" Sometimes the answer is yes, such as strategically planning what I can control about the future of this book, and that recognition creates peace. Your head is likely also filled with an abundance of useful thoughts that might become more useful yet when the volume of the negative goes down. This same question also creates peace when something less positive comes to mind. Positive or negative, you can establish mental habits that create calm on the stormy ocean of the mind; memorization makes these tools part of the entire ecosystem that is you and your surrounding environment.

One of the biggest barriers people face when trying to create distance between themselves and their thoughts is attachment to the outcome. They want to know:

- Will it work for me?

- How long will it take?

- What if I make a mistake?

- Do I have the time?

- Do I have the discipline?

Many more such questions might emerge. Notice that they all tap into one of the past, present and future tenses, often weaving all three together. A future-oriented question like, "Will it work?" arises out of the memory of past failures. On the other hand, some people will suffer from overconfidence because their memory tells them that they've heard this stuff and tried it before. An underlying belief in free will only makes it harder to accept why these questions are problematic, and this person will struggle to take action and receive the benefits of trying something again from a different angle. You can't will a certain outcome. All you can do is take action within the constraints of the laws of physics and build new habits based on existing competence.

Here's a challenging exercise Weber mentions that can help you wrestle with your existing competence by engaging in *acts of will* that demonstrate just how much power other forces of mind have over you.

The Number Skipping Meditation

In any position you prefer, preferably one that won't put you to sleep, settle in and count your breaths from 1 to 10.

Next, try "suppressing" the even numbers. The way I do it is to think "one" on both the inhale and exhale of the first cycle. In other words: inhale and think "one." Exhale and think "one."

Then, as you take your second breath, deliberately suppress the thought of "two." Also suppress the count when exhaling.

Allow yourself to count the third breath: inhale and think "three." Exhale and think "three."

See if you can get to an "invisible" 10. When you're able to do so, try to come back down by suppressing the odd numbers and allowing yourself to count the even. Link each count with your breath.

1-1,	3-3,	5-5,	7-7,	9-9
10-10,	8-8,	6-6,	4-4,	2-2

This exercise will feel unusual at first. It's related to the negation technique taught in hypnosis, which teachers illustrate by saying, "Don't think of a red cat." Although some people will say, "no problem," most of us will need to think of a red cat in order to follow the command not to think of a red cat. Likewise, when beginning with this exercise, you will likely experience the need to think of "two" in order to practice not thinking of two. This outcome is actually desirable because you've positioned yourself as the observer of how your mind creates and experiences ideas against your wishes.

With more practice, you'll soon be able to conceptualize a space that is empty of the number you would normally represent despite trying not to represent it. I believe this exercise creates many benefits, such as developing a greater ability to deal with distractions while juggling multiple pieces of information. In *The Wise Advocate*, co-authors Art Kleiner, Jeffrey M Schwartz, and Josie Thomson explain:

> The ability to inhibit distractions and remain goal-oriented requires input from working memory. In turn, the inhibition of distractions is essential for inhibitory control. This type of mental activity involves not only holding back intrusive thoughts and memories, but also focusing attention and controlling impulsive behavior. (The inhibitory control of attention is sometimes called executive attention.) Together, working memory and inhibitory control enable cognitive flexibility—the ability to be creative, to see a situation from multiple perspectives, and to switch from one approach to another. (81)

What better way to improve at negating distractions—or, in their words, to practice inhibitory control—than by developing the ability to stress and release your focus on deliberately selected mental content and the absence of that content?

Kirtan Kriya Meditation

If you find number skipping difficult, learn Kirtan Kriya meditation first. Also taught by Gary Weber (in this case on his YouTube channel) it is a nice memory and concentration exercise. In their book *How Enlightenment Changes Your Brain*, neuroscientist Andrew Newberg and Mark Waldman demonstrate that it will change the structure of your brain. Kirtan Kriya means "song movement-forms." It is a meditation from Kundalini yoga that combines the notion of "infinity-life-death-rebirth" with singing and finger movements.

Personally, I dismiss the esoteric explanations that relate the sounds to chakras, gods and other mystical elements no one can falsify. You may find them useful, but to me the real value comes from giving your mind training wheels so you can guide yourself to greater focus instead of thinking random thoughts. All you do while sitting is chant "Sa-Ta-Na-Ma." You can coordinate each sound with "mudras" or hand positions to add an additional point of focus on your position in the here and now.

It doesn't have to be Sa-Ta-Na-Ma. It can be Ah-Me-To-Foa, as my wife April tells me some prefer in China. You could also just make something up. Even if there is something to the mouth-tongue-sound connection, that doesn't mean any of these words are magical. The "alchemical transformation" comes from the knowledge of what your mind really is more than the materials of practice. As stated in the second passage of the *Atma Bodha*:

> Just as chopping wood is the indirect cause
> and fire the direct cause of cooking,
> spiritual practice is the indirect cause
> and self-knowledge the direct cause of liberation.

As with numbers, you can apply the number-skipping exercise to these sounds. After reciting Sa, skip Ta while holding an empty space for it, then recite Na and skip Ma. For a variation, invert the process by reciting Ta and Ma while suppressing Sa and Na. You can run this routine both out loud and silently in your mind. You also don't have to perform Kirtan Kriya alone. April and I often sing it together. It's a routine worth memorizing.

How to memorize Sa-Ta-Na-Ma and Ah-Me-To-Foa

When I first watched Weber's video on Kirtan Kriya, I knew I would forget both the term and the sounds if I didn't dedicate intention to memorizing them. Using the main bedroom in my apartment as the Memory Palace, I imagined my friend Edan Kertis with a First Nations member of the Cree tribe shouting "ya!" This took place on the curtain.

> Kertis + Curtain = Kirtan
> *Cree + ya! = Kriya*

I placed this image at the top of the blinds and let my mind pretend there are curtains in this space. Then, just below this mental space, I imagined an Anton LaVey-type figure for the Sa-Ta-Na part (i.e., Satan). He was sitting atop the Chinese character for horse, Ma.

To be honest, this image was not the greatest choice. Albeit effective, it did not feel great to have decidedly dark and somewhat uncouth imagery like this in my mind for the short while it took for Recall Rehearsal to "massage" the target information into my long-term memory.

However, as four-time USA Memory Champion Nelson Dellis and I have discussed on the Magnetic Memory Method podcast, the powerful outcomes more than warrant making short-term sacrifices. Even the crudest imagery stays around only so long as needed. After it's done the deed, the fire of use burns the "training wheels" away. Nonetheless, it is important that each person who comes to the art, craft and science of memory training develop discernment. Aspects of the mental tools you find yourself creating may challenge your morals, ethics and sense of humor.

After I started feeling the Buddha Smile in its new form, post-*Happiness Beyond Thought*, I worried for a time that generating all of this mental imagery stood contrary to the goals of achieving mental peace. Didn't all of this dipping and double-dipping into my powers of Human Random Access Memory essentially equate to bringing myself closer to the dumping grounds of my ego, rather than distancing me from it? I expressed my concern about this several times, but ultimately applied self-inquiry to it and resolved the issue completely. Indeed, if it's true, what changes? If it isn't true, what changes? The reality is that these tools help me create mental peace because I can memorize long passages and recite them. They serve their purpose and then disappear, after annihilating themselves from any hope of retrieval.

This fact is an odd consequence of using memory techniques. You'll often find that you have no problem accessing the target information, but cannot for the life of you remember your Magnetic Imagery. For example, I don't quite recall what I used for Ah-Me-To-Foa, so I can't give you an exact example. I only remember that it had nothing to do with Anton LaVey or Satan. Even if it were, in my experience, the images never poison the target information. They are tools that dissolve once the job is done.

As you work with these techniques, you may notice they interact seamlessly with your breathing. Or you may find yourself paying closer attention to your breath as we've covered in this book. It seems to me that much of the pleasant experience of chanting comes from a kind of breath withholding that occurs naturally as you sound the verses.

Ramana Maharshi notes as much in his *Upadesa Saram*: "Lasting absorption of the mind can be accomplished by first stilling it through breath control, and from that state, contemplating That" (*Happiness Beyond Thought*, 90).

Gary Weber suggests different patterns for the breath while reciting these passages. In my personal experience, this focus was better directed at the Magnetic Imagery in my Memory Palaces used to memorize the Sanskrit and its meanings. In combination with the breathing routines, dreaming and diet optimization, yes, all of this is very much worth it.

Remember the breathing patterns discussed in the chapter "Breathing, Walking, Remembering"? For example, while silently reciting the sounds "Sa Ta Na Ma" in your mind and following the finger-thumb patterns (mudras), you can complete four cycles on a left-nostril inhalation, hold for four cycles and exhale through the right nostril for four cycles. Then repeat the process.

If you've memorized a deck of playing cards, a new set of foreign language vocabulary or phrases in Sanskrit, you can mentally recite the information while following this kind of pattern. I often recommend that students focus on memorizing a quarter of a deck, rather than full a deck if it's just for memory exercise (as opposed to card magic or memory competition). This practice helps develop speed of image generation, the ability to reuse Memory Palaces with ease, and dexterity with similar kinds of information that involve multitasking with multiple layers of information in the same mental movement. I realize it might sound odd to mix playing cards in with Sanskrit for meditation or language learning as if they're the same thing. Yet, there's reason to believe the brain treats them the same way. And from the perspective of a mnemonist who uses memory techniques, information is information. The information might change, but the approach remains largely the same.

As you inhale, focus on just one Magnetic Station in your Memory Palace for cards, vocabulary or Sanskrit phrases, etc. and bring the Magnetic Imagery you've created to mind at the same time you recall the specific location in the Memory

Palace. Hold the breath for as long as you please or include Pendulum Breathing. Call the next card or piece of information to mind as you exhale. Using the mudras can add a level of challenge or of presence to the practice depending on your current ability with these memory techniques.

Just take action

These exercises are challenging, and thoughts may arise that try to talk you out of even making the attempt. But remember this: mastery is living some part of your life the way most others *won't* so you can spend the rest of your life enjoying benefits most others *can't*. This is as true in preparing for exams at school as it is in running a business or using meditation to reduce your thoughts. Believe me, if I allowed myself to be swayed by thoughts about the book you're reading now failing on the market, my will to create it would be shot. I do experience these thoughts. I would eliminate them completely if I could! But I don't have free will. The reality is that I am still on this journey and due to my regular meditation practice, I see these thoughts for what they are and keep moving forward. It's like the obscure poem sometimes mistakenly attributed to Dr. Seuss goes,

> Hostesses who fret about
> Who sits where will find
> That those who mind don't matter
> And those who matter don't mind.[7]

Sure, it's easier to keep cliché quotes in mind than follow them, but that's where practice comes in to *override* the need for will. The more you can rely on practice and simply following fruitful procedures, the less the stuff of the mind will throw you off course. Remember that Ministry album I told you kept playing through my mind during the horrible drug trip that fractured my mind for decades? Its title is helpful. It's called "The Mind Is a Terrible Thing to Taste." Indeed. But with consistent practice enabled by *remembering to practice*, you can taste it less and less.

Further evidence of the absence of free will in my own life is the fact that I am writing this particular book at all. Here's why: my first introduction to meditation was in Mr. Esdale's English class when I was 16 years old. This wasn't when I started meditating daily, mind you. That would come in Saarbrücken, once I started chasing after the strange wonders of the Buddha Smile and its help in warding off the incessant urges for death, which still seem worse than death itself. Mr. Esdale was a Poseidon-figure if ever there was one, but instead of controlling storms and creating islands, he had preternatural control over the garbage can. You see, Mr. Esdale was the strictest anti-gum chewing teacher in my entire high school. He was also a competitive curler. If you don't know the sport, it's basically lawn bowling on ice. With his hawk-like eyes, Mr. Esdale spotted the cud-chewing jaws of his students with laser intensity. Then before you knew it, the garbage can would slide between the desks to stop in perfect position for receiving the gum from the offending student. It was majestic to watch and took place at least once a month.

In all of his strictness, Mr. Esdale was calm and friendly and used actions instead of words to rid the class of gum, and this demeanor, combined with his curling dexterity, made him a force of nature not to mess with. And yet, as with disruptive thoughts, gum kept appearing between the jaws of his students. No matter what, he was never agitated. If he'd ever been angry a day in his life, nothing about him showed it.

One day, Mr. Esdale revealed the secret of his calm. I don't know why, but he announced that he would be taking us through a guided meditation. He explained what meditation is and the results it creates and proceeded to have us close our eyes. It was the most amazing experience in a high school I have ever had without the assistance of alcohol, pot or LSD. That experience has stayed with me throughout my life. It laid the foundations for me to notice the topic of meditation in the future in the ways that I have—with interest. I've been warm to it ever since. Yet, I still had no choice in the matter. Mr. Esdale simply introduced it by chance one random day in 1993.

Years later, I found myself teaching memory techniques. People started asking about my habits. Meditation came to mind and fingertips faster than I could consciously make space for it or chose to intervene. Next thing you know, I'm making a random decision (perhaps like Mr. Esdale's) to make YouTube videos about it.

These videos eventually ranked in the search algorithms and started getting thousands of views, complete with a healthy percentage of shares, comments and thumbs up. Mr. Esdale waved a butterfly wing and I felt it. I responded to it substantially enough to blow a small ripple onto the ocean of the world. The ripple came back and now we are a perfect circle of mutual influence directed at creating a common benefit for all. Then I wrote the first outline of the book you're reading now with a live audience on YouTube. Literally everything included in this book was vetted by our community first. I then rehearsed a revision of this book's outline in a private webinar to substantial applause and received feedback that helped refine the writing plan. I didn't do this out of some need to impose my free will on this book. I did it to combat the limits going it on my own have imposed on previous works.

The human species is fusing with technology, which is helping us find and influence each other. The more we assemble, the better things seem to get. Only ego, territorialism and the desire to control outcomes gets in the way, even though these aspects certainly play a role in creating success. But no one is responsible for the outcomes. Don't hang onto a belief in free will—it is an illusion supported by your trying to control outcomes. This is what causes the suffering that reduces so much success in life. To help you escape this pain, we will next turn to meditative journaling. If you follow the exercises, you'll soon find that your mind is cluttered with lies you didn't notice, creating space for a brighter truth to guide you by the force of obviousness when the clouds of what you thought you and your "will" want are blown away.

7 MEDITATIVE JOURNALING:
NAVIGATE YOUR WAY TO CALMER SEAS

Why write in a journal?

Although it might not seem like it, journaling is a form of meditation. If nothing else, it can be enjoyed as a highly beneficial supplement to your practice that speeds your progress. As I share the different kinds of journaling I have used (and continue using), you may find that the difference between the presence of will and the absence of free will becomes clearer, if you're still struggling with the concept.

The power of journaling first became clear to me when I read *59 Seconds: Change Your Life in Under a Minute* by psychologist Richard Wiseman. In this book, Wiseman presents evidence demonstrating that people who journal not only remember more but experience time differently—they feel like they have more of it. Journaling helps make time feel less scarce, which makes sense. When you reflect on where your time went, you behave differently and make different choices. Plus, if you use journaling to help yourself focus on more positive thoughts, you can create feelings of happiness and well-being. After reading *59 Seconds*, I developed a simple habit of writing down 10 things I'm grateful for every day. Some people like to be specific, others just write single words or sketches. My preference is to use keywords like "water," "food" and "home." You might benefit more from greater specificity in sentence form, such as, "I am grateful for Tim, Allie and Stephanie and their dedication to my cause." I usually just write *Tim, Allie,* and *Stephanie* and mentally reflect on the specific things they do, but you should split-test and see what works best for you.

In *59 Seconds*, Wiseman also explains the science of habit formation, findings echoed in many other books. If you really want to develop a habit that lasts, you need to commit to approximately 90 days. There are different numbers thrown around, but this one seems the most likely, both based on research I've read and my own experience.

In my own practice of doing journaling consistently since 2011, I write on real paper with a real pencil, based on the strong recommendations presented in Wiseman's research. Typing, or merely thinking about your gratitude, just doesn't seem to create the same results. This lack of impact likely stems from the fact that writing by hand uses approximately 150 muscles, each of which connects to pathways in your brain. The more muscles you use, the more of your brain gets activated, allowing the exercise to create more impact.

This next point might be far fetched, but I cannot help but think that the brain is also more receptive to an interaction with organic material. We know that lack of access to nature harms us and can lead to depression and other mental disorders, and that spending time in nature is restorative. In our modern world, interacting with trees in the forms of paper and wooden pencils might reconnect us with nature in a basic way that typing into computers cannot (even if the traces of nature are tiny). Relatively speaking, our brains and sense organs are a lot more chemically related to pencils and paper than the materials that go into iPhones.

Also, when we use paper and pencil and read over what we've written, we are representing something in the world that is then re-represented in our brain chemistry. The truth of the things we write on paper or into a computer may be exactly the same in terms of the content, but the brain may in fact perceive some things as "more true" when they interact with more organic materials and are made by the self that perceives them. Obviously, the chemicals that make up computer screens are just as real as the chemicals that make up pen and paper. Nonetheless, we've spent many more years as a species evolving our communication processes with paper and ink than we have with computers. I don't think my speculation on this matter goes too far.

Looked at from a neurochemical viewpoint, assuming you take up this activity in a way that positively impacts your life, you are likely creating more dopamine and myelin when using more of your body. These positive changes relate to neuroplasticity as you literally create new neuropathways and strengthen them over time. That's at least the view reported by Wiseman, and other authors back it up with more studies in books like *Atomic Habits* by James Clear and Daniel Coyle in *The Talent Code*.

Can you really jot out 10 things you're grateful for and realize what an amazing life you have to produce a dopamine spike? If you do it long enough will it really cause myelin sheaths to wrap around your neurons with such intensity that this new habit will make it difficult for you to forget to write out your gratitude list? Will you really have changed your brain from the inside by assembling with an external practice? I've seen it play out in many lives, including my own. *Genchi Genbutsu*, as a Japanese phrase runs, go and see for yourself.

If all the science these influencers report is true, it's the explanation for why things get even better on the dopamine front when you stack your habits in ways that compound the value of every other habit you complete. Examples of these are meditation routines and other forms of self-care. We'll explore these later. For now, I suggest you kick off your daily journaling with a vision statement.

Begin by crafting a vision statement

A vision statement is a clear, succinct and specific expression of how you want your life, learning experience and quality of mind to be. Why do something like this? As Joe wrote to me after completing one of my lessons around this process:

Hey professor :)
I just wanted to say thank you again for putting that vision statement video out.
If you want to see what I ended up with for a vision statement, I attached it to this email. There's 18 pages of work I had to go through to get it boiled down to this. It was exactly what I needed at the time I needed it.

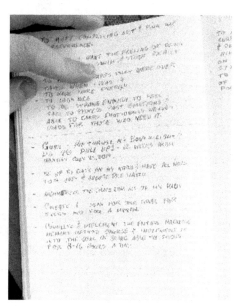

Joe's vision statement

Just as the "magnetic" properties of memory techniques will help you stick the things you want in place while repelling those that reduce your focus, a vision statement will keep your eye on the higher-order desire you're really after. For example, my vision of the Magnetic Memory Method initiative is:

To provide inspiration and strengthen the esteem, memory and mental abilities of people around the world by providing demonstrations and examples of how mature learners operate.

Why craft a vision statement? Well, "Life is a series of exchanges." That's how my Uncle Eddie put it as we exited a baseball game and reflected on all the different things that would happen over the next 24 hours to the vast numbers of people leaving the stadium. As a professor of criminology, he was trained to run the numbers off the top of his head based on current statistics. Everyone is going through transition and negotiating on multiple levels of social interaction on a daily basis. Everyone's life is filled with randomness, and all the more so when you meet for sporting events, and as my uncle speculated, the number of drunks on the road goes up, increasing accidents, while at the same time, more pregnancies can be expected as sports fans work off steam in creative ways when they get home. (I don't know if any of this is mathematically true, but Eddie seems to have had a distinguished career.)

The point is that life is a giant pinball machine filled with activity. But how much of this activity is grounded on clear and focused intention? Before I had a vision for my life, I once went to a Raptors game on the dime of a company I was working for and got so drunk I woke up on a train in Manitoba before I knew what happened to me. Later, my co-workers told me I'd downed 12 shots of whiskey at the bar *after* guzzling who knows how much beer at the game. I think I quit the job in a vulgar slur and vowed to leave Toronto for British Columbia on some bizarre quest for indescribable greatness.

Believe me, when I first heard about writing down a "vision statement," I thought it was the stupidest thing in the world. And it's not necessarily easy to get yourself to start doing it, especially if you're a control freak who needs to know the outcome of things before you get started. But now, even my vision statement for reducing thought has the goal written down—and I believe it works because it reduces having to think about the goal and reduces the endless negotiation that goes on with myself and others—all unnecessary barriers between myself and getting consistent traction. For example, many mornings I have no interest in going to the gym. I try to rationalize sleeping in, I want to exchange my long-term physical maintenance for short-term comfort. But, because I have a vision statement hanging on my fridge, this "contract" stops the negotiation in its tracks, I find myself in the gym, habitually, without having to do battle with myself or anyone else. To my surprise, I just seem to appear in the gym lifting heavy things three times a week. Likewise, I appear on my podcast, YouTube and blog mostly on schedule for years now, as if on autopilot.

Now, how powerful is that? Because my vision statement for my life, health and work has become such a fundamental part of who I am, it's not a matter of choice vs. selection to show up. It's drilled to the point that it happens automatically, or I itch to get it done. Life just doesn't feel right without hitting the necessary standards for realizing the various visions I have for achieving the biggest goal of all: lasting peace of mind.

I do not believe there is a one-size-fits-all method of creating a vision statement and journaling to support it. But here are some guidelines I've found helpful.

Ask yourself, "If I could have what I want now, would I actually *take* this vision?" If everything you envisioned for your future could happen in a snap, would you truly want it?

If yes, you're well on your way to crafting your vision statement. If not, then what you're thinking is probably not your ideal future. Really examine whether all of these elements are things you want, and not the desires of others for your life. Are you being influenced by a partner or your parents? Understand this is not their vision for your future, but yours. It should be something you truly want. If it's not, revise it.

Once you're satisfied, pretend that the vision you've come up for yourself has become reality. Ask yourself "What does having this state bring me?" and "What does it bring others?"

Share this vision and brainstorm with a partner to cultivate at least five answers to these big questions. Their insight can be so valuable for understanding what your vision can bring to your community. Do take time to think about how the vision serves others because only serving yourself is almost certainly going to lead to emptiness. But serving others with your vision can help you realize your highest possible self due to the benefits of "assemblage" we've been talking about in this book.

Pump in your personal values

The next stage is adding the element of your personal values. Think about what you value the most and add this to your vision-statement process writing. Literally ask yourself, "What do I value the most?" or complete the statement, "What I value the most is..."

It could be:

Accomplishment. Things that produce actual outcomes. Many people confuse activity with accomplishment. Action without a goal and a destination, or at least a system to support an outcome, is just activity. You don't want to simply be spinning your wheels, but actually making progress to a destination.

Creativity. This doesn't mean you're creating something totally new. That's probably just added pressure you don't need. As a musician, I know that there is nothing new under the sun. There are only so many notes in scales and so many combinations of chords that make sense together in a key. Every song is simply an assemblage of possible outcomes. But that's not a bad thing! Your contribution is your spin, your take on something that exists and interaction with the rules that govern its existence. It is valuable not just because of the novelty of feeling new and different, but because of the fact that it's "yours" in an interesting sense. That sense acknowledges that "original" means "of origin." Remember that, and as Tony Buzan says, "the rules will set you free." (Yes, it's worth repeating so you can remember it.)

Knowledge and Wisdom. Knowledge can have many meanings, but, in part, it is the ability to say what you mean and mean what you say. You test your theories before putting a final judgment on things and flaunting an understanding. This is not only knowledge, but true wisdom. This is only possible by having a plan in place to know more about everything. You're aware and cognizant of the fact that you cannot know what you don't know. Knowledge and wisdom are rooted not just in what is known, but in your humility toward the things that are unknown.

Collaboration. You value the idea that we are much stronger together than apart. You value dialogue and discussion, that you can teach others and be taught. Others can help you fill in the gaps of what you do not know as you do the same for them.

Finally, the things you value most may be *integrity* and *contribution*. Or perhaps *transparency*, *honesty*, and a *giving of one's self to the greater good* may be the things most important to you.

Whatever it is you value, really drill that down.

Energize using elimination
Once you have this list in place, now comes the fun part: drilling down. Select the top three whys, the top three values you've listed and start eliminating the rest by asking yourself: "What exactly do these mean to me?" "Why are they on this list?"

At this point you can channel your childlike scientist. Be like a kid with all those endless "Whys" kids use to bombard parents and teachers. Repeat "Why? Why? Why?" and "Why else?" If you can't come up with five reasons why something is on your list, it probably doesn't deserve your time, energy or effort to be on your list.

Victory over roadblocks
Repeatedly asking "Why?" does risk creating some roadblocks. You may have a hard time with coming up with any *whys* as you give your motivations a long, hard look. If you're absolutely stopped by this challenge of discovering your whys, step back and think about why this block may be occurring.

Are there life events in your memory that are holding you back?

Look for current internal patterns of behavior that may be to your detriment. You could be running patterns through your mind that simply don't serve you. Think about how you can release this from your memory, or change it, and take those steps to do so.

Examine your life for external systems of control that may be blocking you from realizing your vision. These can be everything from the way your family operates, the flaw of others not respecting your boundaries (because they don't have access to your vision statement), or your job. You could be held back by a problematic boss, or you may be in the wrong profession entirely. Identify those problems, look for alternatives, and stubbornly push for solutions.

Finally, what are those mental models that aren't serving you? What are the recurring beliefs that limit you and hold you back?

Harness the power of planning

Once you've identified these things that may be blocking you, what are you going to do about it? The point of identifying those roadblocks is to move beyond them, but you can only do this if you have identified action steps to do so.

Set some new goals and create new systems. Think to yourself, "This is my goal. Is it right?" and "Do I actually have the competence right now to accomplish this goal?" Constantly be your biggest cheerleader and critic. Find that balance of being real about where you are in relation to where you want to be and what you need to get there. This is working from your existing competence.

Identify the steps you need to reach your goals, then establish a plan to follow through with those steps. You've identified the *why*, but this is your *how*. Make these steps super simple, but take care not to dumb them down. Just simplify them so they correspond to your existing competence.

Most importantly, show up consistently and refer back to your vision frequently. Put in the work, and keep your focus on your vision. Always have this in the back of your mind, the motivation behind why you are putting in the work. Think of it as a treasure map, the culmination of all your effort. If you are honest, concrete, and specific with all these elements, you will find your vision, taking ownership of your future. You won't be a servant to the future or an actor in someone else's story; your future can truly be yours.

April and I keep our vision statement right where we can see it: magnetized to our fridge. I'll keep our shared vision private, but to give you a quick example from the past, let me share with you the story of how I first discovered the portal into what I think of as the Perfect Present.

The Perfect Present

A few years after I started habit stacking, I would add another kind of journaling to the practice either before or after jotting down the gratitude list. At the time, a few different teachings fused in my head and I started writing down a short description of my perfect day either before or after writing my gratitude list. It was 2011, and the Mercator research and teaching grant that afforded me the ability to live in Germany had ended. I was back in Canada, this time living in New Westminster, British Columbia. I could trace the decision to come here to a trip to the dentist in Berlin a few months before.

For years, I'd had a troublesome tooth right in the middle of my grin, and, after three root canals had failed to fix it, I finally went to the dentist to pull it out. Despite the existence of superior technology, this German dentist installed a horribly arcane replacement tooth. The prosthesis, which was the size of a hockey puck, caused intense irritation and disrupted my sleep. My exhaustion led me to make a string of decisions I don't regret now, but which I probably would not have made had I been better rested.

A few days after this trip to the dentist, I was in Pankow, Berlin and speaking with a teacher who'd helped set me free from one of my biggest issues. I decided then and there I would return to Canada. Although I'd won the lease on an extremely beautiful apartment made inexpensive thanks to a government program that helped scholars like myself, I actually had no practical job prospect at the end of my research grant. I also needed to do something about my dental situation with a dentist I could communicate with more effectively.

Less irritating than my tooth, though, were matters of the heart. I'd first met Olivia while teaching at the University of Saarland. To make a long story short, the attraction was as mutual as it was obvious, so I told her in my point-blank manner that nothing was going to happen until she was no longer my student. And that's exactly how things played out. She eventually joined me in Canada on a visa limited to a film studies-related internship that I'd helped her arrange.

While living with Olivia, it quickly became obvious that she experienced depressions far worse than I ever had. Instead of attending to her internship, she sat in her pajamas most of the day watching sitcoms while I stayed away as much as possible working on my budding career as an author of memory books and applying to go back to school. I'd completely thrown in the towel on being a professional academic after zero results from three promising job interviews at universities in the Vancouver area. For reasons beyond my ability logically to understand, not one of them wanted a film studies professor—despite the fact I had two MAs, a PhD and a fancy Mercator to boot. It also didn't seem to matter that I'd written two books about screenwriting and was completing the odd story consulting gig on movies and a TV series that actually got made.

While I was growing my business, Olivia and I decided despite our personal issues that it would be best for me to keep teaching. To do that, I would need to get a teaching certificate. In for a penny, in for a pound, I applied to go back to university at Simon Fraser University and hiked up to the campus several times to get the proper forms stamped while also working as a volunteer, teaching at two schools in New Westminster. It was absolute madness. I could not connect with the age group, but it was all happening somehow—just as everything that exists is always doing just that: happening.

All the while, I was rationalizing the numbers in my head. I would take out loans to get my teaching certificate. I would work as much as possible to keep the loans low and surely it would not be long before I was making money. Yet I knew something was wrong and needed to get out of it. The office I was working out of came to me through the grace of Haydee Windey. An amazing entrepreneur, she owned a training facility called ELIT that helped school students add or supplement the core skills they weren't picking up in public school. After contacting her three times to see about working at her school (persistence still works), she not only found work for me but took me under her wing as I made the shift from scholar to business owner.

I wrote curricula for Haydee's programs and sometimes taught classes. In fact, it was in those very classes that I first shared the memory techniques that went into my first book about mnemonics, *How to Learn and Memorize German Vocabulary*. This book would never have been written if Haydee's students hadn't asked me to write down the roadmap to creating multiple Memory Palaces that I'd shared with them one afternoon.

At this time, Haydee was helping me through a business idea I had created that would offer mentoring to students instead of tutoring. I despised the idea of tutoring in every possible way because it seemed like selling learned helplessness instead of equipping students with the skills they would need to solve their own problems. Mentoring, on the other hand, would give students additional, tailor-made exercises that would strengthen their writing and critical thinking skills so they didn't need tutoring. They would also learn how to deal with university professors when they entered higher education and had to be as self-sufficient as I had been.

Despite the fact that it would be selling my time and energy, I still see it as a decent idea for anyone who fancies themselves playing the role of Aristotle to the next Alexander the Great. After working with a few students Haydee helped me find, it was clear that adding more essays for students to write so they could develop better skills only made sense if they wanted to become writers. Finding such people was even more difficult, so I was soon back focusing on other business ideas, writing curricula for ELIT and preparing to become a high school teacher with a useless PhD hung around his neck like an albatross.

Haydee and I also spent many hours talking about how I could help her grow her business. In addition to helping her, I was siphoning tons of business training into my brain and starting to practice the fundamentals of direct response marketing. She listened kindly to me relate concepts I learned from the *I Love Marketing* podcast and just about every book they recommended. Because talking about what you're learning is so fundamental to remembering the big picture and the small details, I absorbed everything I was learning even quicker. Haydee and I also shared an interest in meditation and the great spiritual leaders, even if we didn't see eye to eye on what I often call woo-woo. Haydee was, however, also a great teacher of life. Her ethical approach to human existence as a whole rubbed off on me and shines on in everything I do.

While this wonderful mélange of business and spiritual learning was happening, it was obvious that Olivia had no interest in spiritual liberation. I meditated and kept my gratitude journal nonetheless, even after the day she punched me when I suggested she go back to Germany if she wasn't going to take advantage of her internship. At that moment, my heart knew our relationship would never succeed, even if my brain hadn't caught up to reality yet.

Fortunately, I had added the Perfect Present exercise to my habit stack. The idea is that you simply describe your perfect day in three to five sentences. As taught to me, it was a one-off exercise in a business training course. By adding what I knew from Wiseman about doing anything you want to make a habit for 90 days, I kept repeating the exercise and started writing my descriptions in pencil. Albeit painful, the exercise quickly revealed the maze I had built around myself. It also quickly revealed the solution.

Olivia and I had talked about where we wanted to live in Vancouver if we married and bought a house. So I worked out in my mind how much I would need to earn and started to write about having that amount of money per year and described the location of the house. I must have been both a poor mathematician and geographer because it was unlikely we would have been able to see the ocean from that neighborhood on a salary of $80,000 a year, but that's what I wrote. I must have known this on some level, because every time I wrote this passage in my journal, something in my heart broke. I wrote it everywhere, on the Skytrain, on the bus up to the university, on the way to see friends in the city and drink my woes away.

The most beautiful outcome of the exercise was discovering that what I had hypnotized myself to believe I wanted was not what I wanted at all! Instead of helping me get anywhere, the exercise was a serial dopamine killer! So I embraced it for another of its aspects: a destroyer of illusions.

Knowing the power of daily gratitude journaling and generally showing up to large projects like PhDs and dissertations with grit, I started to ask what I really wanted. The answer was the same as it had always been: to write, play music and travel the world. So I decided to make the shift. Instead of abandoning the exercise, and instead of writing down what I knew Olivia wanted, I wrote down what I wanted instead. It went like this:

I wake up healthy and strong. The worth of my being is great. I live in joy and abundance. I meditate, exercise and eat well. My passive income exceeds my lifestyle by 10x. I write and play music every day in joy and abundance.

I also created a visual "treasure map" version of the statement and posted a few printouts around our living area. Within a few short months of making this shift, I was back in Germany. I had a new dental implant and was on tour with a band. Even better, I was completely supported by two bestselling books for Kindle and an email list of nearly 1,000 people I wrote to every day. The two dreams I'd had since I was a teenager had become a reality and it felt like it happened overnight.

My first visualized vision statement in the form of a "treasure map"

Why did it work? Once I realized that trying to become a high school teacher was a trap, I could shift all of the energy I was spending onto what I really wanted. This revealed an obvious path to pursue it. If you want to write, you've got to write things that people actually want to read. If you want to play music, you've got to play music that people want to hear. No free will, remember? There are rules to follow based on what the world wants that make giving so easy, if you can shut up and chant the thought silencing chants in this book long enough to listen. Since I was steeped in all kinds of business knowledge at the time related to the rules of "making it online," I was very busy listening to the world and it was suddenly clear to me that the little Memory Palace pamphlet I'd written at the request of Haydee's students *was* something that people wanted.

When I followed the light the world was trying to show me, I soon had all the resources I needed to live the life of my dreams. Before that, I had been busy trying to foist upon the world the things I wanted for the world. Why mentoring? Because I thought the education system was broken. Wrong reason and doomed to either failure or misery due to constantly rubbing up against people who aren't on fire for knowledge and who are looking for a quick fix instead. When I simply allowed myself to explore my existing competence and what was right in front of my eyes, it was all too clear what needed to be done and how to do it.

Now, I don't know for a fact that any such journaling will help you go on tour with a band or launch a writing career. After all, I'd been playing seriously in bands since I was 14 and self-publishing zines and books since around the same age. What happened to me was a serious case of preparation meeting opportunity. This is the magic of the Perfect Present exercise.

We're often so filled with mental efforts that cause us to focus on the needs or wishes of others that we don't realize we're doing it. This means we can't contribute to the world as our best possible selves. So this Perfect Present journal meditation is like a giant pattern interrupt. First you see how you're deceiving yourself and then you use a new truth to put better wind in your sails.

In my case, I was lucky for a few reasons:

1. My second attempt at Perfect Present was completely true to what I really wanted.

2. I had the existing set of competences needed to make it happen.

3. Technologies had created devices like Kindles and online marketing platforms like Amazon.

Free will? Not a shred. I was just following the light of truth revealed by the sparks thrown off by taking the right actions.

Now here's where your existing level of will comes in. You're probably reading this book based on a set of experiences not unlike how I found Wiseman's and every other book we've all read. You saw an ad, clicked some random link on the Internet or otherwise bumped into my website. The question is:

*Are you going to do this exercise yourself and meditate over
who you really are and what you really want?*

The trick is not just to complete the exercise, but to match what you want with what you actually *can realistically* achieve based on your authentic desires, your existing competence and how your competence assembles with the current historical context. Robert Greene talks about this in terms of *amor fati*, or loving your fate. As he recently wrote his email subscribers:

Be at one with your fate and give your actions the weight of eternity. Stop wishing for something else to happen, for a different fate. That is to live a false life. The power that you can have in life of accepting your fate is so immense that it's almost hard to fathom. It gives you real stillness and clarity and perspective. You feel that everything happens for a purpose, and that it is up to you to make this purpose something positive and active.

In collaboration with Ryan Holiday, Greene has even created an *amor fati* coin you can carry with you to remind yourself of this principle. The coin is a *memento*, a word which in its original Latin is a second-person directive meaning: *remember*. As you'll soon learn, carrying a coin that you can either physically grab onto or mentally revisit exemplifies the same Memory Palace principle I used to memorize multiple tools of self-inquiry. These tools finally enabled me to break through to durable mental stillness beyond what I imagined possible.

Guess what? You're living in one of the best historical periods ever because, so long as the Internet remains as it is today, you can achieve just about anything you want provided you meet the conditions Greene mentions and enjoy the ride without destroying yourself by trying to control the outcome. Keeping a gratitude journaling practice should help with that.

Now, I use a variety of journals, ranging from blank page journals to structured journals that come with a plan. As someone who works to avoid learned helplessness, my preference will always be just journaling. That said, I love to use *The Freedom*

Journal and *The Mastery Journal*, both created by John Lee Dumas. Both of these journals look like Bibles and they're hard to not notice in any room. They both start off by helping you define a goal that you:

- Want to achieve

- Can achieve within 100 days

You are also walked through a simple process for fact checking yourself so that you're not stacking the chips against your progress. The journals include daily guidance for tackling your projects and quotes that I've come to think of as mindset adjusters. Each day, the quote at the top of the page causes you to reflect on the nature of accomplishment and remember that many people just like you have achieved their dreams before. *The Mastery Journal* is a bit more advanced, in that it helps you break days down into four distinct missions and helps you create a graphic progress readout at the end of each week. John's journals have been so successful he now even has *The Podcast Journal*, which helps people go from idea to launch by harnessing their focus and developing the habits for success.

Indeed, there are many journals like this on the market. Arthur Worsley's *Tracktion Planner* walks you through a "wheel of life" tool and Yanik Silver's *Cosmic Journal* helps you discover your "oneness" with everyone and everything else using randomization, thought experiments and doodling. Whether you choose a structured journal or just work with some blank pages and the principles discussed in this chapter, never forget, n=1.

Stop and complete this exercise now.

Exercise: Perfect Present and gratitude journaling

1. **Get a journal solely for your gratitude journaling and Perfect Present writing.** Any journal will do, even one that already has notes in it. Just get started, even if it's on an old writing pad you took home from a hotel. You can upgrade later.

2. **Write down 10 things you're grateful for. Don't overthink this step.** My list usually starts with my wife, water, food, having a home and the names of the people closest to me during the week. I sometimes also include the habit of keeping the journal itself. Why not? It's provided me with so much.

3. **Write down the Perfect Present vision you have of a day you would cheerfully repeat if you had to do it again and again.** As you've seen from my example, it doesn't matter if it's honest or not. The process itself will help you find the truth.

4. **Treat this exercise in the spirit of meditation.** You are meditating on who you really are and what you really want. Let the process reveal what is true and what isn't.

5. **Repeat for 90 days or until you've determined that this exercise is not for you.** Don't write it off completely if you abandon it at any time before receiving the intended results. You could well benefit by coming back to it again later.

It only took a while for daily journaling meditation to reveal my own lies to me. By this, the light of truth revealed what I really needed to be doing to serve the world. This meant my journey with the technique was hardly over. I clearly needed to continue with the practice because, once back in Berlin and playing with my band, I soon found myself in an intense relationship burdened by suffering. Haydee would come to my rescue, however. Thanks to fine tuning my mind with meditation and meditative journaling combined, I was open to her wisdom.

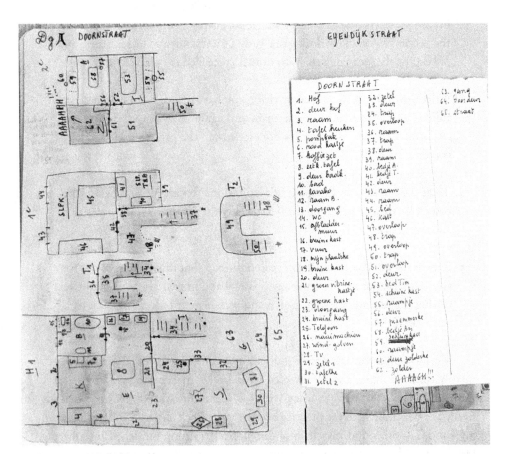

Pia's Memory Palace drawing

8 MEMORY PALACES

I F YOU HAVEN'T BEEN through the twin hells of suicidal depression and chronic pain, then my gratitude for the ancient Memory Palace technique might seem exaggerated. However, I want you to imagine a memory-based shift that releases an unwitting victim from the black jaws of death to a life of abundant access to needed information, even as hell carried on around me. The Memory Palace technique without question sparked a transformation so singular and focused that I've been talking about it ever since—and the best part is that the biggest change happened literally overnight. Even if you aren't suffering, a simple drawing and a game you play in your mind with information can rapidly improve your current life in ways that cannot be anticipated or even understood until after the deep brain structure changes have taken place.

In this chapter, I will help you create the best possible Memory Palace Network and then start using it as a way of life.

Now, this is important: We're going to get into a lot of technical detail about creating both simple and complex Memory Palaces. All of the guidelines make sense and I'm confident you'll see why as part of your practice. "Practice" is the key word here. People who put these techniques into action and give them the attention they are due get results. Pia is one; she has sent me many images of her Memory Palace drawings, a key part of the process for most of us who struggle to see images in our minds.

And practice is key because I assume one of the reasons you are reading this book is that you want a better memory. Moreover, you want the peace of mind needed to focus on the tasks of memorization—and generally experience mental calm as much as possible. And you're intrigued by the idea that memorizing a particular kind of text will help you experience even greater mental peace through memory-based meditation.

Practice is what will get you there, provided your practice is based on the fundamentals of how your brain works in relation to memory. Why is practice so important? I believe mentalist and mnemonist David Berglas put it best in his book *A Question of Memory* (42):

"Memory is not a thing with a unitary mechanism between retention and recollection. Memory is a behavior."

Berglas's observation means that memory is not something we have: *memory is something we do.* Having a Memory Palace Network that you regularly use will become the equivalent of taking your body to the gym a few times a week and working all the major muscle groups.

In this case, your "memory muscles" start with the foundation of spatial mapping and spatial memory. Exercising it will unlock:

- Autobiographical memory, or your own life-story as it goes in your head

- Procedural memory, or how you know how to do things like tie your shoes or drive a car

- Episodic memory, or context-specific experiences—memories of events in a time and a place

- Figural memory, or pictures and visual representations (also tied to iconic memory, which people confused about the "photographic memory" myth should investigate)

- Semantic memory, or your memory for words, concepts, numbers and common knowledge...and other kinds of memory that need stretching and maintaining like every other part of your body.

As you learn more of my story, you'll discover that the "bipolar disorder" that led a kind stranger to grab me back from the subway edge asking, "What the hell are you doing?" likely had a lot to do with the malfunctioning of these layers of memory. Part of my depression surely stemmed from my inability to focus and concentrate, creating a downward spiral as depression interfered with my memory and lack of memory exacerbated the depression. Yet, discovering these techniques and putting them into practice seems to have revived everything, and the spatial memory governing the Memory Palace technique provided the foundation.

Escape from Hell through Memory Palaces

I'd always had dark times. During my high school years, I would leap from being the crazy kid with orange and green hair dressed in pajamas who knew dozens of songs and played in bands to the dark poet with long, jet black hair who for days spoke to almost nobody. I was the kid about whom my dad's friends would call him up asking, "Is he alright? That kid looks like he hates the entire world." Sometimes they were right. My pen and typewriter blasted out violent poetry I arranged into handmade chapbooks for distribution to zine fanatics all over North America. Any learning I did during these dark periods in high school was done with deep resentment. Unless, of course, it was during the many days I skipped school to hang out at the local library where not a single adult ever asked me why a person of my age wasn't sitting behind a school desk.

Other times, I loved the world so much, tears of joy would come to my eyes. With friends, I climbed in the mountains and walked out on frozen rivers, laughing with pleasure at the imminent danger of it all.

Switching between blackness and bliss eventually collided well into my academic career, during my first year of PhD studies in 2003. The subway episode that opens this book was a complete psychotic break that took place much earlier, during a BA that spanned three universities. I spent three months in hospital and another nine in near-comatose "recovery" on anti-psychotics before drumming up the courage to go back to school. Now, rattled from years of testing anti-psychotics, emergency visits to the Clarke and self-induced issues from booze and pot, winter was coming. Worse, I was completely married to the idea of being a manic-depressive.

If my first master's degree had gone relatively well, it was due largely to the kind wing of Susan Swan. One of Canada's most prominent novelists, she'd given a seminar course on the memoir as a literary form. I wrote a traditional essay for the first part of the course, but her encouragement to write an actual memoir brought about a great deal of healing. Later, her recommendation letter was pivotal in my acceptance to the Humanities PhD at York University where I ultimately became the first Canadian to earn the degree. The only problem was that her letter made a big deal of my accomplishments as a person with mental illness. I don't hold it against her, but thinking of myself in these terms did not help my mood. Having earned my BA and MA and successfully entered the PhD program felt great, but the idea that an illness had anything to do with it felt like a fly gradually poisoning the ointment.

When the darkest depression of all hit, what I struggled with the most was the firm conviction I held that mental illness *was* my identity. And all of the progress that followed wouldn't have happened without Memory Palaces. Lots of Memory

Palaces. In these remembered places, which people have been using for thousands of years, I could identify with far better things. I could become one with information itself, rather than with illness. The need for these Memory Palaces and the associated mental tools we use to rapidly remember difficult information landed on my lap because one exceptionally cold winter's day, I couldn't get out of bed. I couldn't get out of bed the next day either. Nor the next. The depression I experienced that year was like nothing before. If previous depressions had been a black dog on my back, this was Godzilla standing on my throat.

Despite my desire to become a well-prepared professor, I was in ruins—completely incapable of caring for myself. I did not groom either myself or my apartment. When I did leave, it was either for cheap pasta, beer and ice cream or to drag myself to the Metro Reference Library. There, I would stare at open books, unable to focus long enough to read a sentence. I remember staring at this passage from Nietzsche in *Also Sprach Zarathustra*:

> *Du kannst dich für deinen Freund nicht schön genug putzen: denn du sollst ihm ein Pfeil und eine Sehnsucht nach dem Übermenschen sein.*

My interpretation and personal translation of this line was and remains:

> You cannot possibly enhance yourself enough for your friend (who represents all people). You should fly like an arrow that longs for the best possible outcomes of humanity.

That's what I wanted to become. The best possible friend to whomever I might teach. Now, I even use the Metro Reference Library—including the top floor—as a Memory Palace, but I had a very hard time concentrating in it back then. In the open-concept, multi-story building connected by staircases and elevators, each floor hangs from the wall like a cliff. Anyone at any time can run, jump the internal balcony railing and sail out into the void to hit center stage, flat on the main floor.

I don't know how I contained myself, or by what act of will I got myself into the library in the first place. I remember confiding with friends about this. Jennifer said it was *L'Appel du Vide*, or the "call of the void." She said Edgar Allen Poe wrote about it (I've never found the reference), and maybe it was what Nietzsche really meant when he said, "if you gaze long into an abyss, the abyss also gazes into you." Some people call this experience "high place phenomenon," and say it stems from the brain's distorting perceptions. At that time, I didn't care about the explanations or another reference in a book I couldn't concentrate on enough to read. I wanted a cure.

Due to paying approximately $70 each time I visited the pharmacist for yet another bottle of ineffective cures, I needed to save money on the transit, and this meant walking across the Bloor-Danforth Viaduct. You may have read about this monumental Toronto bridge in *In the Skin of a Lion* by Michael Ondaatje. These days, this monolithic structure hanging over the Don River is adorned with an anti-suicide barrier called "The Luminous Veil." Back then, a suicidal person took the 12-story plunge about once per month. The walk over the bridge terrified me every time as my story about being mentally ill compounded the call of the void. What other exit was there, if every moment of my future was destined to ratchet up the pain yet another notch?

The suicidal impulse manifested paradoxically: I was terrified of taking the plunge. Yet, at the same time, horrible impulses seemed to force me towards the edge. No wonder some people think they are possessed by evil demons. The sensation *is* something like that. Or worse, they can feel like angels seducing you. If the previous voices urging me to jump back in 1999 had been strangely soft and angelic, the new messages, four years later, came hard and fast, like the brap of nightmare music from industrial groups like Skinny Puppy and Ministry.

"Get up, get on your feet... The mind is a terrible thing to taste."

The urge rarely left me in peace. I would wring my hands thinking about the next time I needed to put in some research at the library. As I sat there among the books on the days I managed to get myself out of bed, the idea of leaping consumed me. As the movie played over and over again, I could only wonder how long it would take before it wore me down and I was eating a library carpet sandwich for the rest of eternity.

Not one to accept suffering forever, I looked at my bottles of lithium and anti-psychotics one morning and knew that whatever they were doing for me, it still wasn't enough. I contacted the Clarke, the same hospital I'd already spent so much time in, and eventually found my way into the office of a new psychiatrist. It's astonishing to me now that, like all the rest, this "professional" asked nothing about diet, but rapidly bounced out another drug cocktail I should try. I tried to decipher his scribbles, and desperate for release from my misery, performed some hasty research on what the words looked like and fulfilled his prescription. If only Jonathan had been around then to help me "super learn" what I was really about to send into my system.

Everything got worse. Not only did I feel more impulsive than ever before, but I spent the better part of a week thinking he'd slipped powder from magic mushrooms into my grab bag of antidepressants and anti-psychotics. The walls around me seemed to turn red and sweat with violent anger as I writhed on the couch in fits of anxiety. I felt like I was a teenager again, back in a basement, inhaling a sword forged of fire and ice.

Magic on the Internet

I don't know how long this depression lasted and the exact chronology is not clear. I only know that my mental state was far from ideal because, along with teaching duties and graduate course work, I had the first of two field exams looming. Before proceeding to the dissertation and its defense, I was responsible for massive reading lists of approximately 150 books and articles for each exam (totalling around 300 texts, 500 when you add dissertation research). These lists are decided upon in advance by the graduate student in collaboration with the examination committee. The examiners are not only well versed in the material, they have views on what those texts mean. The candidate must juggle those views with specific reference to critical details and argue their own conclusions.

While sweating over how I was going to even *start* reading in my shattered state after what felt like an eternity of staring at blurry pages, a letter about my student loans appeared in the mailbox. You're normally not supposed to be responsible for them until after you graduate, but a policy had changed and the letter's fine print—littered with symbols not even Einstein would dream of using—threw me into a fit.

I decided at that moment I needed to either quit, accept that I was going to fail the exams or jump off the Bloor-Danforth Viaduct. I still don't know why I didn't take the easy route. Residual fear of Biblical hell, I guess.

A few days later, I was on campus and still brooding over what to do. In York Lanes, which gathers the campus bookstore together with gift shops and restaurants, I was stopped by a magician. His routine was impressive. It planted a seed. In elementary school, I'd loved magic and watched Doug Henning on TV every chance I got. I gave magic performances from a magic kit during show-and-tell and read books filled with all manner of devious routines one can perform with cards, coins, elastic bands and everyday pens and pencils.

YouTube was just entering the scene and before I knew it, this strange new platform was providing better relief from my torment than any pill could ever offer: watching and learning magic from the Internet. While the dense philosophy, history and "critical theory" I was responsible for fascinated me, my reading list would have been a struggle to read and understand even on the most cloudless days of the mind. Sleight of hand with cards was also difficult for me to learn from books because my mind's eye was limited at the time, but in video format, I could follow along and mirror the teacher. I could *focus* on the knowledge because I could *see* it playing out in the magician's hands as they spoke in clear terms. Plus, many magicians are also philosophers. They care for the traditions of the craft and its intellectual history. Like nearly any group of people who share a common interest, you find comrades, rivals, outcasts, rogues and defectors among magicians. And here's the very best part: in each of these camps, there is always at least one magician who loves *memorizing* playing cards in addition to physically manipulating them.

The card memorization technique is easy enough. What changed everything for me was the combination of memorizing cards and matching them with stations in a Memory Palace. It's an astonishing feeling when you can think of a corner in a room and experience a samurai from a favorite movie leap into being to battle Johnny Cash before throwing ninja stars at a former girlfriend's dog—all for the purpose of instantly remembering the Queen of Diamonds and the 2 of Diamonds. None of this image-making happens for the fun of it—though the process is incredibly fun. It happens because you practiced "elaborative encoding" in conjunction with your Memory Palace and then a reverse process of decoding that helped you get the information back.

From the Internet to Memory Palaces of the ancient rhetoricians
It is said that James Joyce brought the Greek word "epiphany" into common parlance (minus its religious connotations) in his posthumous *Stephen Hero* where

characters experience change through sudden recognition that stimulates monumental change. When I realized that the difficult texts I was studying could easily be translated to index cards and then memorized using the same process I'd learned for playing cards, I remember feeling that sense of epiphany. It was not a moment of instant transformation, nor did my depression crumble into dust, but a new future seemed to open before me.

From that point on, I battled my inability to focus by reading books out loud. It's not a perfect solution, but it helped me get through them and identify the key points. By inscribing the key ideas on index cards, I was able to understand them even better and pause to embellish them with bizarre images. I didn't know nearly as much about how to create effective pictures at the time, but I intuited that they weren't images in the true sense. I placed these images in Memory Palaces based on York University campus, my apartment and dozens of buildings I was familiar with by thinking through my life. I even tried using the Clarke Institute, though negative associations with its corridors forced me to work with other options.

As I placed what I would eventually come to call "Magnetic Imagery" into my Memory Palaces, I deliberately added multisensory elements. Our community calls these the "Magnetic Modes"—which are represented in the acronym "KAVE COGS":

K = Kinesthetic
A = Auditory
V = Visual
E = Emotional

C = Conceptual
O = Olfactory
G = Gustatory
S = Spatial

Although I didn't fully conceive of it at the time in terms of this convenient acronym, I came to use it for every image I create; I simply run through each category, kind of like allowing the pins to fall into place when spinning the dials on a combination lock. Once the Magnetic Imagery has been composed—ideally while also thinking about the Memory Palace station—they play out in little theatrical vignettes against landscapes built from homes and journeys through them.

The Memory Palace is spatial, and this is key to maximizing the volume of information you can remember at a rapid pace. **But each image is also inherently spatial.**

As you work with these techniques, you'll find that using Batman in a Memory Palace opens the opportunity to *turn* Batman's body itself into a Memory Palace by dividing his body into Magnetic Stations. The fact that everything you use in a Memory Palace is characterized by space and unlocks its possibilities is interesting because as Thales, often considered the first scientist and the first philosopher, told us in Greek:

Μέγιστον τόπος ἅπαντα γαρ χωρεῖ /Megiston topos hapanta gar chorei/
Space is the ultimate thing, as it contains all things.

This concept can be seen at work in neuroscience: our brains do not merely store and retrieve information; they chemically encode our memories in different brain locations. Moreover, as neuroscientist Stephen Kosslyn demonstrates in *The Case for Mental Imagery*, our memories move around in the space of our brains as we age. Memories literally change location over time and as we manipulate them. Kosslyn even suggests that there may be a 1:1 correspondence between space in the world and how the brain encodes it spatially in our neural networks. This notion suggests that our brains chemically encode information about rooms in such a way that the relationship between the front wall and the back wall of a room are reflected in where the brain stores its estimation of the spatial relationship.

I don't share all of this science to frustrate or discourage. Magician and memory expert Harry Lorayne once kindly mentored me in how to teach memory and told me to be careful about talking about memory science. He suggested that it only confuses people and bogs them down: people only care about getting results. I have generally found this to be true, but my own interest in science has given me many ideas that guide my own practice using memory techniques. I still share the science with caution and with the understanding that not everyone loves it as much as I do, but I can no longer resist spreading the good news in short bursts of technical detail. As I hope this book makes clear, to use memory techniques, or to meditate, *is* doing science. The more you guide your n=1 adventures based on the scientific conversation, the more you'll get out of it. And if you struggle to understand the terms, use memory techniques to help you memorize their meaning. If you're as fed up with the current anti-science sentiment as we are in the Magnetic Memory Method community, you'll come to love how memorizing some of these wonderful terms opens the door to understanding more, one term at a time.

I believe learning scientifically is key to progress for every community. In *Skeptic: Viewing the World with a Rational Eye*, a collection of Michael Shermer's writings for *The Scientific American*, the writer points out "the facts never just speak for themselves: they are always viewed through the lens of theory.

The two—observations and views, data and theory—are the conjoined twins of science" (2). This passage is particularly important because it helps us understand why everyone who succeeds with the Memory Palace technique, Magnetic Modes and Magnetic Imagery, must become like a scientist of their own mind. The theory suggests that if you create a Memory Palace and "magnetically" couple your bed or kitchen table with some zany, multisensory image interwoven with information you want to memorize, followed by a strategic period of review by revisiting the bed or kitchen and the imagery, then you should be able to remember it. Everyone who understands this basic theory about memory techniques and puts it into action has the chance to successfully reproduce the experiment in the laboratory of their mind. Those who don't put the theory into action are locked out of the discussion. They can only speculate, but won't have the chance to experiment or make observations about the results.

When I started back in the library, memorizing cards was easy. For tough information and languages, I needed to run many experiments because of an absence of contemporary theories at the time. So many of the memory-technique books written during the 20th century are by memory competitors or magicians who use memory techniques as part of their performance to win prizes or enthral audiences. But I was in a life-or-death situation and couldn't care less about winning accolades. I wanted to know *exactly* how people memorize *entire* books. For that, I needed to dig, find theories and run experiments with them in order to get university-level results. I needed a PhD so I could accomplish my goals of sharing knowledge, not the laurels of a competition or more tips from a restaurant gig as a magician.

As I continued to read, I discovered ancient texts on memory techniques, almost all of them devoted to rhetoric. In *Rhetorica ad Herennium*, one of the oldest books on rhetoric from the Roman era, I learned that you must start with the art of memorizing words if you want to progress to higher-order skills. Further, your Memory Palaces must be as physical as possible (the K in KAVE COGS). Many writers on memory talked about creating associations in your mind like inscribing words on wax tablets. The idea I got from the memory parts of *Rhetorica ad Herennium* was to imagine my Memory Palace walls *as if they were as solid as wax*. At the time, I couldn't see these Memory Palaces in my mind and needed to draw them on paper. But imagining how they *felt* physically made them so much easier to use.

Even better, this ancient text advises that you must become a student of how your own mind creates mental imagery. It doesn't matter how the process works for anyone else or how much theory you consume: you learn by doing *and* analyzing your practice (n=1). In fact, the unknown author of this ancient tome (some mistakenly attribute it to Cicero) holds a stern warning for those who seek Easy

Street: "I believe that they who wish to do easy things without trouble and toil must previously have been trained in more difficult things."

The author also warned us against what I call "mnemonic example addiction." Thousands of years ago, this author about memory techniques must have noticed all kinds of students in danger of learned helplessness when he wrote:

> It is the instructor's duty to teach the proper method of search in each case, and, for the sake of greater clarity, to add in illustration some one or two examples of its kind, but not all. For instance, when I discuss the search for Introductions, I give a method of search and do not draught a thousand kinds of Introductions. The same procedure I believe should be followed with respect to images.

Thousands of years later, the Internet is filled with books and software selling mnemonic examples by the ton. Although I must acknowledge that some of these offerings come from a good place, they often create the problem of learned helplessness the author of *Rhetorica ad Herennium* knew we must avoid. Teaching people to fish must be paramount to just handing out food for free. You cannot help people who will not help themselves, and yet I get emails day in and day out asking for more examples from people who are swamped in more than they could ever consume. Some people ask me how much I would charge to create Magnetic Imagery for them. I turn them to the teaching every time, knowing full well that the best solution is for them to learn how to create their own after going through a handful of mnemonic examples at most. Don't confuse activity with accomplishment.

All that wisdom from just one text was only scratching the surface. Not free of mnemonic addiction myself, I wanted more and, in the ancient world, I found it. From Aristotle's treatise on memory, I learned that you must do more than become a student of your own memory. You must build the skills and then *tend* them. He suggests caring for the memories you gather like birds in an aviary, but I now think of it as tending to *multiple* gardens. As the caretaker, you must develop an understanding of when to leave a field fallow, when to till the soil, when to plant the seeds, when to reap the harvest and what to do when a storm arises and seems to tear everything down.

Aristotle also urges us to ponder the contents of our memory as if objects, people and places really were alive, each with a history that emerges from a larger field. I've come to believe that he is encouraging us to nurture not only ourselves, but the community as well, by sharing our memories with others. Aristotle's observation implies a general truth we often forget—that we are not isolated individuals but are formed by and connected to everyone else, and we can experience this by attuning ourselves to our memories in this way. I now always urge people to teach memory skills as soon as they can to tap into this communal aspect, which in turn helps them learn the techniques better. Next to consistent application, teaching is the best teacher.

Another important tip came from Thomas Aquinas, who points out in his *Summa Theologica* that we will struggle less if we avoid abstractions when creating our images and instead make every image more concrete. This links back to the suggestion in *Rhetorica ad Herennium* that we base our Memory Palaces on actual places and *experience* them physically. It is tempting, for example, to take shortcuts and just use a "cup" for the number 79 (using a technique you'll learn later in this book called the Major Method), but a specific cup that you've actually seen, held and ideally drunk from is more effective as a mnemonic object or Magnetic Image.

As I continued to put these theories into practice, the full range of KAVE COGS helped me, because I stopped inventing new images and focused only on content already in my memory, including places to make into Memory Palaces. In sum, as I explored the art, craft and science of memory, I realized the images were not images at all. They were multisensory spools of thread with which one stitches existing mental content into well-known spaces, such as the corners of rooms, furniture and appliances.

Now, with all these principles in mind, let's learn more about how they play out in one of the most valuable stories of all time. Although certainly the stuff of legend, it contains important clues about how to use memory techniques. Let's go back to Ancient Greece.

It's the 6th century BCE, and Simonides of Ceos (c. 546–468 BCE) found himself giving a speech at a banquet before a group of distinguished guests in a large and impressive building. Perhaps Simonides performed a memory demonstration by naming each of the attendees during his talk, as many of us who teach memory techniques tend to do. Since he was known as a poet, it's likely that he recited some of his own verse too.

After concluding his speech, Simonides thanked Castor and Pollux, two mythical boxers who represented heroism and were given immortality by Zeus. When Simonides asked the host to pay him the speaking fee, however, the host expressed annoyance that Simonides thanked gods instead of him.

"Go ask Castor and Pollux to pay you," the host said.

At that moment, a servant told Simonides that two men were outside and asking for him.

"I'll get back to this matter of the fee in a moment," Simonides assured the host and then went outside, where he saw two men on horses. They beckoned him over.

It was none other than Castor and Pollux themselves. Next, without warning, the building Simonides had just left collapsed and everyone inside died.

Later, as the dust from this shocking event settled, using his incredible memory abilities, Simonides helped the authorities identify all the bodies so they could be properly buried by the mourning families who would never have experienced closure otherwise. He did this by visiting his memory of the building in his mind and recalling where each guest had been sitting. This parable now serves as the foremost legend about the art of tying information to location in order to store and "revisit" it.

But I believe there's more to the story of Simonides than most renditions pull out of it. In fact, the legend contains key elements of the memory techniques you'll want to use in your own practice:

- The legend takes place in an *actual* building, not one Simonides imagined. The banquet hall presented a number of locations, or stations, arranged in a certain order (the seating plan) on which to place memorized information (people's names).

- The memorized information—people's names and features—was *important* to Simonides. He paid attention to these details.

- The story contains *exaggerated* and *dramatic* action. Each of the Magnetic Modes are accounted for when you *feel* the building crumbling to the ground (kinesthetic). You can *hear* the rumble (auditory). Even if you don't see pictures in your mind, you probably have an idea of what a collapsing building looks like (visual). Emotions are par for the course when something majestic is lost (emotional). The tale contains notions of squabbling over fees and the feeling of poetic justice (conceptual). You can almost taste and smell the food and wine, if not the dust coming up from the rubble (olfactory and gustatory). Even without knowing yourself where the attendees were sitting, you have a sense of people in rooms at tables, not to mention Simonides' movement from the interior to the exterior (spatial).

As we proceed in this book, I will guide you in how to use Memory Palaces and create Magnetic Imagery using these Magnetic Modes. You will learn the skills most important to the story of Simonides overall: the exponential power of combining location, image, and action with information of importance to you—on a grand scale—for memorability.

Two very beautiful MMM student Memory Palaces mapped out in a Memory Journals

Creating Memory Palaces

"Memory Palace" is really just a sexy term for a "location-based mnemonic device." I love it. Some people hate it. But let's zoom out far beyond our preferences and look at the term "mnemonic" itself. The word refers to anything that helps us remember information, including acronyms, rhymes and basic associations that connect one idea with another in our minds. In other words, a Memory Palace turns space itself into a kind of mnemonic, one that uses mental images of the interior and exterior features of buildings or other features of the world as "hooks" upon which we hang other images. These hooks are typically placed along a "journey." Other terms for this location-based mnemonic are:

- Mind Palace

- Mental Palace

- Memory Castle

- Journey Method

- Roman Room

Why do some of us love to call these mental devices "Memory Palaces"? There are many potential answers. My favorite appears in Augustine of Hippo's (354–430 ACE) *Confessions*:

> *"And I come to the fields and spacious palaces (praetoria memoriae) of my memory, where are the treasures of innumerable images, brought into it from things of all sorts perceived by the senses."*

This passage is important to mnemonists who use Memory Palaces because Augustine is pointing out that, for Memory Palaces to become useful, we need to combine locations with *all* of our senses to create memory "treasure." By joining sensations with locations, we can make information Magnetic so that it will come back to us whenever we wish.

For this reason, it's helpful to think of locations, like the homes of all your friends, not merely with your mind's eye, but with *all* of your senses. For example, I had a friend named Ryan in elementary school whose house I sometimes went to during lunch hour. Although I only vaguely recall that home and don't have a visual picture, I remember the table, the tomato soup and crackers and some basics of the yard—how things smelled, tasted and felt.

For those who don't like the term "Memory Palace," don't turn preference into a mental block. It's not difficult to find a replacement. I once coached an 88-year-old man who went on to memorize hundreds of lines of poetry using the Magnetic Memory Method. He soon revived his dormant German to the point he could re-read old love letters from a time of separation during WWII. But these results arrived only after he finally decided to call his Memory Palaces "apartments with compartments." The lesson here? Don't let the terminology get in your way!

The same goes for the terms "Magnetic Imagery," "mental image" and "mental picture." We use these to describe what we're doing when setting up and using these location-based mnemonics, but this vision-centric terminology is a fault of English. We are really talking about using this level of memory in all of its multisensory elements—infused with the KAVE COGS Magnetic Modes.

You might also find it useful to know that location-based memory techniques appear to have existed before people like Augustine and Simonides worked with them roughly 2,500 years ago. Lynne Kelley shows in *The Memory Code* that many prehistoric cultures used location-based mnemonics. In her book on the Buddha, Karen Armstrong mentions the use of memory techniques in yoga that involve locations. The Buddhist instructor Michael Roach has spoken in great detail about how various meditations were remembered by the monks by placing imagery in different parts of the temple. In an ancient meditation I learned from one of Roach's audio recordings, he asks us to remember that death is always behind us. To encode this part of the meditation, he explained, monks were advised to place a black dog at a particular part of the temple to remind them of this principle. Later, religious traditions like Catholicism would take such ritualistic reminders out of the imagination and externalize them in the form of reliefs or paintings on the walls of their churches. They call these images the Stations of the Cross. In our lingo, they are location-based mnemonic structures housed not in churches but in Memory Palaces.

Memory Palaces are really mental constellations

The principle we learn from historical practices around memory is that we can divide any Memory Palace into "Magnetic Stations." These are strategically chosen places that form the stops along a mental journey based upon actual journeys you remember from the real world and could actually take. For example, one of my Memory Palaces involves my desk, the four corners of my office, various parts of my kitchen, my living room, the exit from my apartment and ultimately the hallway leading to the elevators. My desk is a Magnetic Station, the four elements on the stove are Magnetic Stations and any place that I leave information is a Magnetic Station. Some people might ask: Isn't it better to use a place I'm not currently living in? What if I bump into my Magnetic Imagery? What if I move my furniture? What if I want to add new things to my Memory Palace? What if I memorize something and later find out it was factually untrue and need to make a change?

It's challenging to provide useful answers to these questions. Often, people ask them before taking action. Because *Genchi Genbutsu* (go and see for yourself) is often the most direct and only answer, I often ask people to consider *why* they are asking these questions by examining their learning style. "What if?" learners often lock themselves out of achieving their goals by getting hung up in issues that only matter if you face them. Think of Systema. Imagine if, rather than practicing in the gym, I had asked, "What if I am in Harlem one day and someone points a gun at me?" We could spend all day speculating, but the only answer Systema has is to train your instincts so that you're prepared to execute the best possible move when the time comes. Not the *right* move, because no one can know in advance what that will be. We practice these techniques to be prepared with the optimal moves because we are skilled practitioners of the craft. That's how I was able to perform decently at a memory competition even with jet-lag, arthritic pain and one of the worst hangovers of my life. I'd never even competed before and yet I held my own. Anyone can.

There are countless other questions that will be interesting to consider along your journey and you can find me answering them pretty much every week on my livestreams or download a massive library of answers from my blog or podcast. For now, let's move forward and consider how to use Memory Palaces efficiently. Over the years, I've come to think of Memory Palaces as nothing more than "constellations." They are squares collected in space. In those spaces, I've begun focusing mostly on the corners of rooms so as to increase the speed of my Memory Palace journeys. You can see this approach of using corners reflected in this Memory Palace drawing of the school where I attended grades 8 and 9:

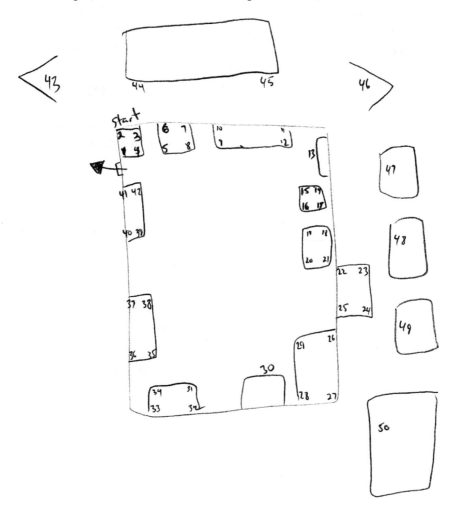

Memory Palace made from a school I attended—the same one with the LSD church parking lot

To increase my speed of recall, I suggest we avoid recreating the entire Memory Palace. When I work with this school, I focus just on the Magnetic Stations. It's like looking up in the night sky. I don't want to see a giant spoon when locating the Big Dipper. Rather, I want to see the star pattern. Likewise, I draw the Memory Palace to sort out a journey I can experience at a glance, focusing just on its parts like the stars. As in *The Matrix*, "there is no spoon."

The idea of a Memory Palace journey resembling a constellation emerged during a conversation I held on my podcast with USA memory champion Nelson Dellis. Like many memory competitors, Nelson has shared his approach to the techniques in books like *Remember It!* and I've been honored to be able to speak with him several times about his process. Nelson is a special kind of competitor and author, however. He's founded the charity *Climb for Memory* and been part of large initiatives to help scientists gather much needed research data in the quest to cure Alzheimer's. His work is "assemblage" writ as large as the mountains you can often find him climbing and vlogging about on his YouTube channel.

To make the journeys inside Memory Palaces as linear as possible, I personally impose a mental sea shell structure that spirals like a Nautilus. Like this:

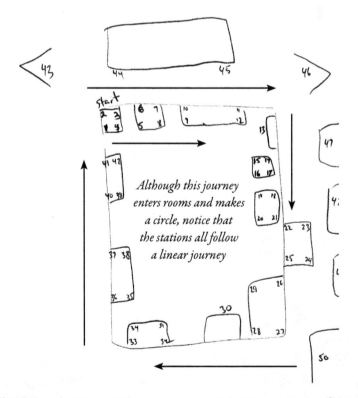

Sea-shell path through a Memory Palace using corners only for Magnetic Stations (Micro-stations)

This approach makes it easier to reduce any Memory Palace down to this constellation style. Again, just as you can see the Big Dipper without imposing the image of a spoon on it, you can experience the journey of your Memory Palace without having to render it beyond one point in space at a time. To get there, however, the journey must:

- Be well formed in advance;

- Use only the most obvious Magnetic Stations that don't require you to memorize them;

- Follow a logical order that doesn't create cognitive load.

In my experience working with hundreds of Memory Palaces personally and advising thousands of students, its unlikely one can achieve these outcomes with any speed or integrity of outcome without drawing the Memory Palaces. Plus the goal is to minimize cognitive load and have each Memory Palace operate as a lean memory machine so you can focus on "Magnetically Weaving" your images into space. Every ounce of preparation is worth a pound of ease later.

Using your life to find Memory Palaces

Before we get into the theory and techniques for creating well-formed Memory Palaces, you might like to know why the tool is so powerful when you take certain best practices into consideration.

First, spatial memory is a *free* resource. Even if you don't see pictures or can't play movies in your head, how much work is it to call your elementary school to mind? If I ask you to draw a square based on your living room, how much effort is that really?

The name of the game is to *start* in a way the keeps the cognitive load low. Some people can imagine their way through Memory Palaces without much effort, but others really struggle. Even those who don't need to draw their Memory Palaces tell me they benefit from the planning stage because they create better journeys and make fewer mistakes when using them. Plus, you'll learn more about how your mind experiences space and start to remember space differently.

To get started, get out your Memory Journal. It doesn't have to be fancy, though you can potentially signal to your brain higher levels of intention and that you value the outcomes of the activity by getting a luxury journal. I sometimes use

The Freedom Journal because of how it includes space for a quick Memory Palace drawing. Whatever journal you choose, label it "Memory Journal" and decorate the cover or inside page somehow. Personalizing it increases your intention and bonds you more closely to it.

In your journal, go through your life and list all the buildings associated with your friends and relatives. This list will form the basis of your first "Memory Palace Network." However, not all Memory Palaces are created equal. That's why I'm going to ask you to create at least 26 of them.

Don't be alarmed by that number. Unless you're very young, chances are you can easily complete this exercise. If you'll just consider each classroom in your elementary school as an individual Memory Palace, you'll already be a quarter of the way to the goal. I suggest that you make a note in your mind regarding the name of the teacher you had in that classroom. For example, a teacher named Mrs. Thomas would make that Memory Palace a "T" Memory Palace. This simple mental "tag" can be tremendously useful for using the Memory Palace for learning.

As you create your inventory of potential Memory Palaces, add your high school classrooms, your home, the homes of friends and family, your place of work and your favorite restaurant. You don't have to complete the list all at once; come back to the exercise often. I create a new list about once a year and am always astonished by how much more of the past I remember. It is a rewarding activity, and you'll be surprised by how working with your memory continually provides you with "new" aspects of your life that would remain forgotten if it weren't for self-conscious memory excavation.

It's possible, and even likely, you will never use them all. But the more you have, the more you *will have* to choose from. Even those Memory Palaces you do not use contribute to the integrity of your Memory Palace Network, thanks to the 80/20 rule. The 80/20 rule, also called Price's Law or the Pareto Principle, is a concept that is used in many ways. For our purposes, we want to think about our Memory Palace Network as the soil from which rows of nourishing plants like tomatoes grow. Although only 20 percent of the space in your garden of Memory Palaces will likely ever produce tomatoes you need, its strength doesn't come from nothing: the surrounding 80 percent of the soil in a garden is important to the success of the 20 percent involved in growing the plants.

Please don't get hung up on these exact numbers. The distribution probably won't be a clean 80/20. I'm sharing this principle because many people report concern that there is no purpose to the Memory Palaces they're creating through the spatial abundance mindset I teach. They worry that they'll be wasting time. The reality is that the gardener who takes care of the entire field of soil gets the most out of the 20 percent that actually grows the harvest. Without that comprehensive care, the most active parts of the soil are bound to underperform and disappoint.

It's also important to note that the exact placement of the rows in a garden may, and likely should, vary over time. Sometimes this means leaving entire portions fallow for a season. Likewise in our memory training efforts, we want a large field of Memory Palaces to draw upon so we always have them when we need them and so we can leave some fallow from time to time.

To sum up the steps:

1. Get your Memory Journal.

2. Think of your life, starting with preschool or grade one. Think of what the room was like. Settle for anything. No matter how vague or ghostly the image, if you get something, hang onto it, cherish it, let it be a treasured artefact of your memory. Write it down. If nothing comes, don't get frustrated. Never associate any memory activity with frustration or any particular need for an outcome. Just move on through the years until you find a room that you remember significantly enough to write down in your journal.

3. When you find your first room, draw a simple rectangle. Like this:

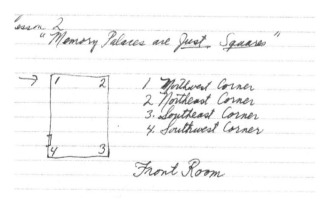

The simplest of Memory Palace drawings, sometimes called by our community a "Magnetic Square."

4. Continue listing Memory Palaces and drawing them. List out the Magnetic Stations using numbers. Make the journey as linear as possible.

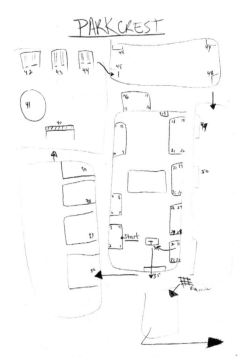

Parkcrest Elementary Memory Palace

As you continue to create Memory Palaces, consider using:

- Homes of relatives

- Libraries

- Movie theaters

- Hotels

- Grocery stores

- Churches

- Cafes

- Restaurants

- Museums

As you compile these lists, mentally note the letter of the alphabet that starts the word. Allan's home becomes an "A" Memory Palace, Parkcrest Elementary becomes a "P" Memory Palace and so on. You don't always have to use them alphabetically, but it's useful to start thinking in terms of these kinds of associations. For example, when I started memorizing the *Upadesa Saram*, I thought of my Uncle Lloyd because U = Uncle. The basement apartment where he died mercifully in his sleep didn't feel quite right, but instead of hemming and hawing about an option to use, I instantly had at least one idea I could potentially use thanks to alphabetical association. I quickly found a better Memory Palace, but without the alphabet strategy, I might have hemmed and hawed over what to use and never bounced to something better. A lot of students resist this alphabetical strategy, but like space itself, it's a free resource. The alphabet has been stewing in your head for years—use it!

I recommend you spend as much time as you can milking the alphabet and your current memory of space from your life in your Memory Journal. Go for gold, as much as you can in one go. Then revisit these lists over time to continually develop new Memory Palace ideas, followed by drawing them out with simple stickman sketches. Although it might seem like you are stretching yourself for ideas and it is all too much effort, this stretching is, in fact, a good in itself. You need as many canvases as possible upon which to paint in order to fully experience the magic of the Memory Palace technique. And you need the practice of associating one thing with another, in this case, people with places, and places with names you can sort alphabetically.

The two kinds of Magnetic Stations in a Memory Palace constellation

Let's now add a layer to the powerful use of "constellations" of Magnetic Stations. There are two types of stations that I have used for different purposes at different times. It will be helpful for you to understand them:

- Macro-stations—an entire room, e.g., bedroom, kitchen, living room, bathroom

- Micro-stations—an element inside a room, e.g., a bookcase, bed, appliance

It's important to recognize the difference because, at the beginning stages of using Memory Palaces, it's often best to use only macro-stations until you get the hang of the techniques. By using one room to store one piece of information, you'll get a feeling for how to hold a location in mind while creating Magnetic Imagery that connects with information you need to memorize. It's kind of like playing "mental Lego" as you let the process attach the different pieces into place on the grid of your Memory Palace.

For example, let's say I wanted to memorize the Swedish word for tree: "träd." (I recently memorized this word based on a question that came during one of my livestreams from a YouTube subscriber who goes by the excellent screen name of Rasmus.) To use a single room as a Memory Palace, I would forgo all the opportunities to use the corners and tables and bookcases. Instead, I would focus just on the idea of the room itself and generally aim for the center. Then, I would imagine something like a silver tree exploding up from the floor, covered in silver trays. The tree would be trading the trays with itself to help me remember the pronunciation of the word along with its meaning.

Here's the most important point when selecting your Magnetic Stations:

Do not select stations that you will have to think about later.

For example, if you have three couches, two chairs, the rugs underneath them, the 15 books on your coffee table and every bottle of booze in your liquor cabinet, you're begging for a struggle. The point of the Memory Palace is to reduce the cognitive demands of following your journey by focusing only on the most obvious location assets that require little or no thought. If you make the Memory Palace creation process a memorization exercise itself, the technique will work against, and not in favor of, your ability to rapidly memorize new information.

Memory Palace best practices

1. Draw your Memory Palaces by hand in your Memory Journal.
Many people prefer to use technology in the form of drawing apps, but there are many reasons why doing so will diminish your results. For one thing, unless you're skilled with imaging tools, using software will probably take much longer to create a simple Memory Palace. You'll also likely be using far fewer muscles and thereby fewer neurons connected with spatial memory.

(I haven't got the budget to rent the brain imaging machines needed to test my certainty that hand drawing your Memory Palaces on paper works better than software. Until such budgets are available, Richard Wiseman presents research on the benefits of handwriting in *59 Seconds* that relates here, as does common sense and your own practice. If you test both options for long enough to create a big enough data set, you'll know the truth of what works best for you, and that's all that matters.)

2. After numbering each station, write a top-down list of all your stations.
This process of seeing your Memory Palace spatially and schematically represented will help tap into both your visual imagination and your conceptual, organizational imagination. When you navigate the Memory Palace, both of these "pre-visualization" strategies will make it easier for you to mentally manipulate the space. Taking the time to draw and list your Magnetic Stations will also help you be sure that you're selecting the right stations.

Remember: If you have to memorize the stations, they are not Magnetic Stations. If remembering that you have both a couch and a chair in a room requires memorization, neither one should become a Magnetic Station. Just focus on obvious spots that are completely logical, such as the four corners of the room relative to the door.

Can you memorize new locations for use as Memory Palaces? Certainly, but I never do this for the simple reason that spatial memory is a free resource. Rooms typically have four walls and corners and the layouts of dozens of buildings magically appear in the memory of most people. Obviously, there are exceptions to every rule, such as when I might deliberately memorize the location of a painting in a gallery knowing full well that it will be moved during the next exhibition. It's a trivial matter to use that painting as a Magnetic Station in a Memory Palace *and* the next layout of the same gallery for different information later. Master the fundamentals first and you'll be delighted by how the rules set you free to use this memory technique in many alternative ways.

3. As you construct your journey through the Memory Palace by identifying your stations, consider following two additional key principles:

- Do not trap yourself

- Do not cross your own path

This is why the "sea shelling" technique is helpful. You want your Memory Palace journeys to be linear for the same reason you don't want to memorize furniture in order to gather stations. Linear journeying makes it easier to follow the path in your mind and you will spend much less mental energy when using the Memory Palace to store and recall words.

Example of a Memory Palace

Let's look now at a real set of micro-stations from a real Memory Palace that I have used for several purposes. This is the office where I used to write my books and blog posts in Berlin. This is the same room where I recorded the first episodes of the Magnetic Memory Method podcast and video courses. This is also the room where I first thoroughly explored using what I call a "Magnetic Bridging Figure" for more than vocabulary, which has been the topic of most of my previous books and courses.

Berlin MMM Memory Palace—Photo by Alan Haig-Brown

We use Magnetic Bridging Figures because sometimes you want to link your Magnetic Stations together to make them more navigable. For example, instead of memorizing a random pile of words in German, I used to organize them alphabetically. I would place *ab* words in an 'A' Memory Palace and tag along as Abraham

Lincoln—the Bridging Figure—spit on Mona Lisa (*abartig*) or bite into a tin of chemical solvent (*abbeitzmittel*).

Likewise, I followed Ezra Pound around a Memory Palace to memorize the Japanese hiragana. On one station, for example, I imagined Pound threatening fellow Modernist Wyndham Lewis while pronouncing a "se" word to help me remember how a character sounded. Their bodies literally took on the shape of the character as much as possible. A quick sketch in my Memory Journal and a number to represent the Magnetic Station in the Memory Palace was all I needed to mentally revisit it later. In this case, I chose Ezra Pound not on the basis of a sound association, but because I knew of his work with Asian languages. Thanks to working with a figure I'd read, heard on a recording and generally thought about philosophically, I could draw upon several Magnetic Modes from KAVE COGS. In addition to sound, I could guess his height, what it felt like to be Pound interacting with Wyndham Lewis as he *sed* something to him and the conceptual realm of why he and Lewis might be in an altercation in the first place (it's a long, but fascinating story if you're into the history of modernist poetry and art).

As with all of the considerations I'm sharing, the point is to use multi sensory representation based on the KAVE COGS formula to ultimately reduce the mental management while maximizing the value of each trigger. This process works because all of the material is already in your memory and snaps together well with the new material you want to learn. Here is some more finesse on why these steps work so well for reducing cognitive load, even if your initial training experience might feel like you're increasing it:

As a film professor with a bit of theatre background, I've known for years that every time you change scenes, you have to "start the engine" again, something that is also true of fiction, as noted by Sol Stein. The Magnetic Bridging Figure allows you to keep the energy flowing and avoid having to start cold on each station because it *must* involve the Magnetic Bridging Figure if you're consistent with this aspect of the discipline.

One of my favorite uses of this Memory Palace principle played out when I wanted to learn a song Marlene Dietrich performs beautifully, "Wenn ich mir was wünschen dürfte." I used Marlene as the Magnetic Bridging Figure and simply followed her throughout the apartment as I sang that song. It begins:

Man hat uns nicht gefragt, als wir noch kein Gesicht
Ob wir leben wollten oder lieber nicht

The lines, laced in war-scarred tragedy, basically mean, "As we still had no face, they did not ask us if we would prefer to live or not."

To memorize the sound and meaning of the lyrics, I encoded everything with Magnetic Imagery on a word by word basis. For *man hat*, I imagined Marlene Dietrich taking novelist Thomas Mann's hat. I felt it as if the hat was my own (Kinesthetic Mode). For *uns nicht gefragt,* I thought of how Cormac McCarthy uses the word *uncials* in his novel *Child of God* (Conceptual Mode). For *Ob wir leben,* I thought of my friend Aaron Obst getting a lobotomy with Dietrich as the surgeon.

The Thomas Mann Magnetic Image took place at the first corner. The next Magnetic Image "happened" over the bed. Using Marlene Dietrich as a Magnetic Bridging Figure to help reduce the amount of unique imagery I needed to create, I followed her throughout the apartment and out into the street. Within about 20 minutes, I was able to sing the entire song. And I did sing it many times in many bars to the astonishment of many a German. I might slip on a line or two all these years later, but I'm confident I could sing most of it now should anyone want the distinct... *experience*... of hearing me crooning away *auf Deutsch*. Many people know just how fulfilling it feels to sing songs from beginning to end. The Magnetic

Bridging Figure in a well-formed Memory Palace provides a fun and easy means of memorizing more songs without the tedious hassle of rote repetition.

Keeping the journey linear and free from path-crossing to prevent trapping myself makes the biggest difference to this practice. It's part of what makes it possible to encode so much, so quickly, because it eliminates confusion about what comes next along the journey and therefore keeps the expenditure of mental energy to a minimum.

So now you've had a look into just one of my many Memory Palaces. Do you see the power of separating places that you already know into individual stations? Do you understand how you can use them to drop pieces of information so you can access them later?

I certainly hope so, because there is literally no other memory method this powerful... and there is still so much to learn about it.

Specify, specify, specify

To be truly successful when using Memory Palaces to store and retrieve large amounts of information, select each Memory Palace with care. Your Memory Palaces should be project-specific and respond to specific needs. As mentioned, I started learning Japanese hiragana before switching to Chinese. To deal with the hiragana—the phonetic lettering system—I needed a Memory Palace with 48 stations that were tightly linked together, but not overwhelmingly so. After some thought, I drew a quick sketch of my girlfriend's apartment. Within five minutes, I had 48 stations written out in a list and 15 minutes later, I had memorized both the sound and the shape of 15 characters. Most of the Magnetic Imagery involved Ezra Pound with a guest, but I sometimes switched to Homer Simpson or the Grim Reaper. You can even add features to a Magnetic Bridging Figure, such as giving someone like Ezra Pound Superman's strength and an enemy to represent another part of a symbol or character:

It really is this simple. However, if I had picked a Memory Palace that was too small (or even too large) and tried to work with it for this particular set of information, results would not have come nearly as fast or as easy. Likewise, without having prepared my Magnetic Lists in advance and developed the ability to rapidly come up with ideas to use, I would never have thought about using Superman with Ezra Pound to create a solution for the *ka* hiragana. Superman's birth name, after all, is Ka-El.

I know that all of this can sound confusing, and for many people it will stay that way if you don't dive in and start using these techniques. In the Magnetic Memory Method community, we sum this principle up with DOC: Doing is the Origin of Confidence. We get a lot of power out of this formula, which makes for a fun chant to rattle off during livestreams:

Doing is the Origin of Competence
Doing is the Origin of Consistency
Doing is the Origin of Creativity
Doing is the Origin of Courage
Doing is the Origin of Clarity
Doing is the Origin of Control

Yes, "control," even in the absence of free will, as paradoxical as that sounds. Especially if you can get control over the mnemonic example addiction that holds so many students from just diving in to experience DOC.

As the unknown author of the *Rhetorica ad Herennium* seems to have known, all the mnemonic examples in the world cannot replace the value of creating your own. Just getting started is important because it helps you work towards developing an *economy of means* in your Memory Palaces. This term comes from the theater and refers to drawing upon the *bare minimum* needed to express certain features of a story. In film, for example, a character who is depressed is often cramped by the camera to show isolation and despair. A character who is happy or free is given more space. Space is never wasted and has deep metaphorical value in most good movies. In the world of Memory Palaces, too much space can lead to "decompression," which in this case is negative. Pack your Memory Palaces tightly to maximize not just the amount of information you can store in them, but also the energy efficiency in using them. Remember, you don't want to have to re-start the engine over and over again.

Another reason you want to specify your Memory Palaces to the information you're trying to memorize is because it helps you track your results and make educated guesses about how long learning projects might take. For example, when I memorized the 32 passages of the *Ribhu Gita* we'll discuss in detail, the sound and meaning of the Sanskrit became knowledge faster because the planning stage helped me decide in advance how many Magnetic Stations I would need and then chose my Memory Palace for appropriateness before even getting started. It's not a bulletproof process, but does help you proceed faster and experience more success.

A Magnetic recap

We've just covered a lot of Memory Palace theory, so let's review:

- **Use known locations.** Choose your first Memory Palace by identifying a familiar location. Many people suggest that you should use your own home as a beginner, but I think you can be more adventurous if you wish. Use your school, church, workplace—nearly any indoor location will do. Keep in mind that you want to make it indoors to maximize the effectiveness and you want to be familiar with the location to the point that, even without revisiting it, you can create a journey throughout the location in your mind and divide the journey into stations.

- **Start with macro-stations.** When working with your first Memory Palace, decide first whether you want to start with macro-stations or get right into using micro-stations. My preference is for people to start large with macro-stations—such as room corners—and then narrow in to using micro-stations, but I leave this to you. Ideally, you'll try both, but there's only one first time and it's important not to frustrate yourself if you feel that using micro-stations might be too much.

- **Follow a linear journey, and don't cross your own path.** Make sure you create your first Memory Palace journey in a way that neither traps you nor causes you to cross your own path. Admittedly, this can be tricky in some buildings and may mean you need to pass over features you could use as stations in order to keep a linear journey. If you rely on the principles I've given you in this chapter, your journey will be streamlined, easy to navigate and effective.

- **Don't sweat it.** If you find you're not using all available space and you've left a number of micro-stations unused, don't worry about it. In the long run, it is always worth it to lose a few stations in favor of having journeys that are clear, linear and easily navigable. You do not want to lose mental energy, certainly not when you'll be using your Memory Palaces for the purposes of passing exams, memorizing scripture or learning a language—or all three at once!

- **Have an economy of means.** This is why it's important to focus on developing an economy of means, a tight and focused approach to getting what you want when you want it without having to remember anything about the journey you created. This concept of the economy of means works in film and it will work in your mind to create compelling journeys that help you recall all the information you'll ever need to memorize.

Exercise: Create your first Memory Palace
Do this now:

1. Get your pencil and Memory Journal but don't use them yet.

2. Close your eyes, and mentally create your first Memory Palace using a familiar location. It doesn't matter if you use a house, an apartment building or a trailer. If you're reading this book in prison, you can create a Memory Palace using even the darkest pit of isolation as a location. (I know this for certain because both convicts and guards have written to me to tell me about their experiences using prisons as Memory Palaces!)

3. Give it at least 10 macro- or micro-stations, or a combination of the two. Don't fear the adventure if you want to go whole hog! This brief exercise helps ensure you can follow the journey in your mind almost without thinking about it. We base our stations on familiar things for the precise reason that we don't have to think about what comes next along the journey. We just mentally *go there*.

4. Make sure you don't trap yourself or cross your own path as you mentally journey through the Memory Palace and lock those stations down.

5. Pick up the pencil and draw the Memory Palace.

6. Keep a top-down record by listing the stations by number and name beside the Memory Palace.

7. Rehearse the Memory Palace journey in your mind to ensure it works for the steps to come. I suggest you mentally "travel" it forward, backward and in patterns we'll discuss later in the Recall Rehearsal section.

9 MENTAL LEGO, OR THE SECRETS OF ENCODING ANY INFORMATION USING MAGNETIC IMAGERY

Y OU MIGHT BE WONDERING, "How the heck did you come up with Thomas Mann? How do you even remember you have a friend with the last name Obst?" The answer is simple: I create Magnetic Lists. Often.

The best part? It's really simple if you let the alphabet do most of the heavy lifting. In my practice, I just get out a notebook and start with the letter A and don't stop until I reach Z. If you practice this technique once a month for a year, you'll be astonished by how many figures start emerging.

It's the same with gathering new Memory Palaces. Your Memory Palaces and Magnetic Stations are physical locations that serve as placeholders for information you want to remember. To help us remember that information, we'll encode it with Magnetic Imagery initially derived from the alphabet. In order to have an ample supply of this imagery, we need to:

1. Gather a bunch in advance of needing it

2. Develop the ability to create spontaneous Magnetic Imagery

In this case, one hand feeds the other. The more you develop the Magnetic Lists we're about to discuss, the more you'll be able to spontaneously come up with Magnetic Imagery. Likewise, the more you experience image creation on the fly, the more robust your Magnetic Lists will become.

In fact, if you've been following along, some of these lists will have already been developed. Remember when I asked you to keep note of the names of your teachers? Each and every one of them can potentially help you encode a new piece of information. If you need to memorize some words that start with "T" in a new language, you have Mrs. Thomas and her classroom ready to go.

Adolfo's incredible success story!

Just as you can divide your Memory Palace lists into categories like schools, homes and churches, you can divide your lists into types like actors, artists, musicians, friends and teachers. Adolfo Artigas, a Navy vet who decided to go back to university, has developed many robust Magnetic Lists—he's even used me as a Magnetic Bridging Figure to help him land 101% on his World History exam. The best part is that one of his sons is following in Adolfo's footsteps and was recently accepted at just 17 years of age to the prestigious Harriet L. Wilkes Honors College of Florida Atlantic University.

To get started with your first Magnetic List, I suggest you get out your Memory Journal and pick a category. Then, list A-Z down one side of the page. Let's say you go with actors. You'll next start filling out the list, perhaps something like this:

- Al Pacino

- Bruce Willis

- Cory Haim

- Derren Brown

- Eric Estrada

Let your mind wander and don't get hung up on perfectionism. If you can't find someone for a letter, move on and come back later.

Having these lists prepared will help you immensely. For example, let's say you're studying for an exam and you need to memorize the word *peripeteia*. Instead of rolling your eyes back into your head or screaming with frustration, you relax and the letter "P" at the beginning of this word takes you to a Magnetic List. You think of Peter Gabriel or Peter Pan or James and the Giant Peach. You remember your friend Paul and using the first Magnetic Station in his home Peter Pan "rips" Paul's pet dog, who is wearing a tie. The dog shouts "ya!" while walking in reverse. Why is the dog walking in reverse? Because *peripeteia* means a sudden reversal of fortune or change in circumstances. By having your lists prepared, all it takes is a second to encode the sound and meaning of even the most difficult material into Memory Palaces. These steps will only be difficult if you're not prepared with your lists. Even if you ultimately don't use the tools in exactly this way, you'll still be better able to innovate if you begin with a focused strategy that fuses the alphabet together with pre-existing mental imagery and pre-remembered space.

Axl Rose
Bill Murray
Christian Bale
Dennis Hopper
Eric Stolz
F. Murray Abraham
Gordon Lightfoot
Harry Maclean
Ian McKellen
Jack Nicholson
Katharine Hepburn
Lemmy
Michael McKean

Nick Nolte
Owen Wilson
Pee Wee Herman
Quentin Tarantino
Rick Astley
Susan Sarandon
Tommy Lee
Uwe Boll
Vino Khamez
Whitney Houston
Xavier Rudd
Yasmine Bleeth
Zane Grey

Now, you may have noticed that I've drilled into the individual syllables of this word. Our community calls this process Magnetic Word Division. It is very useful for encoding information into Memory Palaces. Sometimes you'll need three images for a single word, sometimes just one. Other times, it could be more. The principle is more important than any specific iteration and you'll enjoy hours of mental adventure as you continue to draw upon your lists and snap elements from your lists together with information into your Memory Palaces.

In essence, you're creating more than just imagery when you develop Magnetic Imagery. You're creating vignettes that "encode" the sound and/or meaning of the target information you want to memorize. Then, when you strategically visit it later in one of your Memory Palaces using Recall Rehearsal, you need only re-experience the image, break it down into its component pieces and "decode" the parts to retrieve the memorized information and thus experience it in its original form. As you'll discover in the chapter on Recall Rehearsal, you will benefit most when you use highly specific patterns for revisiting this information. These patterns will relieve you from thinking about the process and let the science do the work of getting the target information into your long-term memory.

Over the past few sections, I've given you a broad overview of creating Magnetic Imagery. However, there's a bit more to be said about this process, so let's dig in deeper and explain more about exactly what's going on when I suggest that you learn to make images like these so that you can spread them around your Memory Palaces with ease. You're going to learn to combine imagery and action in a particular way that will ensure your success each and every time you sit down to remember information.

The power of Magnetic Imagery

Imagery is... well... imagery—mental pictures that you create in your mind. For the purposes of memorization, these pictures and vignettes need to be big and colorful. The larger and the more colorful, the better. Exaggerate the size and colors because that will make the image more memorable. This will strengthen the associations.

Some of my students tell me they're not particularly visual in their imaginations. I understand this completely, and it's nothing to worry about. If you search "Magnetic Memory Method" and "aphantasia" up on the Internet, you'll find me debunking the idea that people who lack a "mind's eye" cannot use memory techniques. You'll be introduced to some people with aphantasia who have extraordinary memory abilities, exceptional creativity and have in common just one requirement for all success in life.

Although I don't think I have aphantasia myself, I'm not speaking from ignorance. I was personally very low on the visual threshold and still would not say that I draw very much on my visual imagination when using memory techniques to encode and decode information. In fact, when I used to read a novel, I rarely saw images in my mind. I read the descriptions as much as I could tolerate, but overall, my mind kept the imagery conceptual. It's possible that I had something called Imagination Deficit Disorder or IDD, but labelling these things is of limited utility. In fact, there's little time for fantasizing about why you cannot do things when you're busy experimenting with how to get them done!

If you're a person who has experienced a low visual threshold, you're in luck. Not only am I able to give my non-visual students in the Magnetic Memory Method Masterclass quite a few suggestions based on my own experiences, but Lynne Kelly, author of *The Memory Code, Memory Craft* and, at the time of writing, Australia's leading competitor in her age category, identifies herself as having aphantasia. Alec Figueroa of AphantasiaMeow has been helping people see images in their minds, but as he and I have discussed on both our channels, Lynne's case and my own experiences demonstrate that you don't need to have a visual imagination to succeed. Wherever you currently stand, just dive in and explore these suggestions.

First, if you can't think in color, don't force it. Try thinking in black and white. If you see nothing, work with *whatever* shows up in your mind when you think about black and white conceptually. Then, exaggerate the black and white just the way it shows up. How black is the black and how white is the white? Is there an opportunity to use gray in some memorable way?

In the event that black and white patterns don't show up or are not useful for you, another tactic is to associate certain prefixes with actors or fictional characters. Having your Magnetic Lists prepared in advanced will make you skilled in rapidly producing useful associations. For instance, the Spanish prefix *cachi-* is associated in my mind with Charles "Chachi" Arcola, who was played by Scott Baio in *Happy Days*. The words don't sound exactly the same, but I am able to visualize Chachi and make the association to *cachi*. Thereafter, every word that begins with *cachi* gets automatically linked with Chachi.

Another option is to use paintings you are familiar with in your imagery—even if only at the conceptual level. For example, although I've never seen the following Magnetic Imagery in my mind, let's return to an example I've already mentioned. The following illustration gets the idea across of how I memorized *abartig* in German, a word that means "abnormal":

Rather than "seeing" the Mona Lisa, all that happened in my mind was recognizing that the Mona Lisa belongs to the conceptual category of "art." That's the *art* part of *abartig* taken care of, again almost entirely on the conceptual level (the C of KAVE COGS). Mona Lisa is a visual object, but I had yet to see it with my own eyes in an art gallery when I used it along with Abraham Lincoln. *Ab* derived from Abraham and *art* derived from the Mona Lisa go a long way. The idea of him spitting is easily felt and heard in the imagination using the K and A of KAVE COGS.

Now, there's an element missing from the illustration that I've left out intentionally for teaching purposes. To get the tig sound into memory, I used Tigger's tail (from the Winnie the Pooh series). If you don't know Tigger, imagine a tiger instead, ideally one you've seen at a zoo or in a book or movie. An example like this need not be purely conceptual. The tail can be felt or heard in the mind slapping away, as if it was your own. As you descend into the multi sensory possibilities, imagine your Magnetic Imagery interacting with this image somehow—without having it illustrated for you. When you do so, the magic of memory techniques can start to emerge as *ab* + *art* + *tig* combined with this "abnormal" action from Abraham Lincoln leads you to see how and why this Magnetic Imagery created such a powerful association for me. I've not forgotten the word since. As Ian Taylor wrote to me:

"I can never see the Mona Lisa painting again after your image association of Abraham Lincoln spitting all over the painting and now I also remember the word *abartig* in German. Just shows that your technique worked too well just by giving an example of yours."

I'm not so convinced that my Magnetic Imagery will translate so well for everyone, but learn to create the imagery for yourself, apply it consistently and you'll soon have an unshakeable memory. With Memory Palaces providing unlimited space for placing such images, all you'll need next are the Recall Rehearsal processes you'll learn later.

In sum, looking at art matters, and you don't have to use it visually. Draw upon the art you already know, even if it's only the words you can bring to mind. The next time you are in an art gallery or looking through an art book, pay closer attention to what you are looking at. The material could become fodder for better associations with the information you will be memorizing as you use the Magnetic Memory Method. I must mention a small problem with artwork, however. Paintings and statues tend to be static. Unlike actors you've seen on television and movie screens, painted figures don't move. You'll need to add motion yourself. That said, if you can imagine the Mona Lisa walking like an Egyptian outside of her frame, or Michelangelo's David doing the moonwalk even just by using words, then you should have no problem.

You can also use toys that you remember in the associative imagery you create. GI Joe, Barbie, My Little Pony... anything goes. As with paintings, the most important factor here is that you can put these figures into action.

With all these concepts in mind, there are a number of things you can do, starting today, to become more visual:

1. **Examine how you read.** Do you actually "see" what you are reading? This question applies to both fiction and non-fiction. If you are primarily a non-visual reader, then make a determined effort to *see* the characters and environments in the material you are reading. Pause, close your eyes and literally build the imagery in your imagination if it isn't coming to you with the desired ease. Don't rush through the pages. Work at this with deliberation. You can start with an imaginary wire frame and pile on the clay (if you find a sculpting metaphor helpful), or you can imagine that you are painting the scene. Personal experimentation will demonstrate what works best for you.

2. **Examine how you watch films.** Are you absorbing all of the visual material, including the backgrounds? By paying closer attention to what can be called the "deep *mise en scene*" (a fancy term for "background") you will start seeing how filmmakers fill the visual field with hidden imagery meant to shape your viewing experience.

3. **Visit art galleries.** I used to hate art galleries until I realized how useful they were when it comes to developing the visual imagination. Art galleries are also excellent for developing Memory Palaces. One of the great things about art galleries is that you can see the brush strokes in great detail, something that very few art books allow for. Since so much of memorizing is about experiencing images in process, looking at paintings is an interesting means of seeing movement as a special effect produced by a motionless canvas. You also get to see the paintings and other artworks in context. You see how they've been framed, how they've been placed in relation to other paintings and how other people are perceiving them as they move around the art gallery. The more consciously aware you become of these elements, the more visually aware you will be.

4. **Look at art books.** Good art books are great for looking at paintings and other artworks you can't physically visit. You can also spend more time with the images, revisiting them again and again to study their intricacies.

5. **Pick an image from a novel.** For example, if you're familiar with *Lord of the Flies*, you could choose the conch. Using an imaginary version of the room in which you currently sit, close your eyes and recreate that object in vivid and intense detail.

Exercise: Visualize an object

Let's go a bit deeper into this last suggestion. It's very important you create the image in a room of a Memory Palace you've created. Why? Because using mentally reconstructed locations is the key to all Magnetic Memory Method efforts. You're going to use the Memory Palaces to memorize information, so why not practice making images in the same location as part of your practice drills? In effect, the rooms of your Memory Palace are the canvas upon which you will paint moving objects and figures—those vignettes mentioned above—in your imagination.

Once you have vividly created an image, be it a conch or some other object from a novel (a sword, ring, piece of characteristic clothing or treasure), do the following:

- Increase and decrease its size. Make it so huge that it presses up against the walls of the room in your Memory Palace (crack the walls if you like). Next, make that image so small that it practically disappears.

- Spend time working on the speed of the transformation from big to small. Focus on actually seeing the object change sizes.

- Spin the object in space—left, right, in every possible direction. Spend time seeing every detail of the object in your mind from every perspective.

- Mentally push the object around the room, both forward and backward.

- Shine light on the object. Reduce the light around the object, again experimenting with the speed at which you imagine the transformations.

- Change the colors of the object. Change the outer colors by working with the surface of the object, but also the inner glow. Work with all the colors you can think of. For bonus points, study a color wheel to become more educated about color combinations.

In this exercise, you've used an object from a novel. This means that you had to invent what the object looked like based on your general understanding of what such a thing should look like. If you chose a fantasy object from a science fiction novel, for example, then your creative work was that much more cut out for you and more rewarding.

You can extend this exercise to an object from a movie. Doing so allows you to relax your visual creativity because you don't have to build it based on an author's description. Borrowing an image from a movie doesn't make the exercise any less challenging, but can make it more rewarding. Follow all of the same steps you used for creating and manipulating an object from a novel with the object you've selected from a movie. A side benefit of these exercises in my experience is that people start paying more attention in everyday life. This may happen because the use of memory techniques and related developmental exercises does not fundamentally differ from many meditation and mindfulness routines.

Preparation and predetermination

At this point, you've gotten most of the big picture of how memory techniques work. Now, before moving on to some examples, there are two principles we must cover: preparation and predetermination. Don't skip these. They're cornerstones of the process.

Preparation involves relaxing the mind. When the mind is tense, busy or exhausted, it will resist attempts at memorization. Being stressed does not mean that you can't remember, only that you're not in the most receptive state to remember. When your mind is open and relaxed, you'll be amazed at how these techniques will double, triple and even quadruple in effectiveness.

Predetermination involves charting out the memory locations and stations in your Memory Palace Network before making any single attempt to place the words you want to memorize.

I must stress that before populating your Memory Palaces with information, you will want to build the entire system first. Having tried to make up my Memory Palaces on the fly, and having helped hundreds of people who tried the same, I can tell you that not preparing and predetermining leads to frustration and impoverished results. Please spend the necessary time to predetermine the locations you want to use and label the individual stations within them. My Magnetic Memory Method Worksheets make this easy. If you don't already have them, along with the care package I have created to help you get lasting results from this book please download them now using *www.magneticmemorymethod.com/vmm*.

I also want to stress that perfection is not the goal here. It's important not to harm your forward movement by being too particular about every little detail—look at my drawings! You just want to get the basic layout in place so that you can work relatively quickly with the words you want to memorize. Movement is better than meditation in this endeavor, so please take action and build your Memory Palaces so that you can model the examples you're about to discover on the following pages. Always remember this: progress *is* perfection.

The rule of Magnetic Action: Take action!

I'm talking about two kinds of action—the first is yours. Putting these suggestions into action is crucial, a point worth repeating a zillion times if that's what it takes to make the whole world wake up to it. These are some of the finest exercises you can engage in if your goal is to easily and quickly learn and memorize any information.

The other kind of action is for your images. If you're implementing, by now you will have thought about different familiar locations, the macro-stations within those locations and the different ways you can use exaggerated imagery. The next step is to give your images a bit of movement—more than a bit, actually. Just as you want to exaggerate the size and color of your images, you also want to exaggerate their actions in order to make your target information more memorable.

10 HOW TO PRACTICE MEMORIZING TONS OF INFORMATION FAST!

S O FAR, WE HAVE discussed the principles and the terminology of the Magnetic Memory Method and gone through how to create a well-formed Memory Palace. Before we get into a detailed discussion of creating Magnetic Imagery and placing it in your Memory Palaces, let's test out the theory and prove that Memory Palaces are indeed the best and most fantastic way to remember information.

Once you've downloaded the Magnetic Memory Method Worksheets and filled them out, your spatial memory will be humming. That means it's finally exercise time. But unlike so many other memory trainings out there, mine does not recommend using trivial material. Far too many books and articles on using memory techniques suggest beginning with a list of unrelated items or shopping lists. The truth is, you should practice using memory techniques with:

- Information that interests you,

- Information that will improve your life, or

- Information that both interests you and will improve your life.

There's no point in exercising with anything less, with the rare exception of the order of playing cards from a shuffled deck. This highly specialized technique can be incredibly fun for training and can be used to do some stunning magic tricks. Plus, it's great training for learning how to memorize abstractions and reuse Memory Palaces either in the short or long term.

The following descriptions of images and actions from my own imagination are for demonstration purposes only. To achieve real results, you'll need to create your own Magnetic Imagery for the information you want to memorize. Please don't fall for the memory trainings out there that expect you to recreate their images in your mind and succeed. You might experience some results from this, but I'm here to tell you that the results can be total if you use your creativity to come up with your own images. Don't cheat yourself, and the examples given in this book won't cheat you either. Remember, I'm going against ancient wisdom from the *Rhetorica ad Herennium* by packing in so many examples, and am trusting you to see the principles at work behind the examples and then follow through by taking action. My hope is that I'm teaching you to how fish, first and foremost, not just dumping the fish into your boat for the sake of amusement. When it comes to memory techniques and using them well, you risk starvation if you can't cast your own reel. Don't mistake the activity of reading this book with the accomplishment of using these tools to memorize information that will improve your life.

With this warning out of the way (at least for now), let's get started. The following Sanskrit vocabulary examples are small bites you can start to experience vicariously in your mind. They should help you with handling the larger memory tasks I'll teach further on in this book: 32 phrases that have the power to set you free from the tyranny of your mind.

Macro-station 1: Bathroom—abhyasa
This word means "constant practice." It can also mean "continuous effort" or even discipline.

Imagery and action: Abraham Lincoln cutting the "Yahoo" (search engine) logo with a saw.

Abraham Lincoln + Yahoo + a saw = *abhyasa*

Macro-station 2: Bedroom—acharya
This word means spiritual leader or teacher who passes down ancient wisdom—like Gary Weber. The prefix *a* means "toward" and *char* means "to go." It is the root of our word for "car." It literally means that an authentic teacher helps the student go toward the goal by living a life that exemplifies the journey.

Imagery and action: A giant second chin grows from a car as it runs over yams on the way to enlightenment.

A chin + a car + yams = *acharya*

Macro-station 3: Living room—advaita

Advaita means "not two." It also means "oneness with everything."

Imagery and action: Black Adder (played by Rowan Atkinson) plays air guitar as Steve Vai disrupts his song with a tambourine.

Adder + Steve Vai + tambourine = *advaita*

Can you see (or feel, or realize) what's going on here? The more the Magnetic Imagery draws upon readily known figures from popular culture, the less work the brain must do. Now, try this experiment:

After reading the conditions of the experiment, close your eyes. Or, if nothing comes to mind, get out your Memory Journal and try writing down the answers. Ultimately, you'll want to explore all options and continue exploring them over time.

Bring your Memory Palace to mind.

You're in the bathroom.

What do you see, feel or experience?

Is it Abraham Lincoln sawing through the Yahoo logo? If so, then see if you can decode the Magnetic Imagery I shared with you.

Can you reconstruct the word I shared?

How about the bedroom? Do you find a car in there with a double-chin?

If you can remember simple items like these as quickly and easily as I know you can, you can also memorize all the vocabulary in any language.

Again, please take my Magnetic Imagery for what it is: A set of examples. These techniques work best when you develop your own tools and practice with them, while continuing to develop more.

Objection time!

I can't read minds. But I know what you might be thinking right now: "This stuff is easy for you, Dr. Metivier. Your imagination is some kind of turbocharged Energizer Bunny. You used to eat LSD for breakfast!"

Except for the LSD part (don't tell my mom), here's the truth: my mind isn't any more or less creative than yours. My brain is built from the same stuff. The difference is that I've developed it by deliberately engaging in creativity exercises, some of which have been in use for years. The Memory Palace? Ancient! Magnetic Lists? They used to call this strategy "the bestiary" and it goes back at least as far as the 14th century. You can easily use the same developmental exercises to improve your own creativity, always keeping in mind that it's the mind of creativity that draws upon information that already exists. You don't have to reinvent a single wheel. You reduce cognitive load by drawing upon what is already there and snapping in "new" things by observing them as they come in. It's nothing more than an amusing game of mental Lego.

In my view, the most important trick you need is not a trick at all. It's the habit of hitting the pause button. Pause to notice. Pause to follow the steps. When you're encoding information with Magnetic Imagery, take just a second with each image to ensure that you're really seeing it in large, vibrant and bright colors. Run through KAVE COGS in your mind. Focus on the action. Make it zany and crazy. Make it as exaggerated as possible by simply going through a list of what *can* happen.

There are only so many verbs under the sun, so as you go through your lists, think about the possible actions each of your Magnetic Bridging Figures can take: Abraham Lincoln can spit, but also kick, jump, sweat, kiss, bowl, play the tambourine, dig, etc. List out the alphabet in your Memory Journal and gather all the verbs you can.

Again, if you cannot see any of this in your mind, focus on the *words*. This is the ancient advice in *Rhetorica Ad Herrenium* that made it possible for me to see images in my mind without seeing them. Make the descriptions wild, crazy and memorable at the linguistic level alone if that's all you've got. For years, that's all I could do. It worked just fine and I wound up becoming more visual as a result. Heck, just the other day I felt like I could reach out and touch Cobra Commander. Not high on my wish list, but he helped me get the job done and later I performed a decent memorized deck routine for William Gordon, who provided the Memory Palace photographs and main illustration for this book.

Pausing to notice at other times throughout your day will help you, too. For example, I just mentioned William Gordon. As a serious practitioner of these techniques, you'll see a new name as a wake-up call to add a new Magnetic Bridging Figure to your Magnetic List. (Both W and G.) If not him, the next person and the next and the next. This pause to gather and reflect will compound your progress. You will be paying attention to what's happening around and inside you, and you will likely notice things you hadn't before. Remember the large traffic sign I noticed in Berlin—the one I'd passed countless times without seeing? It suddenly became imbued with interesting detail when I paid attention to it, and it became useful to me in a Memory Palace.

If you're still doubtful that this is going to work, consider my friend Daniel Welsch; he went from skepticism to memorizing all 50 Spanish provinces in less than an hour! Amanda Markham used the Magnetic Memory Method to memorize 200 words in Arrernte in just 10 days. Thanks to Magnetic Bridging Figures, she overcame a major hurdle because most of those words start with the letter "A"—and that's in a language with little over 300 words in total. Then there's Eldon Clem, a professor in Israel who memorized 1,000 words of Ancient Ethiopic in six weeks. All of this is achievable, and in all cases, success can compound when you learn from studying how others have applied these techniques. The keys, once again, are: the Principles of Preparation and Predetermination applied to Memory Palaces, Magnetic Bridging Figures and the Recall Rehearsal process you'll learn about in the next section.

Some basics of memory science

One of the main lessons of this book is that you must become the scientist in the laboratory of your own mind and memory. This command is not coming from nowhere.

German psychologist and memory science pioneer Hermann Ebbinghaus (1850–1909) performed many memory experiments. His findings are useful for those of us interested in practicing memory skills at the highest levels because he explained why memory techniques work. You can find his ideas in a book called *Über das Gedächtnis* (or *Memory: A Contribution to Experimental Psychology*). His findings were tremendously influential on me as I worked to make the process of remembering even more powerful. In *Über das Gedächtnis*, Ebbinghaus suggests that learning and retention degrade based on time and position. This came to be called the "Serial Positioning Effect." In other words, the order in which you learn something affects how well you will keep it.

By "order," we mean not only time, but proximity—whether an item to memorize is at the end or in the middle of your list, for example. This distinction is important because it matters a great deal what kinds of information you encounter, when you encounter it and the types of information that one groups together. If you tackle a bunch of unrelated information, then something called the Forgetting Curve will have greater power, no matter how much you've used a Memory Palace to combat forgetting.

These findings influenced me to experiment with the Memory Palace technique in greater depth. I tested using strategically patterned revisiting in order to defeat the Forgetting Curve—the predictable rate at which your memory of any given information will decay over time. My investigations used the power of spaced repetition based on the Serial Positioning Effect. This idea would not have emerged without the self-experimentation of Ebbinghaus. This self-experimentation is something we can all implement through modelling the scientific principles that govern memory, as revealed through his original investigations.

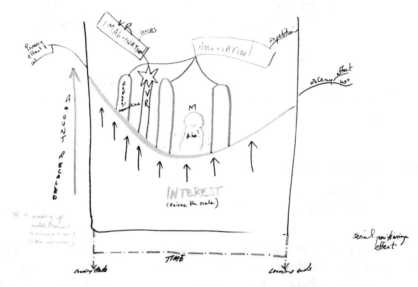

The Forgetting Curve drawn with Tony Buzan as he taught me what he calls "The Most Important Graph In the World"

Now that you know what Memory Palaces are and how to place information inside them, we're going to go into the scientific explanation of what you're doing when using the Magnetic Memory Method.

Why is this all so groundbreaking? Unlike many spaced-repetition mental software programs, which make decisions on your behalf, the Magnetically deliberate process of information consumption lets you rig the game in your favor.

The first insight is that all information is encountered in time. As it happens, the information we encounter first and last about a topic tends to be remembered better almost by default. The fact that we tend to remember what we encounter first is called the Primacy Effect; remembering what we encounter last better is called the Recency Effect.

These are general rules of memory, so please don't take them as dogma. Sometimes you'll also experience something called the Von Restorff Effect—also called the Isolation Effect. It tells us that when a piece of information stands out from other information, it is more likely to be remembered. For example, if a washing machine appears in a list of fruits, you will be more likely to remember the washing machine than the fruits. Now, you might be thinking that using Magnetic Bridging

Figures and gathering alphabetically related words would diminish this effect. I haven't found this to be true, and it still works provided you use KAVE COGS and all the other principles to make each Magnetic Image stand out. Having Abraham Lincoln spit on the Mona Lisa is in no way diminished by having the same Magnetic Bridging Figure biting into a tin can a few Magnetic Stations later. But it is important that you pretend to feel the teeth "biting" into the *abbeitzmittel* to remember the *bite* sound in the word. It matters that you hear the auditory nature of the image, add some emotion to it and all the rest. These tools of the Magnetic Memory Method make your Magnetic Imagery hard to forget and fun to remember.

How to use Recall Rehearsal

What exactly is Recall Rehearsal? The best answer you'll get will be to try it. Here's how: First, find yourself a quiet place and go through the Magnetic Imagery you encoded into your Memory Palace. Start at the first Magnetic Station in any of your Memory Palaces and keep going until you come to the end of the journey.

For example, if your Memory Palace has 10 stations, start at Magnetic Station 1 and then decode the Magnetic Imagery you created there. Once done and you're satisfied that you've decoded the information correctly, move to the second Magnetic Station. Repeat this process until you've reached the tenth Magnetic Station in the Memory Palace. You can perform this process mentally, but I recommend you use a pen and pencil to write everything you remember in your Memory Journal. Write it all down directly from your memory without concern for accuracy. Your goal is to first exercise and test your memory so you can check for accuracy later.

After travelling your Memory Palaces forward from the first Magnetic Station to the last, perform the following five steps to perform a Recall Rehearsal exercise. Following these steps can hack the Serial Positioning Effect and give each piece of information you've encoded equal amounts of primacy and recency:

1. Travel your Memory Palace journeys forward.

2. Travel your Memory Palace journeys backward.

3. Travel your Memory Palace journeys from the center to the beginning and from the center to the end.

4. Travel the Magnetic Stations of your Memory Palace by leapfrogging or skipping over even and odd stations, both forward and backward.

5. Pop into random Magnetic Stations once in a while, e.g., Magnetic Station 7 at one time and then later to Magnetic Station 2.

Diligently using a Memory Palace and Recall Rehearsal will ensure you overcome the Forgetting Curve every time. All you have to do is revisit the information in a particular set of sequences so that you're using the Serial Positioning Effect in a few different ways that lend equal primacy and recency to each piece of information you've encoded. And the Memory Palace, when well formed, is the tool you'll use to rapidly access the information for exposing yourself to the memorable Magnetic Imagery you've created at each and every Magnetic Station.

Why is Recall Rehearsal so important to memorization?

The answer is simple: if you do not practice the information by decoding what you've encoded, you will almost certainly forget it. The fact of default forgetting follows the old "use it or lose it" principle. It affects everyone, memory master or not. You simply cannot expect information to enter long-term memory if you don't revisit it in the ways your brain needs for long-term encoding to occur. Our challenge is to make what our brain needs easy and fun while still being realistic and avoiding the digital amnesia and distractions that arise when we tie our brains to addictive apps. Never forget: *you* are the ultimate memory app!

Here's what happens with information that you don't encode: your brain splits it up into many small pieces, scatters it like buckshot and stores the pieces in different chemical locations. As this dispersing of the information takes place, your brain is literally "cooking" up the small crumbs of information related to the whole (which itself was never truly whole, but always dynamic and composed of parts) and changing it into something else during the process.

Then, when you try to recall the information, your brain has quite a task before it. It must not only access the information from hundreds (or thousands) of locations, but also relate the new chemical structure of the information crumbs with the other pieces. Sometimes this isn't a problem, especially when the neuropathways have been well laid and maintained. However, if you've ever had trouble recalling a name you heard seconds before, then you know just how quickly a neuropathway can be built and then decay.

It doesn't have to be this way. To increase your accuracy of recall, simply encode the information effectively, store it in a well-formed Memory Palace and then revisit the information strategically. Do this and you will create powerful highways between the neighborhoods and cities of your brain.

The wrong way to think about Recall Rehearsal

A lot of people think of using a Memory Palace and Magnetic Imagery as replaying a movie in their minds. This is an incorrect and potentially harmful metaphor.

Why?

The answer is simple. Movies are exactly the same every time you watch them. The only changes are in how you and your life circumstances evolve between each viewing. But when it comes to moving through a Memory Palace, the Magnetic Imagery you created during the encoding process never stays exactly the same. This is due to the fact that your brain breaks the information down into smaller pieces and stores it in a variety of chemical locations.

The better you get at using memory techniques, the more you play a role in deciding how and where the information is broken down and stored. Your Memory Palaces are more like theaters for the staging of plays. You use these theaters as locations for manipulating Magnetic Imagery and Magnetic Action to trigger recall and decode information. This process lets you literally "restage" the Magnetic Imagery you've created in your Memory Palace.

To quickly review, your effectiveness relies heavily on:

- Having created your Magnetic Imagery correctly and according to established principles, such as KAVE COGS, that make information memorable.

- Placing the Magnetic Imagery in well-formed Memory Palaces using the Magnetic Memory Method principles.

What if I make a mistake during Recall Rehearsal?

Should you find any flaws in your recall when assessing your recall accuracy, make corrections to the Magnetic Imagery. This simple process will not only strengthen your memory, but also give you additional, highly conscious exposure to the information. It doesn't take long and you'll become a better Magnetic Mnemonist and work the information deeper into long-term memory.

When correcting your Magnetic Imagery so that it's stronger, use what I call the Principle of Compounding. This simply means you add new material, reduce unnecessary or confusing elements and make the Magnetic Imagery bigger, brighter and more colorful while going through KAVE COGS again. Remember the demonstration for remembering the Sanksrit word *abhyasa*? Abraham Lincoln cut the Yahoo logo with a saw. If for some reason this image did not work on its own and

I struggled to recall it, I would add more detail, such as Abraham flexing his abs and a yak to strengthen the *ab* and *ya* associations for better recall.

But the Principle of Compounding shouldn't be needed if you follow the steps the first time around. Often you'll find that the only reason the Magnetic Imagery did not perform is because you did not fully follow the Magnetic Memory Method principles.

Practicing the practice

Even when you're satisfied with your accuracy and no longer feel you need to correct the Magnetic Imagery, still keep practicing Recall Rehearsal by revisiting your Memory Palaces and decoding the Magnetic Imagery. How often and for how long must you do this? The honest answer frustrates some people, but here it is anyway: it depends.

The number of times and how long you need to revisit the Magnetic Imagery you've created depends on:

1. The level of Magnetic Memory Method ability you've built up through practice.

2. Your use of the techniques to help you memorize information that actually matters. Memorizing trivial information with little or no consequence to your life tends to lead to less than spectacular results. Make the time you spend with these techniques count.

3. Your understanding of the science behind accurately remembering with mnemonics and use of Recall Rehearsal. Practice using this approach to ensure that the Primacy Effect and Recency Effect are being equally applied to all of the information you want to remember, by rehearsing backward, forward, and at different starting points.

4. The nature of the information. We don't know why in each and every case, but some information resists memorization. In language learning, for example, polyglots have a term for the small percentage of words they can't seem to memorize no matter what they try: The Stubborn Quintile. (Luckily, if you create a Memory Palace and buckle down with the Magnetic Memory Method, even these resistant words can be memorized fast.)

5. Your physical and mental state. Maybe you lack personal interest, or your Memory Palace brings back negative memories that interfere with the process. You might be eating poorly or have or a physical illness, or you might simply be tired. All of these factors can affect your ability to effectively concentrate and remember.

Rules of Five: Dominic O'Brien's 5 or the MMM 5?

Keeping in mind these five factors that determine the effectiveness of your practice will serve you well. There is also a good rule of thumb—which coincidentally has five points—that you can follow or should at least know about even if you don't use it. "The Rule of Five" is a review pattern developed by World Memory Champion Dominic O'Brien, who is also an incredible educator about memory optimization. His Rule of Five says to review as follows:

- First review: Immediately

- Second review: 24 hours later

- Third review: One week later

- Fourth review: One month later

- Fifth review: Three months later

Personally, I think you'll benefit more by reviewing much more often than this. Even so, O'Brien's basic layout is valuable, and you should keep it in mind, experiment with it and make changes based on the discoveries you make about yourself and your memory.

I follow a more rigorous Recall Rehearsal pattern than the Dominic O'Brien Rule of Five. Here's what I do:

- First reviews (notice the plural): Immediately, then one hour later, three hours later and five hours later. If there is enough time in the day, a minimum of five Recall Rehearsal sessions on the first day is best.

- Second reviews: The next morning, two times during the next afternoon, two times during the next evening and once before bed. More reviews should not be necessary, but they will not harm you any. Further, the more you review, the more practice you will get with the Magnetic Memory Method.

- Third review: Once a day for each day of the following week. In other words, after you've done five reviews for the first two days, practice Recall Rehearsal at least once a day for the next five days. You may find that you don't need this many exposures, but, as a beginner, follow this principle anyway to experience the effect. If you find that deviating from this pattern causes your accuracy rates to sink, then you'll know more about the Forgetting Curve and can come back to this chapter to revisit how to combat it.

- Fourth review: Once a day for a week the following month.

- Fifth reviews and beyond: Keep reviewing the information at least once a month, if not more often, for as long as you want to keep the information intact. Or, if you're 100-percent confident that you've encoded it for life, you can stop.

Hold on! Isn't that a ton of reviewing?

Some people write to me with the desperate claim that this process is too much work. Frankly, I often think of the scene from *Reservoir Dogs* involving the world's smallest violin crying out in pity just for one suffering soul. I don't respond this way judgmentally. I also experience these complaints. I have to combat them too. The best weapon in this combat is always the truth.

Here it is: when your ego is out of the way, or at least tempered by realistic thinking, this amount of review isn't hard work. Far from it! When compared to the hours so many people dump into populating spaced-repetition apps, having your Memory Palace Network prepared and then memorizing the information that improves your life will take much less time. Dig your well before you're thirsty.

Yes, software can help with the strategic revisiting of information so it enters long-term memory, but it's less effective than doing it in your Memory Palaces. That's the simple truth. Further, using Memory Palaces properly can reduce the number of repetitions needed and remove the risk of digital amnesia through device dependency.

Anyone is free to cement their opinions into beliefs—some people always will. They're also free to relegate this kind of review process to spaced-repetition apps if they wish, but there is little evidence that those work as well as memory techniques. Yes, study after study demonstrates the advantages of using mnemonics, but the truth is, those studies don't matter. You are the scientist and your brain is *your lab*. If you are acting in alignment with authentic goals and really want to accomplish something special in life, what you're learning now is truly the best way. The only thing that matters is that you're actually doing it. If you follow the practice, you'll experience for yourself how little time is required. In fact, depending on the amount of material, you can accomplish incredible feats of learning by rehearsing just 15 minutes' worth of information each day.

There's another reason Recall Rehearsal is so much more powerful than using index cards, spaced-repetition software or old-fashioned rote learning. Instead of using the "blunt force hammer" of repetition to attempt to permanently stamp out memories from nothing at all, you'll now be using your Magnetic imagination. You'll be constantly exploring connections and developing your creativity. Plus, the more you use your memory, the better and faster you get. You'll learn more and the more you learn, the more you *can* learn. This will happen to you almost on autopilot when you're using the Magnetic Memory Method because you'll have more stored information in your long-term memory with which to make more connections.

You don't have to take my word for it. As Hugh Blair recently posted in the Magnetic Memory Method Mastermind group:

> For a few years I had many thousands of flashcards for language learning running in my deck and ran through a few hundred per day and ran up against two walls:

> 1. Using them as a crutch for information storage method simply became rote learning on steroids, which is merely a somewhat stronger version of a weak approach. Anthony has talked a lot over the years about the problems of storing "in the void", which equates to me as learning without any "hooks", like spatial + image (e.g., memory palace), numbers (e.g., pegs) and so on. This void/no-hook approach is far too hit and miss for me. I eventually came to feel that climbing up the hill of the Ebbinghaus curve every time was an unnecessary struggle.

2. Once you're practiced at using cards, moving through the material on cards can become slow compared to other methods. Station hopping in my mind's eye can feel slow at the beginning, but can become quite fast with practice, just like the first ever G-major chord on a guitar feels slow and unfamiliar, but before too long you're shredding. In my personal experience using cards without a solid method of storage involved an additional step of referencing and dereferencing which I found sometimes hard to accelerate with practice, although some improvement is possible. I became what you could call a good rote learner, but at some point it just felt like a hassle.

What was the way forward for me? Well, in the end I associated the use of cards with the MMM "recall rehearsal" stage and used it as a kind of game to move across my stations in an unexpected and cross-sectional way to undermine the serial positioning effect. Just like Anthony says, without feeding myself the answers, but rather using the cards as triggers for the magnetic imagery in virtual space. I often took just the one card and used it as a starting point to, for example, leapfrog backwards through the stations all the way through the same palace. Then I would change the game regularly to keep the exercise novel.

Two things became evident to me as a result:

- many of the cards quickly became redundant since they became not the information storage mechanism, but rather a fresh axis to perform recall rehearsal and those cards could often be parked fairly quickly, and

- the novel order of rehearsal resulted in me quickly identifying weak Magnetic Imagery since I was doing a "commando drop" into a Memory Palace and was often coming at the stations from an unexpected direction.

Thanks, Anthony, for sharing your insights into the strengths, weaknesses and relative merits of flashcards over the years, it helped me navigate through a frustrating part of my "learning how to learn" journey.

In sum, Recall Rehearsal is one of the most important elements of the practice. Don't miss it!

11 LEARN MINDFULNESS BY
MEMORIZING NAMES

I F YOU DON'T HAVE a memorization goal, learning to memorize names is the most mindful thing you can do... Here's a story that might show you why.

I had just finished a workout at my gym in Kelvin Grove, when I heard someone shout out my name. At first, I thought it might have been Lawrence or Kyle from The Boys House of Coffee across the street, but they were inside their cafe. I scanned around until my eyes fell on an older gentleman stepping out of his car.

"You calling me?"

"Yes," he said, "I've been trying to find your office."

"Oh, are you trying to deliver something?"

"No," he said, "My name is Abraham. Like you, I'm also an online educator and I want to bring you to India to help millions of people learn."

An entrepreneur in manufacturing, Abraham had decided to help his fellow Indians learn better. He did some research online and kept running into my name. When he saw we live not merely in the same city but also the same borough, he figured he would say hello.

I offered him coffee, but inside The Boys House of Coffee Kyle told me they were closing for the day. We sat on a bench outside and Abraham started laying out his plan until his son, Lem, arrived. Then, as we were talking, a woman arrived and asked me if I'm Anthony. She had taken one of my courses and introduced me to Ruby, who was with Lisa on a walk. There were a lot of names to keep track of—a perfect application of MMM.

Lawrence and Kyle in The Boys House of Coffee are names I've known for a while. Lawrence is forever associated with Laurence Fishburne who played Morpheus in *The Matrix*. Kyle is in a battle with the character Kyle Reese from *The Terminator*. I immediately associated my new friend Abraham with Abe Lincoln and his son with Lemmy from Motorhead. When Lisa and Ruby came along, I associated them instantly with Lisa Simpson and the ruby slippers from *The Wizard of Oz*. Later, Abraham's daughter Amy showed up and I wrapped her in images with my cousin Amy and with online marketing expert Amy Porterfield.

You can talk about memory at a very complicated and mechanical level, but at its core, making these associations is almost like withdrawing from a bank account filled with associations instead of cash. You put information in through continual observation of your mental content and then you draw the information out to make rapid associations. The more you focus on training your memory, the more associations you have to draw on. For example, I don't believe that I've met a Ruby before, but now that one Ruby is encoded with Dorothy's slippers, the "interest" starts to compound deep in the vaults of this brain's memory bank. But most importantly, you're *one* with the internal contents of your mind and the external world. You assemble with it all, becoming the wealth of information, its flow and exchange, one name and its owner at a time in the great unified field of society.

Yet, without these techniques and the mindfulness needed to remind us to use them, everyone—and I mean everyone—has an inclination to almost instantly forget the names of new people they meet. As names are one of the most common things people want to remember better, it's worth looking at the practice more closely.

Why everyone forgets names

Don't you wish you could remember the names of new people you come across? I know I've often wished that memorizing names was easier. Forgetting names sucks, especially at events where you're meeting important new contacts. Business cards are fine and dandy, but you want to be looking that new person in the eyes and connecting, not constantly peeking at the sweaty piece of cardboard stuck to your palm. Instead, you want to hold each person's name with the certainty that can only come from mastering your memory.

The good news is that this instant forgetting is not your fault. The first step to remembering names is to understand why you forget them.

1. **Abstraction.** Unless you're a philologist (one who studies the authenticity and meaning of written texts), most names only function as abstract labels for people, not as meaningful words in and of themselves. There are, though, some ways that the meanings of names can be manufactured to help your memory. As Lynne Kelly demonstrates in *The Memory Code*, memorizing even the most abstract names is a skill that has helped the human species survive for thousands of years. We wouldn't be here without memory skills.

2. **Attention.** When we meet people, we might hear the sound of their names, but we're not paying attention to sound. Instead, we're both *looking* at them

and *feeling* social pressure. We're dazzled by their good looks, thinking they resemble a celebrity or horrified by the food dangling off their faces. Worse, we're also thinking about what we're going to say next. Our concentration is directed inward instead of outward.

3. **Overstimulation.** Most often when you meet someone new, it is in a highly social setting. You're bombarded by stimuli. The room is filled with noises. You may be drinking alcohol, suffering jet-lag or moving around. All of these elements distract you from fixing names to faces.

You know how you sometimes go to the kitchen from the living room and then forget why you're in the kitchen? This happens because the instant you leave the living room, the movement and change of locations floods all of your senses. Your intention isn't so much forgotten as it is suddenly pushed out to sea like a message in a bottle.

The same thing happens when you're introduced to a person. You hear the name, but then you ask where they're from and what they do. In combination with all the activity in the room, it's the same effect. Waves of information push that bottle out to the margins of your mind and the new name you just learned falls out your ear.

These are the reasons your brain doesn't grasp names and hold onto them like treasure. Yes, treasure! Every name is as valuable as a rare coin. Nearly everything— if not absolutely everything—we memorize is the name for something that points to something else. So name memorization is a top-of-the-line skill.

While forgetting names is not your fault, you can eliminate the problem with practice. You'll make a mistake from time to time, but even slip-ups can become powerful assets. It's better to mistake a Kristen for a Kirsten than to draw a total blank.

The super simple mechanics of memorizing names

Let me tell you a story. In early 2016, my friend Max Breckbill of the *Starting From Zero* podcast held one of his great entrepreneur dinners in Berlin. I was glad to be in attendance. His dinners are amazing: they are events where a bunch of people get together to network and just chill out in a relaxed restaurant. As always, Max began this dinner with a round of introductions. As each person said their name, I created a crazy image to help me recall it. For example, there was a guy named Lars, so I saw Lars from Metallica playing drums on his head.

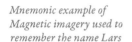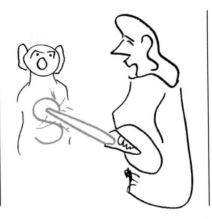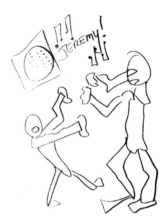

Mnemonic example of Magnetic imagery used to remember the name Lars	*Mnemonic example of Magnetic imagery used to remember the name Lukas*	*Magnetic mnemonic example of using Pearl Jam to remember a name at an event*

For Lukas, I saw Luke Skywalker using his lightsaber to carve an *S* onto Lukas's chest. This was so I would remember it was Lukas with an *S* instead of Luke as in Skywalker.

A bit later, I saw a guy named Jeremy in a fistfight with Eddie Vedder with the Pearl Jam song of the same name playing on the soundtrack.

There were 20 other names and, in a very short period, I created a wildly explosive image for each. I did not connect the names in any particular way with a story, however. You might think that the linking method, whereby simple Magnetic Image associations are made between items in a list, would have been handy in this case. Although some people fare well with it, I personally do better when I use the environment of a Memory Palace to place the Magnetic Imagery. The Memory Palace "space" is the link. But I didn't use a Memory Palace or the linking method in this case, because Max rotates the tables. For this type of memorization, because you rarely see people in the same place twice, each individual needs their own vignette, a mini-story that requires no connection with any other name.

This doesn't mean I couldn't have used the restaurant as a Memory Palace and stored the images with the location of the person when I first encountered them. But the key will be remembering the vignette, not the location. You just want one clear and distinct vignette per person that can travel with them wherever they go. Crucially, these vignettes must be *insane*. The good news is, it's easy to make images that really pop in your memory (we have already talked about the use of cartoonish violence in memory imagery). Just use KAVE COGS to make them...

...brighter than the sun...

... and more colorful than the Joker...

When I saw Lars, it wasn't just a humdrum image I thought about. The Metallica drummer was exploding with light and color, almost like a neon sign wrapped around a disco ball. Keep in mind that I "thought" this image, which is quite different from seeing it. It's not like memory wizards have HD television in their minds.

You can develop visually so that you do see things better in your imagination, but you don't strictly need to be a visual person, as we've covered before. You can get started with nothing more than verbal associations. Next ask yourself, "what would this look like if I *could* see it?" Often a simple question like that will move you toward the ability to see in your mind.

Next use...

    ... explosive sounds...

        ... epic sizes...

            ... rip snortin' physical force...

When I saw Luke Skywalker carving an *S* into Lukas's chest, I so fiercely felt the burn and vividly imagined the smell that I almost felt like puking. I even imagined that I could see the smoking embers on his shirt from the searing effect of the lightsabre.

When I saw Jeremy fist-fighting Eddy Vedder, it wasn't music-video sized Vedder the way I've seen him on YouTube. Vedder was massive and his fists pounded down with enormous force. Plus, the song "Jeremy" was blasting at top volume, as if screamed by Vedder with volcanic energy. Again, this happens both in words and visuals with as many other sensations involved as possible. The images feed the verbal descriptions and the words going through my mind amp up the sensations so that everything is tangible, memorable and downright Magnetic.

How long should this creative process take? With practice, mere seconds. You'll be surprised by how quickly you can pick up this skill and do it at a very high level. I've seen teenagers learn the skill in under an hour and win competitions on the same afternoon.

How to practice memorizing names

Since the stakes are high when it comes to memorizing names at events, try practicing at home before taking your new skill out in the field. It's easy: use Wikipedia to get a list of names and use the tools you've just learned.

The important thing is not to make a list of just any old names. Choose names that you would like to have memorized. These names for memory exercise might be:

- Composers

- Scientists

- Sportspeople

- Experts in a certain field

- Poets

- Emperors of Rome

In short, choose names that will make a difference to your quality of life either professionally or in connection with a hobby or personal interest. One of the biggest failings with learning memory techniques is that people practice with material like shopping lists. The problem with these is that the material is uninteresting and the stakes are low.

No matter what kind of names you choose to practice with, start small. Although you will soon be capable of memorizing dozens of names at rapid speeds, don't overwhelm yourself at the learning stage. Start with 5–10 names. Developing the ability to learn, memorize and recall names isn't a competition. Your goal is to learn the technique so you can master it, not frustrate yourself into giving up a skill that amounts to real magic. Memorizing names is, arguably, the most important skill in the world because of how important it makes other people feel.

Now, once you've associated crazy images to each name, go through the list a couple of times and make sure you've really exaggerated each. Next, distance yourself from the list. Take a notebook and head off to a cafe or at least to another room. A lot of people make the mistake of recalling a word and then checking right away to see how they've done. Unfortunately, this bad habit amounts to rote learning and will not serve you in the long run. You need delayed gratification so that you're really exercising your imagination and memory.

As you sit in that cafe, write down each and every name you associated with an image. If you come up blank, place a question mark and move on. Give yourself space and really hunt for the images. Then, as you head home, go over the list and fill in any blanks you managed to excavate.

You don't have to give yourself a score when you get home, but do take careful note of where you made mistakes. Analyze what went wrong and work on strengthening the associative images that didn't help you recall a name. Repeat this practice until you're confident that you can memorize names at an event. Once you're out in the world, don't feel like you have to give demonstrations or show off. This skill can be private, though you will find people noticing your talent and you should teach them how to do it. They'll thank you forever.

In my practice with memorizing names at events, I have learned that there are five conditions that will promote memorization of this kind:

1. **Have your own speech ready.** First, if you're at an event featuring a round of introductions, have an elevator speech prepared. If you're dreaming up your introduction on the fly, you won't be focused enough on memorizing the names of others.

2. **Engineer your position.** Try to be the one who goes last so you don't spend the entire time worrying that your introduction could have been better. Plus, if you go last, people will remember you better thanks to the Recency Effect. If there isn't a circle introduction at the event, you can be the one who suggests it. This strategy is an excellent way to engineer your position.

3. **Always be cool.** Relaxation is essential when memorizing any kind of information—especially in real time. Daily habits like meditation and fitness help a great deal. You can also deliberately manufacture calm using invisible techniques at the event such as Pendulum Breathing and Progressive Muscle Relaxation. No one will know you're doing anything and you'll be as relaxed as a sleeping YouTube kitten. Nothing will rattle your cage.

4. **Don't drink or smoke.** If you want to have a strong memory that works on command, cut out alcohol and stop smoking. I used to get away with it when doing memory demonstrations, but alcohol seriously messes with your working memory. Nicotine withdrawal makes concentration difficult if not impossible all by itself. Better never to have smoked at all.

5. **Let go of the outcome.** You can't control it anyway and wanting to succeed trips up a lot of beginners. Putting all thoughts of success out of your mind leaves your memory free to percolate the images you feed it. Plus, you can play with the names in high spirits. Since you'll want to go through the names a few times throughout the evening to massage them from working memory into long-term memory, you want the entire process to be fun. Racing through your list motivated by the fear of making a mistake only damages the results.

Point 5 bears enlargement: don't get stressed when you flub. At Max's entrepreneur dinner I struggled with a few names. It's all Brian Dean's fault. He's the guy behind Backlinko, a site you must check out if you run a website or blog. That night, I needed to go through my list of names at least once to ensure I could remember them all, but Brian kept asking me questions about memory while I was trying to memorize!

Okay, it really wasn't his fault that I wound up reaching hard for a couple of names. As I explained to Brian while we were talking, there's a reason I struggled: because I had my fat lips motoring away instead of going over the names a few times, I was not working against the Forgetting Curve. I predicted that I would lose 40–60 percent of my potential for total recall every 10 minutes that passed without making a quick pass over the names.

It turned out my numbers were off, though. Thanks to following the five conditions that we just covered, I only struggled with two of the names later. Further, I didn't entirely forget them as I'd predicted I might. With a bit of a push, the images popped up and I was able to retrieve them. Annoying, but passable. (There was one name I got completely wrong, but that's only because I misheard it.)

Anyhow, the point is that despite my dark prediction of failure while speaking with Brian, I had consciously released my need to control the outcome. Yes, everyone in the room knew that I was a memory guy, and that created some high expectations (if only in my head), but mistakes are an opportunity to talk about how memory works. In many ways, mistakes make for better illustrations of how and why the techniques work or fail to work. We're going to look at one of the main culprits next.

Don't be mystifying—either to yourself or others

At Max's entrepreneurs' dinner, one of the names I struggled with was Pascal. Because things were going fast, I picked an ineffective image for him. The philosopher Pascal had famously turned from atheism to religion, so I saw an image of God halfway putting a noose over his head and halfway slitting his throat. Although I did get this name back eventually, it took a fight. There are a few reasons:

1. **Vague image.** I don't know what Pascal the philosopher looked like, and I've never seen God. In retrospect, I could have used Michelangelo's God from the Sistine Chapel, but that still doesn't exactly help get back to "Pascal" at speed.

2. **Cluttered action.** I tried to see two actions instead of just one.

3. **Loose association.** Neither hanging nor throat-slitting have any direct relationship to atheism.

In sum, I created enough vague elements in the image that they acted as obstacles between myself and the target information.

But... I didn't let myself get stressed out about it.

I simply noticed the outcome and knew I would use it as a talking point and teaching tool if called upon to give a memory demonstration. I have given demonstrations, I have made errors and I have won respect simply by keeping my cool and sharing what went wrong. You can do this too. It's why I recommend you follow the "Always be cool" principle while taking time to analyze your mistakes. Just think about how you can do better next time and share the process so that others can learn too.

Let's say you're called upon to give a demonstration and you can't recall a couple of names. Instead of giving up or getting frustrated, just move on the same way you would in practice. As you're finishing the other names, you'll often be pleasantly surprised at how the ones you forgot suddenly spring back. If they don't, you wind up with an opportunity to explain what went wrong and demonstrate troubleshooting on the fly. Whatever you do, don't let yourself get frustrated. It's just like when you're meditating and find yourself long-gone in a thought: don't get frustrated, don't judge yourself harshly, just accept what happened and bring your attention back. You don't want to blow your momentum over what amounts to nothing in the long run. Always be cool and your memory will serve you well.

Follow all these tips well and there is one more effect you have to be ready for: you will be admired. People will be super-impressed by your memory skills—especially if you're humble and can handle mistakes gracefully. By the same token, prepare to be forgotten. I can't tell you how many times I've run into someone and called them by name. They're always shocked and amazed that I remember them. More often than not, they can't do the same. This lapse in their memory can create an awkward moment. Don't let it. Just make a joke or otherwise blow it off and offer to teach them the skill. You'll be able to use their name as an example. Personalized examples in teaching are often the best.

So, assuming you get yourself a list of names and get practicing, you now have a skill that will serve you for life. You never have to be at an event in a sea of strangers again. When you can remember names and assemble them with the existing contents of your mind, you will always be surrounded by friends wherever you go. Now that we have talked about being friends with the present, we are going to look at becoming friends with some very important parts of the past as well.

12 Where to Start? How to Overcome Beginner's Paralysis

"When you realize how easy it can be to fix something inside yourself, you start to hate that you didn't do it sooner, instead of skirting the issue for the past twenty years."
—Daniel Madison to Ian Frisch in *Magic Is Dead*

"When once you have tasted flight, you will forever walk the earth with your eyes turned skyward, for there you have been, and there you will always long to return."
—Leonardo da Vinci

"Better a diamond with a flaw than a pebble without."
— Confucius

I F YOU HAVE BEEN going through this book in a linear way, you've already learned a lot about how to use Memory Palaces and Magnetic Imagery. Now, a common beginner's question is: *what* do you use these tools for? I could say that the most rewarding and productive thing you can do is let go of the outcome, begin your practice and experiment your own way through to a result you value. However, given there are limitless fields of knowledge that you *could* memorize, that advice sometimes doesn't cure beginner's paralysis.

So, if memorizing names doesn't appeal, I'm going to suggest scripture. That might sound weird, coming from an atheist like me, but please hear me out. I thought Ben was crazy when he suggested I loosen my categorical atheism enough to give it a try, but I'm glad I did. Becoming less rigid in this way took everything about my meditation journey to a whole new level—literally transforming the Buddha Smile from a slice of bliss to a full-on nuclear factory filling half my head.

The Upanishads, the Bible, the Torah, the Koran, the Analects of Confucius and on and on—go far enough back and all cultures are enmeshed in scriptures.

Deep thinking on spiritual matters is part of every human tradition and virtually all of them offer some value—even the extinct ones. Strikingly, the most valuable parts of each spiritual tradition are generally those shared by all! Here are some reasons memorizing scripture is always worthwhile:

1. Memorizing scripture creates an internal source of inspiration and, perhaps, resilience.

2. Scriptures are usually organized into small component parts that have evolved over centuries specifically to be memorable.

3. By having scripture memorized, you will become closer to the traditions that got humanity this far. Even if a lot of the ideas in them need to be retired, others are well-worth preserving and having accessible at the drop of a hat.

4. Deeply internalized knowledge can help heal spiritual wounds.

5. Having scripture memorized potentially makes you a better contributor to your community.

With all that in mind, you can understand why this chapter is going to look at how to memorize scripture quickly and how to make it stick for the long term.

What to do before memorizing a single verse

The scriptures of many traditions have been collected as verses—that is, ideas, parables and directives that are highly compressed. These verses are the units of scripture memorization we will be working with. With this in mind, once you know that you're embarking on a scripture memorization journey, it's important to plan how you will do it. Your plan should include three things:

1. A Memory Palace Network and Magnetic Imagery based on Magnetic Lists

2. Practice time

3. An arrangement of the material you plan to memorize on your first outing

Building your Memory Palace Network has been addressed earlier in this book, so we're going to assume you've already done it. Setting aside practice time should be simple. If you don't know which part of a scripture to try to memorize, just think of a challenge you are facing and Google which part of your preferred tradition deals with it. So, now you are ready to begin.

Here's an example of how it works. Let's say the topic of "listening" is a particular challenge in one of your relationships right now, so you look for a verse on listening. We'll take a rather short verse, Proverbs 18:13 (NIV):

"To answer before listening—that is folly and shame."

Magnetic Imagery example for memorizing Proverbs 18:13

I'll offer instruction on how to memorize the book and chapter numbers later. For now, let's focus on the verse itself. Personally, I don't usually spend much time on the meaning of a passage at this stage. Contemplation can come after I've memorized it. So, let's sort out the keywords. In our example verse, they are:

- Answer

- Listening

- Folly

- Shame

The next thing I do after isolating the keywords is ask myself who I know who relates most closely to either the form of the verse or its meaning.

My friend's sister Andi comes to mind. I thought of and chose Andi as my Magnetic Bridging Figure for this verse because I was focusing on the first word "answer." (Remember, a Bridging Figure is one who shows up in each Magnetic Image of the sequence you are memorizing.) The *an* in Andi and the *an* in answer magnetically attract each other. Weave these associations together in a Memory Palace and one will trigger the other.

In a Memory Palace, it's easy to see her typing out an email. What kind of email? An email in response to an episode of *Fawlty Towers* she's just seen on television. She does this before she even heard the end of the sentence that offended her, and as a result, feels ashamed. Why *Fawlty Towers*? Because it has a sound similar to "folly" in it.

By looking for natural parallels that are already in your memory and imagination, you can often come across just the right set of images. This happens much more quickly than if you try to create abstract associations. Avoid abstractions as much as possible: they're difficult to recall, create weak associations and cause more frustration than they're worth.

Once you have the keywords magnetized, you might be wondering how to memorize all the little connecting words. Before you launch into your memorization attempt, stop and think about whether you really need to memorize them. Wouldn't your mind automatically fill in the blanks? In my experience, the answer for most people is "yes"—their minds really do fill in the blanks provided they follow the rest of the steps to come.

If, after experimenting, you find that your mind just doesn't do this, then you really do need to come up with associations for all these little words. For this, I suggest you create a stockpile because these joining words appear in everything you'll memorize. So, for efficiency, if you use a tutu for "to", then always use that same association. If you use a bee driving a forklift for "before," use that every time you need this word. Don't worry. It's unlikely that your mind will mind the repetition. The Memory Palace will provide more than enough differentiation. The important point is that you're drawing upon information, ideas, people and objects already in your memory. That's where the real memory magic happens. And sadly, this is a point that is too often missed by many memory experts who otherwise mean well.

Some ways to remember chapter and verse

It's usually not enough to remember only the words of verse; you must also know its book, chapter and verse. Using Proverbs 18:13 (NIV) as our example again, you have two two-digit numbers to memorize, as well as the book it's from. In general, I suggest that you have one Memory Palace Network per book of the Bible. So if you're working on Proverbs, have a Memory Palace Network just for Proverbs. This way, you'll never have to wonder what your Memory Palace Network is for—it will always be clear to you. Next, you'll want to develop skills with a simple technique for memorizing numbers. The general approach to this is called a PAO list; PAO stands for Person Action Object. I favor the Major Method or the Major System for using PAO lists, which is named after the mysterious 19th-century man who refined it, Major Bartlomiej Beniowski. The Major Method (or System) was refined in the 1800s, but PAO-type approaches are truly ancient. The Katapayadi System, which establishes much of the basis for the PAO approach, is perhaps 2,300 years old.

A PAO list is a collection of meaningful visualizations you associate with numbers. Having one will help you remember numbers faster and with more ease. Although your brain is naturally good at visualization, some people struggle to create their first PAO list. When you are well practiced, associating images with all of the two-digit numbers from 00–99 happens as easily as breathing. Some of these mental images will refer to People, some to Actions and some to Objects.

This is important: by incorporating the person, action, object triad into memorization, and, with practice, collapsing this PAO into a singular event, you are turning the abstract value of a number into a meaningful mental impression. Further, becoming proficient in PAO strengthens your association abilities. To truly excel in developing a PAO you must create your own images, practice them accordingly, and evolve them over time. There is no shortcut, no quick fix, and no substitute for creating your own imagery in a PAO system. As you change and update it over time, this constant state of evolution will help it become as effective and powerful as possible.

In the Major Method, you take a number and associate it with a consonant. This allows you to create word associations more easily because you can choose the vowels that help you make words. Following the Major Method, the digit-consonant associations are:

- 0—soft C, S, Z

- 1—D, T

- 2—N (The two downstrokes formed when writing the letter N correspond to the number 2.)

- 3—M (Rotate your letter M to the right? What do you see?)

- 4—R (Reverse the numeral 4 and it looks something like an R.)

- 5—L (Representing 5 fingers, which you can use to form a letter L with your hand)

- 6—Ch, J, soft G, Sh

- 7—hard G, K

- 8—F, V (A V8 is a kind of car engine and also a popular vegetable drink.)

- 9—B, P (The numeral 9 resembles a backwards P; this, mirrored, also resembles a B.)

When you're committing these associations to memory, you might wonder, "why these associations?" Ultimately, I don't think anyone knows, but they do contain a pattern. For every pairing where you have multiple choices, the sounds are produced by the exact same part of the mouth. Go ahead and pronounce d and then t. Your tongue strikes basically the same position in your mouth. Take ch, j and sh sounds for another example, or b and p. Each of these sounds take place in the same place in your mouth. Simply notice how the mouth movements of many of these letters correspond.[8] If you are having trouble remembering which letter corresponds to which number, do more than keeping these "patterns" in mind: try saying the numbers and letters out loud and notice how your mouth and tongue move to form each one. Many people have told me the combination of understanding this hidden logic and acting it out has helped them remember the system. The Kinesthetic Mode serves again!

What does this have to do with the Sanskrit we'll be memorizing for mental peace? Perhaps nothing, but Gary Weber places no small importance on the value of the pronunciation. Since he seems to speculate that Sanskrit evolved along with humans, it's possible that some of the mental benefits achieved from using the words come from how touching parts of your mouth with your tongue may fire off signals in certain parts of your brain. (As soon as I have the budget for it, I'll give it a test.) Perhaps epigenetics will provide revelations. Perhaps it's as simple as how so many languages have a word like "mama" because the word seems to mimic the opening and closing of the lips when a baby wants milk.

Chances are you don't need brain scans or hours of research to test the relationship between your mouth positions and the quality of your thoughts. Just test. Play with it. Experiment. I read a long time ago that relaxing your jaw and focusing on having your tongue *not* touch any part of your mouth is a great way to slow thoughts. Theoretically, our tongues move around our mouth in tandem with our thoughts. By deliberately holding it in limbo, you give your mind something to do other than thinking. The Sanskrit provided in this book courtesy of Gary Weber via the ancients provides a freeing alternative.

... Zzzz ...

To really solidify the encoding of your number/letter associations, you must practice. I've found the fastest and easiest way is to create a Memory Palace and place each number in a Magnetic Station. As you journey through your Memory Palace you could find a zero-shaped cookie being devoured by Cookie Monster as a sleeping snake snores, "Zzzzzzz...." nearby.

Once you have your Memory Palace and numbers encoded, it can be translated into a PAO. Use your memory journal, beginning with oo. Begin assigning people, actions, and objects to letter combinations all the way to 99. Combine the sounds you've made. For example, 22 could be "nun." You simply add a vowel to the two letters to make a word. Then again, take 235: there are different possibilities. When I get N, M and L the first thing that comes to mind is "animal." What comes to yours for 235?

Does the oo–99 PAO have to be done in a day? Certainly not. Really spend some time encoding your list, creating images that are vivid and memorable. You'll find as you progress through the numbers, imagery starts to flow and becomes easier to create. Always ask: "How can this be more specific?" The goal is to create intense, detailed images that are virtually unforgettable. As an example, my imagery for Proverbs 18:13 begins with using the Memory Palace I have built for Proverbs. Next, using the Major Method, the chapter number of 18 is TV—a concept for which I have several images: Dr. Frank-N-Furter from *The Rocky Horror Picture Show* and the infamous television from the movie *Videodrome*. The number 13 is, for me, the Hoover Dam, J. Edgar Hoover or a Hoover vacuum cleaner. In this case, one level of association leads to others, something you can explore with each of your solutions for 00–99. Hoover in no way contaminates the original association because the original choice of the Hoover Dam was its catalyst. Combining them I picture J. Edgar Hoover sucking the Hoover Dam in through a Hoover vacuum.

For the actual verse—"To answer before listening—that is folly and shame"—I created a sequence of events. I imagine my friend's sister, Andi, hastily sending out an email (meaning she wasn't listening). A bee is covering her email with honey, which is being sent to Fawlty Towers, to an ashamed John Cleese. This is a very small number of images relative to the number of words. The PAO images then support the memorization of the phrase.

This imagery is always a work in progress. I'm always looking for a way to improve my imagery. You should too. Instead of seeking perfection, seek progress. Practice makes progress (and, remember, perfection is progress), and you don't have to look hard to find opportunities to exercise your skills. Use the opportunities that are already present in your life and reward yourself. Invest the time, create your PAO, use it day to day. Try memorizing numbers related to:

- Banking Info

- Anniversaries

- Phone numbers

- Formulas

- Music

- Prices

Once you've understood this technique, it will be simple to create little associations to precede the associations you use for the verses themselves. This process, which will come to flow as if it were one step instead of many, makes memorizing chapter and verse fast, easy, effective and fun. What matters most is that you associate everything with information that already exists in your mind and that is meaningful to you.

Once you have done the work of memorizing the scripture and its numerical location, you get to have fun: a mental walk through your Memory Palaces one at a time. Yes, it's time for the Recall Rehearsal routines you learned about previously. As you develop your skills, you'll find that different verses enter your memory at different rates, and each presents its own form of brain exercise. Variance in challenge is a good thing. It keeps you on your toes and keeps things interesting. You don't want it to be too easy. When memory techniques suddenly become easy, they become boring and you stop using them. Remember the Challenge-Frustration Curve!

As you move through your Recall Rehearsal, you should "trigger" the associations you made and let them bring back the information. If you've correctly planned and organized your memorization activities, this should happen without any mental strain. Further, if you've properly numbered each Magnetic Station as described earlier, then you'll have even more autopilot familiarity with your Memory Palaces. If you are memorizing verse numbers and memorizing the scriptures in verse order, then that itself acts as your numerical clue.

The "Big 5 of Learning" and remembering for the long term

There are five crucial activities that help ensure you encode something in long-term memory. They aren't uncommon or taxing tasks at all, but making sure to perform all five does take intention. Also called the Big 5 of Learning, they are:

1. Reading

2. Writing

3. Speaking

4. Listening

5. Remembering and Recalling

The good news is that these are natural complements to each other. Writing automatically leads to reading, reading easily leads to speaking and so on. If you have your Memory Journal at hand and have someone you can talk to about memory practice, then 4 and 5 come to the fore.

As part of reading, when memorizing verses, it's good to also read various interpretations and commentaries about your verse. These will give your mind more context to help create deeper connections in both your imagination and the physical structures of your brain. With the wealth of media available online, it is also easy to find recordings of the verses spoken by others. Download them, listen to them and recite along with them. If nothing pre-recorded exists, simply record yourself and listen back to your own voice. Where possible, make memorization a family or community occasion. Reciting with others and hearing others share what certain passages mean for them is quite powerful in creating long-term memory impact.

Along with the Big 5, another crucial aspect of memorization is time. You must commit to creating time for your memorization practice. How much time do you need? That depends on you and your goals. Once you start, chances are this question will no longer be very interesting to you. You'll be enjoying the process so much and finding satisfaction that each new verse gets you closer to the goal. The journey will become so much more important than the destination. And when those destinations are reached, you'll be excited and want to create new ones. The benefits for the sharpness of your mind will be very clear to you.

Common questions and answers about memorizing scripture quickly

Does the length of verses matter?
Yes and no. I recommend starting with short verses. The trick, then, is in seeing that longer verses are usually just a connected series of shorter verses. In such cases, it can be helpful to spend more time ensuring you understand the gist of a long verse before committing it to memory.

Should you use flash cards and sticky notes?

No, or at least not until you've completed one project without them. I don't recommend this and shared Hugh's experience in the last section because relying on externals doesn't create the needed skills of memorization that a Memory Palace and association develop. Flash cards and sticky notes don't exercise your brain in quite the same way either. The only exception to the rule is if you're memorizing individual words or terms and, instead of having the answer on the back of the card, you have the Magnetic Imagery you created. In this way, you'll ask your brain to do a bit of memory work and jog itself into action. The benefits of doing this will be incredibly rewarding. And as soon as you can, leave the index cards and sticky notes behind.

Should you memorize from online scripture sources?

Generally, no. Many people want to memorize from online sources and tools, such as *Scripture Typer* or *Bible Memory Kids*. Yes, some of these Bible apps look great—they may be clean, well-organized and perhaps even fun to use. But they also create digital amnesia. If you must source your scripture from a screen, at least write it out in your handwriting and memorize from that. This practice will deepen the importance of the verse to your mind and is a win-win from the get-go.

What scripture should you memorize?

At the risk of being repetitive, I'll say that knowing why you want to memorize scripture does matter. Every time you feel the longing to do so, think about each individual piece you could choose and find your reason why. Remember, long-term memorization is a marathon, not a sprint. Plan, show up consistently and enjoy the multiple benefits as they increase over time, one verse at a time. As I tell my religious students, just pick the scripture that gets you one step closer to God and focus on it, one word and one line at a time. Soon practice and the examples to come will show you how to memorize 11-17 words per Magnetic Station.

13 BRINGING IT ALL TOGETHER

"I am the cause of the remembrance of the scriptures."
— Ribhu Gita, 27.14

Why I'm sharing my Magnetic Imagery

The previous chapters contained a lot of theory, so to help you see how the ideas work I am going to share some of my own practice. I invite you into the mental zoo of Magnetic Imagery I created and placed in a Memory Palace for the *Ribhu Gita* selections in Gary Weber's *Evolving Beyond Thought*.

At the risk of raising the ire of some readers, I have to rehash the point made in the *Rhetorica ad Herennium* thousands of years ago: these are examples of how the process works for a single individual—me. Copying them misses the central point of the Magnetic Memory Method. Plus, they're impossible to copy anyway.

Instead, my goal for this chapter is to take you through an extended example. All of my previous books have limited the presentation of mnemonic examples precisely so that the focus falls on helping people learn to fish so they have the skills for life. It is clear that fishing *for* people tends to impede their ability to take action on their own. As I mentioned at the beginning of this book, and as Weber discusses in *Evolving Beyond Thought*: "The most useful teachers teach others how to learn... by 'abandonment.'"

Abandonment is especially apt when teaching with mnemonic examples because, as you'll see, I have nothing generic to draw upon. I can only use cultural references that already exist in my memory. Rarely do I search on Google for imagery ideas because this violates the number-one rule of association-based mnemonics:

*Don't memorize new information in order
to memorize other new information.*

You should always link new information with your existing mental content. For this reason, the best outcome of sharing mnemonic examples is the *demonstration* of creative selection and combination that encourages you to play with your own special stew of existing knowledge and pop culture references—the stuff that is unique to you and which only you can access.

I've had people offer to hire me to create mnemonic examples for them and many others have promised I'd get a million subscribers on YouTube if I made inventing mnemonic examples the focus of my videos. These incidents have only encouraged me to resist creating them for pedagogical purposes even more, especially since I take no personal pleasure in creating mnemonic examples for information I have no intention of memorizing. That would be worse than producing a counterfeit painting. It would be like producing a counterfeit painting and then hiring an actor to play the part of the painter and hiring an audience to admire both the painting and the actor posing as its creator.[9]

I feel that whether abandonment is a legitimate teaching method or not, we all face abandonment one way or another in our lives, and most commonly where mental skill is involved. No one can see inside the mind of another. All the mnemonic examples in the world won't make how memory techniques work any clearer. These examples are in my mind. The words and images I use to communicate them to you do not convey the entire multisensory and deeply personal natures they have for me.

Yet, I did rethink the rigidity of this stance, after warning people about their "mnemonic example addiction" and criticizing the "mind crimes" of medical mnemonics websites, when I read an article called "Why Minimal Guidance During Instruction Does Not Work: An Analysis of the Failure of Constructivist, Discovery, Problem-Based, Experiential, and Inquiry-Based Teaching" suggested to me by Barbara Oakley of Learning How To Learn (whose influence and own writing in "On Creating a Sticky MOOC" has hugely improved the success of my courses and YouTube videos). The findings of this article boil down to this:

> Even for students with considerable prior knowledge, strong guidance while learning is most often found to be equally effective as unguided approaches. Not only is unguided instruction normally less effective; there is also evidence that it may have negative results when students acquire misconceptions or incomplete or disorganized knowledge.

Personally, in most cases, I have learned best when given an instruction manual and left to my own devices. But I have run a series of experiments by putting my devotion to minimal guidance and teaching by abandonment to the side. In my own mind, I called this series of experiments "Mission Maximum Guidance."

First, I started offering one-on-one coaching, which involved me coming up with mnemonic examples on the fly for clients. In one case, with Lee Escobar on the other side of my Skype screen thousands of miles away, I looked at the corner of my room after he tossed me a name to memorize. With barely a second's pause, Lee said, "Anastasia."

As I explained the process, I pointed to a ceiling corner in my office studio.

"Okay," I said, "I'm *not* going to make a mnemonic in my head. I'm going to consciously think about this corner, right here. And then it's like weaving in my memory of that corner, my conscious memory and thinking about that corner."

As I explained, because I don't know someone named Anastasia, I thought about Cliff Burton, the tragically deceased bass player of Metallica. He had written and performed a track especially cherished by bassists called "Anesthesia (Pulling Teeth)." It's a fusion of classical music-like melodies with snarly noise effects and heavy drumming. No, the anesthesia squirted into your gums at the dentist is not the same as "Anastasia," but it's more than close enough and the mind can see and hear a long-haired bassist and his creations and readily make the connection.

Holding on to that image while searching my mind for someone named Anastasia I'd seen with my own eyes, I said, "give me another one."

"Bertha," Lee said.

I laughed at the convenience of his choice. As I explained, pointing now at the middle of the corner wall, I used to have a bass that I called "Bertha." It was then just a simple matter of having Cliff Burton interact with this bass in a line of action going down from the ceiling to the floor.

As Lee processed my example, he moved his hand around in the air to demonstrate the concept of "weaving" images into space. Then he spontaneously produced his own mnemonic example:

"So Anastasia might be ants on a stage hanging out on a good day in the corner?"

"Exactly."

My only advice from there was to avoid an abstraction like "good day" and make it more concrete—unless the abstraction works for him.

A few weeks later, Lee sent me a video testimonial from the airport. As I knew when we met for the session, his goal had been to memorize 300 names at each of his speaking events. Within a few weeks of our session, he had almost memorized 200 names and was well on his way. This experience opened my eyes to the potential of supplementing my "teaching by abandonment" books and video courses with more in-person training for those willing to invest in one-on-one help.

My second, ongoing experiment in Maximum Guidance involves livestreams on YouTube. I conduct these sessions in a number of different ways, ranging from casual balcony broadcasts to detailed slideshow presentations. In making these presentations, I teach freely, knowing that I am creating a dual reality for viewers. Those who haven't taken either my free course or the full MMM Masterclass will be served with general information. Those who have invested time and energy in the memory training will receive deeper insights, and to my pleasant surprise, these people often help with the teaching.

As a general principle, those less invested in spending time with any level of training tend to ask questions that amount to asking for handouts. They don't seem to understand that no number of mnemonic examples will do the work of creating their own Memory Palace Networks and creating their own images based on both a theoretical and applied understanding of the process. Nevertheless, lightbulbs do switch on during these sessions. Many people report that they've finally taken action as a result of them. That's the most important thing.

My third experiment in Maximum Guidance has been in the form of what is now called the "Memory Dojo." To those students who have taken the MMM Masterclass and gone onward, I've been offering weekly sessions to go through technical questions and use our Facebook group for discussion and accountability. This group gives me the opportunity to more closely observe the progress of students. One, Adolfo Artigas, regularly reports on his school exams and how the MMM has helped him consistently score in the high 90% range. He also posts videos of his campus and gives mini-tutorials based on his discoveries. Another, Yrgalem Solomon, shares mind maps of the Memory Dojo sessions along with her adventures with memorizing English vocabulary. Likewise, Michael McLaughlin has been combining mind maps with Memory Palaces. Michael Swain and Sunil Khatri frequently share their successes with Japanese. As Sunil recently wrote:

> Coming clean—so I took a break over Christmas and New Years from my kanji study. I stopped at 300. After 2.5 weeks of not studying I reviewed all 300 and was able to recall all but 5 of them. Very happy about this!!! Back to studying now.

To this, Pete Halsted responded:

> Very inspiring indeed, I have been doing basically rote learning of Spanish for the last 3 months while immersed in South America. Just getting into MMM. I also took 2 weeks off while our daughter visited.

And feel like I have lost 50% of what I thought had stuck. Looking forward to retention rates like yours!!!

In this experiment, I feel rewarded in that Maximum Guidance has transcended my own efforts and become a family affair. Pete doesn't have to take my word for it. The MMM community nurtures the unified field with examples of their own.

It's too soon to tell how this initiative will grow, but I'm tremendously excited by the potential. For one thing, I know that all the mnemonic examples in the world will not help anyone nearly as much as creating their own. But dozens of us, or hundreds, of thousands, creating in tandem and sharing the results—that will be a flourishing boon of activity for those skeptical about taking the plunge. They won't need a Morpheus to show them just how deep the rabbit hole goes after that: they'll be Morpheus, the hole itself and every traveler in the hole's rhizomatic web of existing and potential channels!

All in all, these experiences have warmed me up to the idea of sharing more mnemonic examples in the hopes that I'm completely wrong about their role in teaching by abandonment. It is still clear and obvious that all who come to the art, science and craft of memory techniques ultimately reside in their minds alone, but it is also now more obvious to me that the presence of someone who can demonstrate and motivate serves some learners who will not find a point of entry in any other way.

Since you are working on building a skill in your own mind, it behooves you to be the one who takes up the mantle and learns the skills by doing. And further, that you do this the instant your understanding is complete enough to cast your hook into the vast ocean of your imagination. Should your ocean feel frozen over, take inspiration from Kafka:

> "A book must be the axe for the frozen sea within us."

Let this book be your axe.

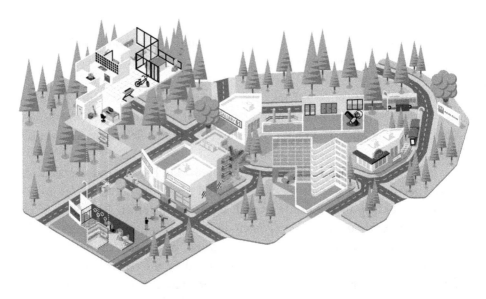

An extended mnemonic example using the Ribhu Gita

Now that you understand the spirit in which I offer it to you, here is the Magnetic Imagery I created and snapped into a Memory Palace—like psychological laundry transformed into mental Legos—for the *Ribhu Gita* selections in Gary Weber's *Evolving Beyond Thought*. For best results, please download the care package included with this book. It contains a full video walkthrough with photographs of the actual locations to fill out the map of Kelvin Grove. I also recite and explain verbally how the techniques work with complex, foreign language text with simple English translations like you'll encounter in this chapter. Get this now at *magneticmemorymethod.com/vmm*

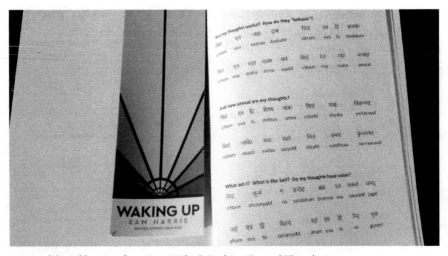

A page of the Ribhu Gita from Gary Weber's Evolving Beyond Thought

I have memorized the sound and meaning of these passages of the *Ribhu Gita* with reference to the self-inquiry questions Weber uses to contextualize them (shown in bold in his book, and which you will read in the next section with the mnemonic examples). Overall, I have found the questions more useful than the translated meaning of the text, but both play a role.

The benefits of memorizing these verses have been greater mental calm and greater frequency of feeling like a light has switched on in my head. In the book, Weber suggests "these verses, learned, and chanted, again and again, and investigated with diligence and perseverance" can create awakening. I have found they have served well toward that end.

The Memory Palace I created for memorizing these 32 verses of the *Ribhu Gita* starts in my apartment before proceeding outside where I strategically pin Magnetic Imagery in the air. Although I normally don't like outdoor Memory Palaces, it seemed fitting in this case. I also used the Pillar Technique throughout, which generally involves starting at the ceiling and "writing" the Magnetic Imagery from the top down on imaginary pillars. Typically, the space is divided into three parts: top, middle and bottom.

Magnetic Station example

All of my personal knowledge of Sanskrit pronunciation comes from modeling Gary Weber's recitation of the text on his YouTube channel. I have not found another recording to compare his with, nor done any Sanskrit study with a qualified teacher. Although Weber suggests that pronunciation matters, I have become a big fan of "close enough," provided I am understood and can understand. It's a position I have come to after having learned and spoken a few languages and found an abundance of possible pronunciations based on regional differences as granular as the exact neighborhoods of a city like Berlin or Beijing.

Speaking of "close enough," I honestly do not recall every last Magnetic Image I created for this *Ribhu Gita* Memory Palace. The majority of these images are indeed what I actually used, but some are inventions and are close enough to what I would have used at the time. (This issue presents yet another reason why I have been reluctant to share mnemonic examples in the past.) Also, it is important to understand that Magnetic Imagery is not meant to be permanent. These tools are meant to be like training wheels on a bike. The sooner you no longer need them, the better. Or think of them like the key to your home. You need the key to get in, but once you're in, you can technically be inside of your home and not know the location of your keys. Once you have the target information, you can develop the ability to never need the key again to access the target information.

People sometimes worry that these images will create mental clutter as well. Put that aside. One would never avoid another vacation for concern that more amazing memories of events and locations will cause suffering. The mental adventure of creating Magnetic Imagery for use inside of a Memory Palace or Memory Palace Network is like taking a mental vacation and comes with all the rewards. You might well remember the key (or keycard) you used to access your hotel room, but all the focus falls on the content of the vacation, which you can access reliably provided you were present to the journey.

Also, note how "memory reserve" builds as we proceed. The more Magnetic Imagery accumulates to deal with words and meanings, the more accumulates. You'll find in your own practice that the more you memorize texts verbatim, the less effort goes into the practice because you develop a pool of go to Magnetic Images.

Presence to the practice, then, means letting go of the endless questions and possible obstructions. Let go of the outcome and always bring the spirit of the beginner and you will succeed without fear or concern.

Because I am not learning Sanskrit as such and have not checked every last word of Weber's translation, I'm not claiming any accuracy for these readings or inviting the criticism of Sanskritists. In each case, I've found that most of these renderings jibe with other texts I've read about Advaita Vedanta when they appear. And anyway, I'm more concerned with the gist of the meaning for self-inquiry purposes. I'm very cautious not to create any attachments whatsoever while engaging in a practice designed to create freedom or liberation (*moksha*) from them. I suggest you at least consider doing the same. Further, on the matter of a translation's accuracy, consider the point Linda Heuman makes in her essay "Whose Buddhism Is Truest?":

> ...built into the traditional account of the First Council is the story of one monk who arrived late. He asked the others what he had missed. When they told him how they had formalized the Buddha's teachings, he objected. He insisted that he himself had heard the Buddha's discourses and would continue to remember them as he had heard them.

Although you really can memorize things with stunning accuracy, it's important to be clear when accuracy on the surface level isn't available. Work instead for acquiring and retaining deeper levels of meaning based on truth. Likewise, and at the risk of unnecessary repetition, my wish is for you to see these mnemonic examples as a demonstration of *ars memorativa* designed to release you from any attachment to mnemonic examples. No one person's Magnetic Imagery can ever be the best or truest and work for everyone else.

With all this prolegomena in tow, I can now begin explaining my practice for memorizing the 32 passages of the *Ribhu Gita* from *Evolving Beyond Thought*.

How I remembered 32 passages of the Ribhu Gita

Gary Weber divides his *Ribhu Gita* selections, which are those I have memorized, into themes. The sections we're using here cover self-inquiry questions that help us explore the nature of the mind, which can help us experience relief from its turmoil. They are tools that have worked for me.

Although there are possibly grandiose claims that the mind can be permanently neutralized, and as we'll see, the final lines of the text assert this as the ultimate goal, it is unlikely that "planning thoughts" will ever leave. So long as a person exists, the mind will need to operate in the world. Planning thoughts will assist in this operation, lest the person become vegetative, as befell the unfortunate Nietzsche.

The passages go through two transitions too. The first passages offer questions about our thoughts. The passages collected after the first transition help us reflect on our ideas and beliefs about the bodies we inhabit. By challenging them, we can experience relief from the suffering these beliefs create. The passages after the second transition present us with questions that help us explore the nature of the bliss we can experience after working down our illusions about the mind and body. The final verses help us explore the benefits of the practice. Weber calls these *capping verses*, and they seem intended to help cement the inquirer's findings in place. They certainly work for me, thanks to the emphatic reminder that all of these efforts are scientific in nature.

1. Are my thoughts useful? How do they behave?

chittam eva mahaa dosham
thought alone great folly

chittam eva hi baalakaH
thought alone is small boy

chittam eva maha atma ayaM
thought alone great soul this

chittam eva maha anasat
thought alone great unreality

The images for these four lines occupy a simple room indicated on the map you can download and watch unfold on video at *magneticmemorymethod.com/vmm*.

In the first corner, I have Chet, a character from *The Hardy Boys*. Although *chittam* appears multiple times throughout the text, I personally only need to encode him once. Other people may need to include their image for a recurring word each time it appears in the text. When some people come to memory techniques, they think they must have one image for every word, but as the Proverbs example earlier in this book demonstrates, this may not be necessary. Even when the text is in another language, you need not encode every last word with an image and can compress in different ways as you proceed.

Below Chet (*i.e., chit*) I have a Magnetic Image of my friend Tam playing a tambourine. *Chet + Tam = Chittam*. Weber translates this word as "thought" so I imagine Tam thinking as he plays the tambourine. Note that these Magnetic Images involve the following Magnetic Modes:

- Kinesthetic: I think of what it *feels* like for Tam to play the tambourine.

- Auditory: I *hear* what this instrument sounds like (or approximate what hearing is like mentally in the absence of sound).

- Visual: Although I don't really *see* pictures in my mind, I am nonetheless imaging what this scene would look like if I could mentally picture images.

- Emotional: Although slight, I have drawn upon my emotional reaction to the Chet character as I read Hardy Boys novels in my youth. His appearances were usually humorous.

- Conceptual: The whole notion of the Hardy Boys as a detective series is a concept.

I am not touching on either the olfactory or the gustatory modes in this example, but if I struggled with the image, I would add them during a second pass.

As it would become onerous to point out the Magnetic Modes in every single example, please refer back to this one if you need to refresh the process. Using these KAVE COGS categories to add different layers to the mental imagery you draw upon really does help make the process faster and more effective.

Slightly below Chet and Tam, for *eva*, I have Eva Perón who rides the Chinese symbol for horse (which is the sound *ma*). This word means "alone." Since Eva Perón had been the first lady of Argentina and only one person can hold that role at a time, "alone" is closely related. Seeing her laughing made the *ha* memorable. *Mahaa* means great, so again being the first lady lends itself to this conclusion rather naturally.

Dosham stretches my brain a little, but Homer Simpson comes to the rescue. Noted for shouting "d'oh!" often during moments of both frustration and insight,

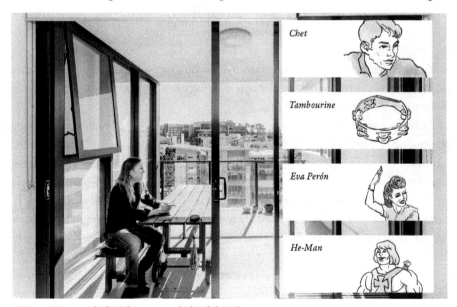

Mnemonic example for "chittam eva hi baalakaH"

I put a shammy in his hand and, since *dosham* means "folly," Homer uses the shammy to clean the sign from the TV show *Fawlty Towers*.

For the second line, I work with the second corner of the room. I could have used the wall between the two corners (as you will see I do in parts of the bedroom), but in this room, I use the corners only because I thought I would use buildings only when I started the text. I later changed my mind and abandoned the prepared Memory Palaces to work with the elevator, lobby and surrounding neighborhood. I follow the general guidelines of what I teach closely, but not to the point of dogmatism. The old line about knowing the rules (through experience) before you break them will put you in good stead in your own practice.

This second station does not need to repeat any of the pre-existing material and goes straight to the new words, *he baalakaH*. Again, you might need a specific Magnetic Image to tell you to repeat parts of the first line, or you might need to create completely new imagery. But if you, like me, go straight into Recall Rehearsal, chances are you will be able to remember calls for repetition with no effort whatsoever.

This Magnetic Image is He-Man wearing a balaclava and laughing. In Sanskrit in this context *he* translates to "is," so I thought of He-Man singing the song "He is" by the band Ghost. Since *baalakaH* ends with a capital H and thus has a "hah" sound, laughing takes care of that. The actual word means "small boy" and, as I interpret the line with the help of Weber's self-inquiry question, the idea is to picture your unchecked thoughts as behaving like a small and out-of-control boy. Don't worry, this line is not prejudiced against child's play.

Weber translates the third line as "Thought alone is this great man" or "great soul." The idea is that we imagine ourselves to be great (or even just imagine that we want ourselves to be great) at the cost of being present to what actually is, which is the present moment.

Chittam eva already stands, so, in the third corner, I "write Magnetically" from the ceiling to the floor. The line sounds more like "ma-hat my-yam", so I have the Chinese symbol for horse *(ma)* donning a hat while sitting on a yam. It is a great man for doing so.

In the fourth corner, the new information is "mah-han-a-sat." My mind doesn't need another horse symbol, so I just see my artist friend Anna sitting on a piece of her art. It is a particularly surreal piece in order to help me remember that "mah-han-a-sat" means "great unreality."

To get this passage into long-term memory as quickly as possible, I diligently run it through Recall Rehearsal. This means I recite each of the four lines in order. Then I recite each part in reverse order. Then I recite parts one and three, followed by four and two. Then I recite two and four, followed by three and one. I do this several times, thereby allowing the Serial Positioning Effect to give primacy and recency to each portion of the scripture.

Thus, in Weber's translation, the meaning of the Sanskrit runs:

"Thought alone is the great folly. Thought alone is the small boy. Thought alone is this great man. Thought alone is the great unreality."

2. Just how unreal are my thoughts?

chittam eva hi mithya atma
thought alone is illusory self

chittam shasha vishanavat
thought is hare's horn

chittam naasti sadaa satyaM
thought is not is ever true

chittaM vandhyaa kumaaravat
thought like the son barren woman

Station 5 falls in another room, using the corner just inside the room and by the door. I imagine a character named Skeeves from the Robert Asprin *MythAdventures* series beating up the Buddha as a symbol for atma. *Mithya* for something illusory (everything we see) is already known to me from listening to many talks given by James Swartz.

Station 6 is the next corner. Here, I use a person named Sasha with whom I've spent some time. In this Magnetic Image, she and I watch the sci-fi series *V* while my friend Anna (the same artist friend from the previous room) pushes horned rabbits into a vat from the series *Breaking Bad*. Why horned rabbits? Because *shasha vishanavat* means "hare's horn," and that is how the meditation asks us to consider the nature of thought—as unreal as a horned rabbit.

Station 7 falls on the next corner and involves a particularly obscure reference. When playing with The Outside in Germany, we performed in the hometown of Thomas Mann: Lübeck. Outside the concert venue I saw a poster for Nasty Jeans, a band performing the following week. *Naasti* means "is not" and thoughts are precisely not anywhere near jeans this nasty, so the work is done.

Below this poster, now transported mentally onto my bedroom wall, Saddam Hussein sits on a yam. Since I'm sure he never did this, the meaning that thought is "never true" sticks.

Station 8 again does not repeat *chittam* and so moves directly to *vandhyaa kumaaravat.* It's one of the more challenging passages, but I finally settle on the actor Vin Diesel smashing a van while shouting "ya!" down on a cow (German for "cow" is *kuh*). Here, I draw upon my 34 from the 00–99 system I created. It is "mare." Just as 13 starts with the Hoover Dam to bring in J. Edgar with a Hoover vacuum cleaner, I move from the word "mare" to "nightmare" and arrive at the nightmare horse from Piers Anthony's *Xanth* novels. This horse is kicking a vat—the same vat from *Breaking Bad* as above—only in this case, it is barren.

For your consideration, as you develop your Magnetic Lists, you'll find that your associations for numbers come in handy for words and vice versa. Drawing upon my Magnetic Image for 34 here was very useful. It saves time and energy.

"Thought alone is the illusory self. Thought is like the hare's horn. Thought is never true. Thought is like the son of a barren woman."

3. What am I? What is the self? Do my thoughts have value?

chittam shuunyaM na sandehaH
thought emptiness no doubt

brahma eva sakalaM jagat
Self alone whole world

aham eve hi chiatanyaM
I am alone verily consciousness

aham eve hi nir gunam
I am alone verily without gunas/attributes

Station 9 starts strategically on a corner of the balcony so I can get into the living room without crossing my own path. I place a shoe that "empties" yams onto my mom's former hairdresser, Sandy, with a high school friend whose last name is Dey. For *na*, I include a former girlfriend who asks me "na?" in German. ("Na" is a word with oodles of uses, but this girlfriend usually used it in a cooing, endearing way that basically meant "So then? How are you?" or "So? What's next?") By this point, the convention of some of these phrases ending in "hah" is alive and well. I do not need to encode an image for it. In terms of meaning, Sandy is opportune, because in my memory, Sandy is a skeptical person.

Station 10 finally releases the *chittam* pattern and spatially takes the next corner, putting a teacher named Mr Kilby in Buddha pose for *brahma*. Mr Kilby taught World Religions 12 at my high school and represents my first memory of learning about brahman and atma. He also offered the kindness of extending me no favors when I told him I'd missed an exam because I'd been locked up in the drunk tank. "Not only have you failed this exam due to absence, but also proven that you've learned nothing from this course." He was right to let me pay the price and fail the exam, but dead wrong that I'd learned nothing. Indeed, I still learn from that course, and from you, Mr Kilby.

Below Kilby, Eva is not necessary, but I have her tossing a sack of lamb into a green Jaguar that I recall a friend of my dad's driving deep in the mists of memory. This man has a giant globe in the car and sings, "He's got the whole world in his hands..." to express the "whole world" meaning of these two words.

Station 11 switches yet again to start with *ahem*. Abraham of the Bible comes first to mind, so I go with that, while eliding the deeply familiar *eva hi* and going straight for the next new piece of information. Below Abraham, I see a cup of tea (i.e., chai) and a guy I know named Tan, who has a yam. Abraham Maslow said a few things about "consciousness" and Abraham Lincoln was conscious of the need to sharpen your axe before cutting down trees, hence that *ciatanyam* for consciousness passes with greater ease into memory.

Station 12 needs nothing more than an image for *nir gunam*. A fellow named Nur created one of my book covers and the band Sonic Youth has an album called *Goo*. Without Nur, the book would not look nearly as cool. 23 in my 00–99 PAO is Sylvester Stallone, who played the Vietnam vet, Rambo. The *gunas* as "ropes" or inclinations that "bind" us to the world is already known to me, so this pre-existing familiarity puts me on easy street this time around.

> "Thought is emptiness—there is no doubt about this. Self, alone, is the whole world. Verily, I am, alone, consciousness. I am, alone, without attributes."

Before going on to the fourth passage, I'd like to dwell for a moment on this point about familiarity, which raises a powerful general note about the role of reading and having multiple teachers. Many of these terms and words were familiar to me in advance of memorizing the text because when I became interested in Advaita Vedanta, I practiced what my friend Jonathan Levi calls "brute force learning."

Basically this term means reading and processing as much as you can, as quickly as you can. I'm not sure if Jonathan is the origin of the term or not, but don't be turned off by its military tone. The reality is that rapid learning is greatly assisted by imbibing information for the purposes of experiencing both the big picture and granular detail at the same time. Thanks to multimedia, the rapid service of eBay and a relentless passion for uninterrupted, sustained, silent reading, my brain had been exposed and primed for many of these words and concepts.

Although we are looking for oneness through the practice at hand and I have felt its grace in my own way, I still stand by my oft-repeated claim that "one is the most dangerous number" when you're trying to learn anything. Read widely, from multiple voices and with reference to your personal learning hierarchies and consumption preferences I've discussed at length in *The Memory Connection*. The more you take in, the more those teachers become part of you. The more this reveals of what "your self" might become when you use the process to move closer to the unified field through making yourself more aware that *you* always already were the unified field—you just couldn't see it. Without continual practice, it's easy to unsee this truth many times over again. Memorizing these passages and reflecting on them will help reduce instances of disappearance from your existence as the field.

On a final, personal note, this passage of the *Ribhu Gita* has been quite useful to me in times of distress. This is thanks to a chapter in *Evolving Beyond Thought* that concerns itself with self-inquiry, titled, "Do my thoughts have value?" When caught in a particularly noisy storm of thinking, simply reciting the four-part line of this part has done much to deterritorialize the clouds of thinking when the memorized question readily came to mind. Of course, such punishing thoughts had no value whatsoever. Nevertheless, without the question I was forced to feel the "jaws of the crocodile," which, according to James Swartz, is sometimes how *samsara* is defined. We'll discuss the memorization of that useful term where it rests in my living room next.

4. How do bondage, sin and samsara arise?

mana eva hi saMsaaraM
mind alone is samsaara

mana eva hi mandalam
mind alone is the circle

mana eva hi bandhatvaM
mind alone is bondage

mana eva hi paatakam
mind alone is sin

Station 13 introduces Moses with Mana. He feeds this to Eva Perón. As mentioned, the word *samsara* for wandering or ever-changing illusion of the world was already known to me. A Magnetic Image you might consider could be Dr. Seuss's Sam-I-Am or Sean Penn in his role as Sam from *I Am Sam*. Stations 14 to 16 do not need imagery for *mana eva hi* because this is established on Station 13. Station 14 needs only a mandala, and I choose the snake necklace from *The Neverending Story* as a solid image of a circle. Station 15 has my former band, The Outside, tossing a hat down on a van. I know internally it is "vam," not "van", and the correction is easily made upon recall. Station 16 has "It's Pat!" of *Saturday Night Live* fame jumping on a camera.

"Mind, indeed, is the worldly existence. Mind, indeed, is the mandala. Mind, indeed, is bondage. Mind, indeed, is sin."

5. Where does the concept of a "body" come from?

mana eva mahad dukhaM
mind alone great sorrow

mana eva shariirakam
mind alone cause of body

mana eva prapanchaakhyam
mind alone is the world

mana eva kalebaram
mind alone is the body

With *mana eva* well-established, Station 17 has the *Mad Magazine* mascot duking it out with a leg of ham. Station 18 sees an old childhood churchmate named Sherry exaggeratedly tending to a rack of lamb. Station 19 involves a preppy student I knew and Peter Pan chalking up a yam shaped like a globe (prep = *prap*,

Peter Pan = *pan*, chalk = *chaak*, yam = *yam*).

Station 20 involves Caleb, whom I knew at York University during my doctoral years. He is pounding on my dad's Dodge Ram (this truck is the same Magnetic Image I use for the King of Diamonds and I mention this here to illustrate how images can be multipurpose).

> "Mind, indeed, is the great sorrow. Mind, indeed, is the cause of the body.
> Mind, indeed, is the world of phenomena. Mind, indeed, is the body."

FIRST TRANSITION: *The Body*

6. Where does the feeling of a "knot" in our heart come from?

dehe ahem iti sankalpaH
body I am this notion

hrdydaya granthir iritaH
heart knot is regarded

kaala trayepi tanna asti
time three periods is not

sarvam brahma eti kevalam
all Brahman is alone

Station 21 involves the high school friend with the last name "Dey" as mentioned in verse 3. *Dehe* is pronounced "day-hey," so I have my friend trouncing on a pile of hay. E.T. (the extra-terrestrial from the movie) emerges to fight with my mom's hairdresser, Sandy (also mentioned in verse 3), and Kal-el's father. Kal-El is the birth name of Superman and I use his father to represent the sound "paH." Actors Marlon Brando and Russel Crowe have both played this character, but I use the concept alone. Remember, you need not see images in your mind in order to link a trigger with target information.

Station 22 is a huge beating heart in the hand of magician Dai Vernon. A tattoo artist I know named Grant finds this irritating—so irritating he is tying himself in knots. As alternative Magnetic Images, you could use Ulysses S Grant tying himself in knots, or perhaps the actor Don Knotts writing a grant in a dramatic way.

Stations 23 and 24: The next passage is repeated multiple times and only needs to be encoded once. I use two corners of the elevator. Kal Penn is an actor: I have him playing an Epiphone guitar (with the bullseye-target design used by Zaak Wylde). The guitar has a huge light "tanning" an Aston Martin car.

If you're new to memory techniques, you might need to add an image for *ah* at the end of a figure like Kal Penn and an image for *tri* (perhaps a tricycle). I do not need images in these cases, and it is not clear why sometimes each syllable needs Magnetic Imagery whereas others do not. I suggest you not judge the process either way and always take Magnetic coding on a case-by-case basis, enjoying shortcuts and instances of "mental autofill" when they appear. Likewise, do not be frustrated or discouraged when extra effort is required. The last line of this phrase was tricky for me until I remembered that I used to live near the Saar River in Saarbrücken.

In the elevator, I place one of the bridges that spans the Saar River. I have a van crash into it (for *vam*). Mr Kilby as the image for *brahma* hovers in meditation pose as E.T. arrives again in a Kevlar vest with a lamb in tow.

"The notion 'I am the body' is regarded as the 'heart knot.' In all three periods of time, it is not so. All is self, alone."

7. Where does the sense of different bodies come from?

> *dehe tri epi bhaavam*
> body three-fold supposition

> *yat tad deha jnanam ucyate*
> that that body knowledge is said

> *kaala trayepi tanna asti*
> time three periods is not

> *sarvam brahma eti kevalam*
> all Brahman is alone

Station 25 is my high school friend, Dey, again, this time with the Epiphone guitar. The lamb is now baa-baa-ing at the van. Station 26 is Weird Al Yankovic ("ya") with the singer of the band Tad, tossing jars of jam and tea (chai) at the wall. The "ewe" sound of *ucyata* automatically encodes without an image, but anyone can readily use a ewe.

> *"The supposition that 'I am the three-fold body' is said to be the knowledge of the body. In all three periods of time, it is not so. All is self, alone."*

8. Where does the sense of "real" and "unreal" originate?

> *dehe ahem iti yad bhaavam*
> body I am this that supposition

> *sad asad bhaavam eva cha*
> real not real supposition verily and

> *kaala trayepi tanna asti*
> time three periods is not

> *sarvam brahma eti kevalam*
> all Brahman is alone

As you may have noticed by now, many of the images can be recycled.

Station 27 is my friend again, now with Abraham, E.T. and Weird Al. *Bhaavam* is in such close proximity, I found no need to use it again. Less is more, whenever possible. Therefore, see if you can find a way to carry images over. If you encode consistently over a few days, this will be a simple matter.

Station 28 involves the satirical professor Gad Saad fighting the tyrant Assad. Since Gad Saad is often questioning what is real versus what is not real, he works magic here.

I do not recall encoding *bhaavam eva cha* with unique images, likely due to the carryover effect combined with listening to Gary Weber's recorded recitation.

> "The supposition 'I am this body' creates the supposition of 'real' and 'not real.'
> In all three periods of time, it is not so. All is self, alone."

9. Where does the idea that there is a world come from?

dehe aham iti sankalpaH
body I am this notion

tat prapancaami hocyate
that world of five elements is said

kaala trayepi tanna asti
time three periods is not

sarvam brahma eti kevalam
all Brahman is alone

As this line is a repeat, station 29 is free. I use my German girlfriend, Olivia, only to indicate this repetition. Station 30 has King Henry from the TV show *The Tudors*. This may seem like a stretch to some, but if you watched the series in German, as I did, you know just how often *In der Tat* was uttered by a variety of characters.

For *prapancaami*, I combined existing knowledge of how the word "five" is etymologically related to *pan*. I added on the pram from *Battleship Potemkin* and had it spilling a globe made of cheese into a hole to trigger *hocyate*.

> *"The notion that 'I am this body' creates the manifest world of the five elements. In all three periods of time, it is not so. All is self, alone."*

10. What is the fundamental source of our misunderstandings?

dehe aham iti sankalpaH
body I am this notion

tat eva ajnanam ucyate
that alone ignorance is said to

kaala trayepi tanna asti
time three periods is not

sarvam brahma eti kevalam
all Brahman is alone

Station 31 focuses solely on the new words, *ajnanam ucyate*. A jam jar has already been in play and it is a simple matter to have a letter "A" throw it down on Sylvester Stallone in his role as Rambo.

> *"The notion that 'I am this body,' alone, is said to be ignorance. In all three periods of time, it is not so. All is self, alone."*

11. Where do our biases and misconceptions come from?

dehe aham iti yaa buddhiH
body I am this that intellectual conclusion

malinaa vaasan ucyate
impurities impressions is said

kaala trayepi tanna asti
time three periods is not

sarvam brahma eti kevalam
all Brahman is alone

Station 32 for *malinaa vaasan ucyate* involves a friend in Berlin name Marina and another van, this time covered in Vaseline. Upon reflection, Magnetic Imagery using the notion of vas deferens in some ridiculous manner might have been easier.

> *"The notion that 'I am this body' is said to be the cause of impurities and impressions. In all three periods of time, it is not so. All is self, alone."*

12. Where does the idea that we are a separate individual come from?

dehe aham iti yaa buddhiH
body I am this that intellectual conclusion

satyam jivaH sa eva saH
truly individual soul that alone is

kaala trayepi tanna asti
time three periods is not

sarvam brahma eti kevalam
all Brahman is alone

Station 33 for *satyam jivaH sa eva saH* brings back Gad Saad, now sitting on a yam. The word *jivaH* is already known to me. *Sa eva saH* has memorable properties built into it through alliteration and rhythm. Had I needed images for this part, I likely would have equipped Eva Perón with a saw.

"The intellectual notion that 'I am this body,' alone is the individual soul. In all three periods of time, it is not so. All is self, alone."

13. How does this belief that we are these bodies manifest in our lives?

dehe aham iti sankalpaH
body I am this notion

maha anarakam iiritam
great hell is proclaimed

kaala trayepi tanna asti
time three periods is not

sarvam brahma eti kevalam
all Brahman is alone

Station 34 for *maha anarakam iiritam* brings together Mahatma Gandhi with Arkham Asylum from the Batman universe. If you've ever seen this horrible place represented in one of the comics or movies, you know that it most certainly is a kind of hell.

Conceptually, I imagine that proclaiming Gandhi is "irritating" the space (or empty air) in Arkham Asylym. This encodes *iiritam* using auditory parallels in combination with the Spatial Mode.

> *"The notion that 'I am this body' is proclaimed as the great hell. In all three periods of time, it is not so. All is self, alone."*

14. Where does our concept of a "mind" come from?

dehe aham iti yaa buddhiH
body I am this that intellectual conclusion

mana eviti nischitam
mind is only defined

kaala trayepi tanna asti
time three periods is not

sarvam brahma eti kevalam
all Brahman is alone

Station 35 for *mana eviti nischitam* revives Moses, pairs Eva Perón with E.T. and brings in my friend and fellow mnemonist, Jonathan Levi. Why Jonathan? Because he and I have spent a lot of time talking about niches and how they define segments of the market. Again, an observational intuition of the language does not require me to encode *tam*, but I can readily use my friend Tam, a tambourine or a combination of the two.

In retrospect, it might have been wise not to use Jonathan here because it often brought business matters to my mind during meditations during the process by which this phrase was entering long-term memory through Recall Rehearsal. On the other hand, some things related to business clearly needed "defragging," so the choice may have been more appropriate than the preferences of the conscious mind prefers to admit.

This point is apropos the entire series of phrases and self-inquiry questions drawn from the *Ribhu Gita*, and so I raise it for the benefit of your own practice. Sometimes the Magnetic Imagery you create will cause a nagging sensation or draw you out of your practice. Such occasions should be embraced and treasured as opportunities for reflection. Rejecting them could slow your progress both in memory and in life.

> *"The notion that 'I am this body' is defined as certainly being the mind. In all three periods of time, it is not so. All is self, alone."*

15. Why do we believe we are different from everything else?

dehe aham iti yaa buddhiH
body I am this that intellectual conclusion

paracchinnam itiiryate
the limitation regarded as

kaala trayepi tanna asti
time three periods is not

sarvam brahma eti kevalam
all Brahman is alone

Station 36 for *paracchinnam itiiryate* involves a can of Para paint parachuting down and spilling cheese over Rambo, my symbol for most things sounded "nam." This cheese limits his spiritual progress.

> *"The assertion that 'I am this body' is the limitation. In all three periods of time, it is not so. All is self, alone."*

16. Where do our sorrows come from?

dehe aham iti yad jnaanam
body I am this that knowledge

sarvam shoka itiiritam
all sorrow described

kaala trayepi tanna asti
time three periods is not

sarvam brahma eti kevalam
all Brahman is alone

Station 37 features my friend Jan with an advertisement for Rambo jam (again, Rambo is the Viet-"nam" vet). Note that in the "grammar" of Magnetic Imagery, the images need not appear in the order to bring back the correct syntax. Jan is doubling here for both *yad* and the *ya* sound of *jnaanam*.

Station 38 starts with *sarvam* already covered by an image from when the repeating refrain throughout this sequence was encoded. I do not distinctly recall what I used for *shoka*, but I have a feeling it was Storm Shadow from *G.I. Joe* to get the "sh" and "oh" sound going. Next, *itiiritam* is basically a variation on previous words and I let the logic of the language help. I could have used my friend Tam, if needed.

> *"The misunderstanding that 'I am this body' is described as all-sorrowful. In all three periods of time, it is not so. All is self, alone."*

17. What is the great mistake that the "I" makes?

dehe aham iti yad jnaanam
body I am this that knowledge

saMsparshamiti kathyate
great (mis)touch talked about

kaala trayepi tanna asti
time three periods is not

sarvam brahma eti kevalam
all Brahman is alone

Station 39 starts with a friend known fondly as Dr. Sam. He has asparagus bunches in his hands, which in German are called *spargel*. He is using these as a shammy for cleaning up E.T., who is feeling mis-touched. *Kathyate* was known to me in a different form because when discussing the Katha Upanishad in a recording, James Swartz mentions that one of the meanings of *katha* is conversation. Given the patterns in the passage, I needed nothing special to render it as *kathyate*, but a cup of yerba mate could work to help one get an image for the basic sound needed here.

"The misunderstanding that 'I am this body' is said to be the great conflict. In all three periods of time, it is not so. All is self, alone."

18. Where does the idea of "death" come from?

dehe aham iti yaa buddhiH
body I am this that assertion

tadeva maranam smrtam
that verily death understood

kaala trayepi tanna asti
time three periods is not

sarvam brahma eti kevalam
all Brahman is alone

Station 40 needs only Magnetic Imagery for *maranam smrtam*. My friend Marina comes into play again, this time with more of a one-to-one correspondence than she had previously. I see a Smurf playing a tambourine with the skull and crossbones on it with a look of understanding on his face to help symbolize the meaning.

> *"The assertion that 'I am this body' is itself understood to create death. In all three periods of time, it is not so. All is self, alone."*

19. What is wrong with the idea that "I am this body"?

dehe aham iti yaa buddhiH
body I am this that assertion

tadeva ashobhanam smrtam
that verily inauspicious understood

kaala trayepi tanna asti
time three periods is not

sarvam brahma eti kevalam
all Brahman is alone

Station 41 needs only an image for *ashobhanam*. Lee Asher has long been a favorite magician. It is was easy to see him making a banana appear. The logic of the language takes care of the rest, though I could have used Rambo again if the "nam" ending didn't fall into place on its own.

> *"The assertion that 'I am this body' is regarded as inauspicious. In all three periods of time, it is not so. All is self, alone."*

20. Just how serious is this mistaken belief that "I am this body"?

dehe aham iti yaa buddhiH
body I am this that assertion

maha apaapamiti smrtam
great sin understood

kaala trayepi tanna asti
time three periods is not

sarvam brahma eti kevalam
all Brahman is alone

Apaapamiti is the only word that needs a new image on station 42. Since Gary Weber pronounces it something like "mahaapaapamiti," rather than two independent words, I had the pope (*der Papst* in German for the "pap" sound) riding the Chinese symbol for horse *ma*. As usual, E.T. storms in for the "iti" sound.

> "The assertion that 'I am this body' is understood to be the great sin. In all three periods of time, it is not so. All is self, alone."

21. Why is this concept so overwhelming?

dehe aham iti yaa buddhiH
body I am this that assertion

tushthaa saivi he chochyate
great prejudiced conception verily is said

kaala trayepi tanna asti
time three periods is not

sarvam brahma eti kevalam
all Brahman is alone

Station 43 involves toilet paper (tushy), Sy Sperling from the Hair Club for Men, He-Man and nothing for *chochyate*, which fell into place on its own.

> *"The assertion 'I am this body' is, verily, overwhelming, it is said. In all three periods of time, it is not so. All is self, alone."*

22. Does the "I am this body" belief cause all of my faults?

dehe aham iti sankalpaH
body I am this notion

sarva dosham iti smrtam
all faults is understood

kaala trayepi tanna asti
time three periods is not

sarvam brahma eti kevalam
all Brahman is alone

Everything in this passage has some kind of existing image. Nonetheless, I place the bridge over the Saar River with Homer Simpson, E.T. and a Smurf for good measure on station 44.

> *"The notion that 'I am this body' is understood to be all defects. In all three periods of time, it is not so. All is self, alone."*

SECOND TRANSITION: *If I'm not this body, then what am I?*

23. What is my nature?

aham eva hi gupta atmaa
I am alone truly mysterious self

aham eva niranteram
I am alone gapless

aanandam paramaM maanam idam
bliss supreme measure all this

dRshyam na kincana
that is seen not anything

  Station 45 starts with Abraham, Eva Perón and He-man. A guppy fish wearing a sweater from The Gap helps, along with the Chinese symbol for "he" (sounded as "ta"). *Niranteram* takes its own station (46). I use the band Nirvana with a tarantula. I'm not sure why that works, and it is probably the least logical Magnetic Image I create. Nonetheless, I did not judge it and allowed it to do its work.

The next passage only needs to be encoded once for use throughout this section. Station 46 sees progressive sitarist Ananda Shankar with a can of Para paint he dumps on Johnny Cash ("the man in black") and my friend Edan for *idam*.

I knew a Trisha once upon a time who is now burdened by a wedding ring from my "na"-saying former girlfriend. They both scratch their chins at the odd predicament (*das kinn* is German for "chin").

> *"I am the mysterious Self. I am alone the gapless. Bliss is the supreme measure.*
> *All this which is seen is not anything."*

24. What is the ultimate teacher?

aham eva paraM brahma
I am alone supreme Brahman

aham eva guror guruH
I am alone the Guru of gurus

aanandam paramaM maanam idam
bliss supreme measure all this

dRshyam na kincana
that is seen not anything

Station 47 requires only the Para paint can and Mr Kilby. Station 48 has Jaggi Vasudev, a.k.a. "Sadhguru," roaring to trigger *guror*. *Guruh* is self-evident and fell into place on its own.

> *"I am, alone, the supreme Brahman. I am, alone, the Guru of gurus. Bliss is*
> *the supreme measure. All this which is seen is not anything."*

25. What is the ultimate happiness?

aham eva akhilaa adhaara
I am alone whole support

aham eva sukhaat sukham
I am alone happiness beyond happiness

aanandam paramaM maanam idam
bliss supreme measure all this

dRshyam na kincana
that is seen not anything

Station 49 has Klaus Kinski in his *Aguirre, the Wrath of God* role. He's trouncing on the "hair" of Frank Kern, an advertising and marketing "guru." Station 50 has Sook-Yin Lee, a Canadian broadcaster I once met at a zine convention. She's sucking on a hat, and then on a leg of ham.

> *"I am, alone, the support of everything. I am, alone, the happiness beyond happiness. Bliss is the supreme measure. All this which is seen is not anything."*

26. What is the transcendental illuminating light?

aham eva paraM jyotiH
I am alone great light

ahem eva akhilaa aatmakaH
I am alone complete self

aanandam paramaM maanam idam
bliss supreme measure all this

dRshyam na kincana
that is seen not anything

Station 51 involves my friend Joy with a cup of tea. The rest is known save for *aatmakaH*, which fell into place naturally. When I say "naturally," what I mean is that sometimes the memory of the word itself holds without need of Magnetic Imagery. This is a good thing. Embrace it when it happens.

> *"I am, alone, the transcendental Light. I am, alone, the Self of all. Bliss is the supreme measure. All this which is seen is not anything."*

27. How does one move beyond the everyday dance of energy?

aham eva hi tRpta atmaa
I am alone truly satisfied self

aham eva hi nir gunaH
I am alone truly without attributes (gunas)

aanandam paramaM maanam idam
bliss supreme measure all this

dRshyam na kincana
that is seen not anything

Station 52 needs only the Toronto Raptors mascot and He-man. All other words were known to me by this point.

> *"I am, alone, the satisfied Self. I am, alone, without attributes. Bliss is the supreme measure. All this which is seen is not anything."*

28. Can we ever fill that "lack," that "incompleteness" we feel?

aham eva hi puurna atmaa
I am alone truly complete Self

aham eva puraatanaH
I am alone the ancient One

aanandam paramaM maanam idam
bliss supreme measure all this

dRshyam na kincana
that is seen not anything

Station 53 has a former pet cat purring, followed by the same cat with a giant @ symbol that he is tossing at my friend Anna on Station 34.

> *"I am, alone, the complete Self. I am, alone, the ancient One. Bliss is the supreme measure. All this which is seen is not anything."*

29. Can we reach a permanent, peaceful state?

aham eva hi shaanta atmaa
I am alone truly peaceful self

aham eva hi shaashvataH
I am alone truly permanent

aanandam paramaM maanam idam
bliss supreme measure all this

dRshyam na kincana
that is seen not anything

Station 55 has Santa Claus and Station 56 has my friend Shannon with the vat from *Breaking Bad* from a previous example as a kind of time machine to achieve permanence.

"I, alone, am the peaceful Self. I, alone, am permanent. Bliss is the supreme measure. All this which is seen is not anything."

30. Does this state extend everywhere and is it stable?

aham eva hi sarvatra
I am alone truly everywhere

aham eva hi susthiraH
I am alone truly stable

aanandam paramaM maanam idam
bliss supreme measure all this

dRshyam na kincana
that is seen not anything

Station 57 brings back the bridge over the Saar River, this time with Frank Sinatra dancing on it. Station 58 has the novel *Das Parfum* by Patrick Süskind. Nothing was so stable as the scent that drove the anti-hero of that novel mad in the end.

This is the conceptual mode in action because I have never seen a portrait of this author that I can recall.

"I, alone, am everywhere. I, alone, am truly stable."

THIRD TRANSITION: *Capping verses for Knowledge of the Self*

31. What is knowledge of the Self?

aatma jnannaM paraM shaastraM
Self knowledge highest science

aatma jnannaM anuupamaM
Self knowledge unequalled

aatma jnannaM paro yoga
Self knowledge highest yoga

aatma jnannaM paraa gatiH
Self knowledge supreme goal

Station 58 has a floating meditator in half lotus throwing a jar of jam down at a Para paint can that spills on Frank Zappa in his "Shah" outfit from the cover of his album, *Sheik Yerbouti*. Since Zappa very much presented himself as a "mad scientist" of music, this association works well both phonically and for meaning.

Station 59 has my friend Anna with the newspaper and my mom (i.e., a ma'am). Station 60 fell into place without need of Magnetic Imagery, but I place an image of myself executing some stretching movements learned from *Happiness Beyond Thought*. Station 61 has a Para paints can again with a cat and the conceptual thought of having a "prerogative" being like having a goal.

"Knowledge of the Self is the supreme science. Knowledge of the Self is unequalled. Knowledge of the Self is the highest yoga. Knowledge of the Self is the supreme goal."

32. Knowledge of the Self

aatma jnannaM cittana ashaH
Self knowledge thought termination

aatma jnannaM vimuktidam
Self knowledge liberator

aatma jnannaM byana ashaM
Self knowledge fear dispeller of

aatma jnannaM sukha avaham
Self knowledge happiness generator

Station 62 brings back Lee Asher the magician. Station 63 has the German filmmaker Wim Wenders on a cow—mooing, this cow pours tea on the Hoover Dam. Station 64 has my friend Jan throwing a banana at Lee Asher. Station 65 has Sook-Yin Lee again, this time with ham only.

"Knowledge of the Self is the termination of thought. Knowledge of the Self is the liberator. Knowledge of the Self is the dispeller of fear. Knowledge of the Self is the generator of happiness."

* * *

Instilling the memories

I suggest memorizing these verses one at a time without pause until they are completed. If you can manage one line per station, you can memorize one passage using the four corners of each room in a Memory Palace per day and be done within a month. You may also like to pause and contemplate a new passage for several days or longer before adding more.

Or, as I have done, you might like to work on two pieces at once. As I memorized these selections from the *Ribhu Gita*, I gave my brain a bit of rest and variety by encoding lines from the *Upadesa Saram* by Ramana Maharshi on the walls of the same Memory Palace. Albeit an intermediate-advanced use of a Memory Palace, it works nicely. I feel that memorizing and working with this second text in a more informal way at the same time enriched my understanding of the first.

For some people, adding a second text, especially to the same Memory Palace, will create obstructions that should be avoided. It's important not to frustrate yourself, as all of this practice is intended to create ease and fun, not hard work and misery.

Once you have the material memorized, one to three recitations daily are recommended (see the section in the previous chapter on Recall Rehearsal). I have not yet tested a period of stopping daily recitations to see how long it takes before I lose any of what I have memorized. I would guess that the staying power will be durable due to the amount of repetition I've put in, but so far I have no desire to discontinue reciting these passages from the *Ribhu Gita*, and the *Upadesa Saram* I have also memorized. If anything, I am continually drawn to adding more and am currently compiling passages from the *Ashtavakra Gita* for future memorization.

As Gary Weber and others point out, no amount of chanting and memorizing will help you attain "enlightenment" or "liberation." Rather, it is the understanding of what these texts are telling you about the nature of your being that makes the difference. In the Zen tradition, it might be said that where there is practice, there is enlightenment. These statements themselves indicate this by pointing out that self-knowledge is the highest form of yoga.

Many people do not think they are either visual or creative enough to come up with so many associations. People often marvel on my livestreams at how quickly I come up with images for the information they throw at me. I believe you can too. Here are two ways of understanding how you can come up with Magnetic Imagery yourself, perhaps faster than you think:

1. Practice

Everyone I've ever spoken with claims they came to the art, craft and science of using memory techniques with no special inborn level of imagination. If anything, it is usually the opposite and they found it difficult at first. In *Fluent in 3 Months*, Benny Lewis talks about how he had to stretch when using mnemonics for language learning, but also how it rapidly became easier with consistent practice. Practice *is* consistency—otherwise it is not practice. Keep that in mind and you will almost certainly find the ease in creating associations you seek. What matters is preparation, predetermination, using Recall Rehearsal and the power of the Big Five.

Jumping into the practice of association for large texts completely raw and without some smaller-scale practice with the systems discussed in this book is not recommended. Long before reading *Happiness Beyond Thought* and adapting its stretching and movement recommendations, my books and courses had detailed the importance of breathing and progressive muscle relaxation for overcoming mental obstacles. The ego is happy to tell you that this form of memorizing is too difficult and that you are not creative, along with mountains of other "blah blah blah." Don't underestimate the power of physical relaxation and the breath for interrupting these patterns so you can focus on the many tools your mind has for use at this moment.

2. Use what you already have

Second, the noise of pop culture I have displayed here is an unusual asset we all have—an asset the ancients did not. I'm just an average trailer park kid who soused himself in network television, rock radio and the pulp fiction of my era. Chances are, you're something like this too. Use this existing content in your mind and avoid reinventing the wheel.

Too many people think they need to memorize their associations and set about creating complex mnemonic systems and stock images they use in rigid ways. In my experience, most people get the best results when they stir down into what their mind already contains. For the purposes of combining meditation with memory techniques, all of this mental chaos is like the lees in wine that add texture and flavor. As ironic as it may seem, I truly have found much peace in all that noise simply by letting it come up without force and then cranking up the volume.

Who Are You Really and Why Should You Memorize Self-Inquiry Questions to Find Out?

"However, I do feel some empathy for those critics, because I do the very same thing myself. Say, for example, when I am reading Nietzsche, I want to fuse with Nietzsche, I wish I had known him, had been able to have a conversation with him, had been able to see a taped interview with him or something. It seems to me to be a very humanistic impulse to want to get to know a creative person in a very deep, detailed way, the way you might know a personal friend and their confidences."

— David Cronenberg, interviewed in *The Modern Fantastic*

"Oneness cannot find otherness no matter how long or hard it looks, because there is no otherness for oneness to find. The definition of oneness could be said to be no-other-to-find."

— Fred Davis, *The Book of Undoing*

B EN'S CALL TO ADVENTURE and reading Gary Weber led me to discover Advaita Vedanta, which seems to center around a concept called "non-duality." The term is fraught with difficulties, but those difficulties are not a problem. They are a solution. Working through them creates all kinds of focus and concentration abilities. (Sam Harris features a non-dual training in his Waking Up app, which is worth checking out.) It's a strange shift that operates like a chemical change on your perspective. Just as toast will never return to bread once it's been transformed, people claim you cannot un-see non-duality once you've experienced it. I'm not sure if that's true, but if you're anything like me, once you reach "the other side" and feel what non-duality is all about for yourself, you'll wonder why you didn't see it all along. Then, before you know it, you'll be back in duality and later wonder why it's so easy to lose sight of the most powerful discovery of your life. And then endless rounds of questions will begin... have you really been "one" with "everything"? Can you be?

The easiest way for me to explain my experience of non-duality is through a story. It begins after I read *Happiness Beyond Thought* and reproduced as many of its exercises as possible, including even heavier memorization tasks than have been discussed in this book. Thanks to the primacy effect, the *Ribhu Gita* passages will probably maintain their hold in my mind as the most important, as will the main self-inquiry question:

"To whom is this experience occurring?"

Quickly after I began practicing, when a thought arose, I would ask, "Who is having this thought?" Or, when performing some of the simple stretching exercises Weber provides, I would notice feelings of deep peace and relaxation overcoming me. Instead of taking them at face value, I would ask, "Who is feeling this sensation?" For a while, I followed Weber's recommendations based on the tradition and answered, *neti neti,* or "not this, this this."

Soon, this *neti neti* answer dropped away. I found myself having experiences similar to the state Douglas Harding discusses in *On Having No Head.* I first read Harding's book, mentioned by Sam Harris in *Waking Up,* a few years before I got to Weber and didn't understand it experientially at the time. The practice of asking "to whom is this experience occurring?" made sense to me on a cognitive level, but nothing in particular changed from either Harris's or Harding's descriptions of using it as a tool. After adding Weber's teaching to the mix, the initial effect was actually quite unsettling.

I first noticed that the familiar Buddha Smile feeling at the center of my forehead started moving to the back of my head. I may have developed this sensation due to the expectation effect. Gary Weber demonstrates this location of bliss on one of his own YouTube videos when explaining the location of the task-positive network in the brain. It's entirely possible that I self-hypnotized myself into a delightful placebo that has created so much pleasure ever since. Yet, even with a head beaming with pleasure, I fell into a "Dark Night of the Soul" shortly after my first non-dual experience. Here's what happened.

One afternoon, I was riding my bike under the bright Australian sun, and the entire world suddenly felt completely empty. There was nothing but silence and emptiness. The sensation of an *I* and the entire field felt the same. The profound silence that was everywhere was not pleasant but, rather, shocking and alienating.

My head beamed with pleasure throughout, but I could not shake the unsettled feeling. I took it with me to meetings, felt it while recording podcasts and worked out with it in the gym. I would be lifting something heavy in front of the mirror with people wandering around and music pulsing. Eveything seemed to play out perfectly, like the connected gears and figures of an elaborate cuckoo clock that was somehow projecting out of my head into the world. I wasn't in front of the projection either. I was just a star in a massive outer space that included the furthest reaches of the universe. I felt aware of everything, like a kid on too many drugs, minus the drugs.

I sat in the bathroom one day, total bliss at war with abject horror. I now felt with certainty that the gurus in this strange new world of non-duality were right: there really is only *One* thing going on and all of it was utterly empty. I could only wonder why on Earth the game was set up this way. I had this amazing beacon of bliss beaming in my skull, an addictively pleasant feeling I never want to live without. Yet at the same time, I felt it was a curse. Here I was experiencing an enormous sense of totality and yet forced to occupy just one position in the time-space continuum until my body died.

This unsettling feeling lasted for nearly a year. It didn't chew up every minute of my day, but I remember having odd conversations with my fellow entrepreneurs. I worried that I damaged one friendship in particular with what must have sounded like babbling on esoteric matters when he just wanted to talk about podcasting. Another friend, Seph, had spent far more time on similar texts and seemed to connect more with the experiences I was describing. He was working on a book about the nature and necessity of meaning, while I was writing this one, about dissolving it. Although we never converged on whether meaning is needed for happiness or not, we had many delightful conversations about how meaning could be defined in a life conducted "beyond" thought. If we experienced meaning at all during these delightful discussions, I do think we would agree it took place in the silences between our words and nowhere else.

During this time, I wrote to Gary Weber about the declarations in other books and recordings about non-duality that said self-inquirers needed a teacher. His answers were helpful and ultimately reminded me that self-inquiry was what I needed more than a teacher. This was useful guidance, particularly since so many of the other texts maintain a hierarchy with the guru at the top. They place the care of the guru in the hands of the student and suggest that devotion, or *bakhti*, requires literally sustaining the teacher with offerings of assistance ranging from shelter to food and money. Weber's reply was a breath of fresh air and reminded me of my favorite Systema instructors who held to the core philosophy that everyone is in it together as a perpetual beginner. The teacher is the student and the student is the teacher. Heartened by Weber's response, when I felt totally alone or longed to follow the suggestion that I needed a teacher, I would simply ask, "Who is it that feels so alone?" When I felt that I needed to send another email to Weber, I stopped myself and asked, "Who is it that feels the need to have a teacher?"

Soon, the tiny seeds of helplessness shrivelled. I realized that the teachers are everywhere. I remember walking among thousands of people on Brisbane's bustling Queen Street with my head blazing. It felt like the sun itself had opened my skull and hopped inside. I felt that I was either going to go mad or about to "wake up" into a completely different reality. If you've seen *The Matrix*, you'll remember a scene where Neo discovers that he's not actually sitting in a room with Morpheus. In fact, everyday life is an illusion and his real body is in fact housed in a vat of pink fluid. As Morpheus and his crew try to locate exactly where Neo is in the vast towers of similar pods housing most of humanity, Neo watches the illusion version of himself being taken over by the surreal fluid of a mirror he has touched. This fluid mirror (which now looks a lot like the mercury-esque substance the Agents will later inject into Morpheus) soon crawls from Neo's hand and up into his mouth. A transition effect shows that Neo has dreamed it all from within his pod and when Morpheus and crew finally find him in the real "matrix" of pods, they blow the lid and cause all the tubes sustaining his body to release. It's a gruesome scene and I think of it often when the bliss gets so extreme that I feel like I'm about to explode.

Of course, I don't think I'm trapped in a pod or about to awaken into another reality. Yet, the feeling has sometimes been so intense that I have visited my doctor and asked for a brain scan to rule out a brain tumor. She diligently checked all my vital signs and ordered blood work. I'm apparently fit as a fiddle. Now that I've come out of the Dark Night, and so long as I don't get freaked out by these experiences, it's all rather amusing. And when I pay attention, the teachers truly are everywhere. They always have been, and there's no denying that sometimes it is useful to spend time in the presence of a leader.

In fact, I have a lapel pin. To you, it might look like nothing special. You might even look right past it. But that lapel pin is incredibly special to me for two reasons that relate to non-duality.

Tony Buzan told me one evening over dinner that "the rules will set you free." For those who don't know the name, he revolutionized many minds around the world when he popularized mind mapping via books like *Use Your Head*, which was also a series on the BBC. Later, he co-founded the World Memory Championships while continuing to develop his ideas about mind mapping and memory training. At some point, we became friends on Twitter, frequently tweeting amongst ourselves in front of the world. When the chance came to learn about teaching memory and mind mapping in 2016, I leapt at the chance and headed for the U.K.

I'd already been teaching memory for years but learned a ton from Buzan about how the minds of students tick—including my own. I also learned a lot about the business of teaching memory at an international level. But Tony told me that he saw this work as more than mere economics, and he seemed so excited by the Internet:

> It is going to be like a super nova. It is going to explode mental literacy around the world, and I am really happy with that because in this modern age, despite the fact that the information age has given us a lot of information overload, it can do wondrous things. One of the things it can do is to spread good news to every brain, igniting every brain to become a flame with a beauty, the magnificence of the human mind.

Although I have no personal interest in the competition aspect of memory improvement, Tony generously helped me mind map the future of the Magnetic Memory Method project as something that would last, and ideally grow. The potential he saw was in the teaching method itself. As he told me, "A real teacher is a beacon. A real teacher is someone who launches others on the exploration of their internal universe. A real teacher is a harvester of questions." Those words were a good sign to me, as I normally teach best not by telling people what to do, but by asking them what it is they are doing and how improving their self-study efforts might be improved so they can do better on their own.

Tony then told me to pay attention, not just to the rules that govern the brain and memory. He focused my attention, as did Gary Weber, Ramana Maharshi, Stephen Hawking and a whole host of characters, on the "physics" of reality. There are rules that govern everything, including the rules of business. It's worth repeating, as Tony did, echoing often in my memory: "The rules will set you free." They will also make your brain cells flourish.

The next day, before leaving Henley-on-Thames, Tony needed some help carrying the Lorraine Gill paintings he used to explain concepts in creativity and the origins of his approach to mind mapping. We walked slowly across the grounds of the Henley Business School, deepening our conversation about these matters. Then, in the posh lobby, he walked up to me, removed a pin from his own jacket, pinned it on mine. He said, "Anthony, you are a 'Warrior of the Mind.'"

Even though I talk a lot for a living, in that moment, I was speechless. I knew about this pin because Joshua Foer makes a big deal of it in *Moonwalking with Einstein*. This is Foer's book about how Buzan gives him a call to adventure that ends in him becoming the 2006 USA memory champion. The pin comes up when Foer talks about how Buzan served as Michael Jackson's creativity coach for an extraordinary hourly fee that only the most lavish "rules" governing commerce could ever make possible. What I didn't know about this artistic rendering of a brain cell is that Buzan gives it out only to a select few for Outstanding Contributions to Global Mental Literacy.

Warrior of the Mind Pin

I don't think Buzan gave me the pin to bolster my ego. I think he gave it to me to assemble me even closer to the memory tradition I'd already devoted so much of my life to promoting. He told me as much when I later interviewed him on the Magnetic Memory Method podcast and we masterminded further about how to encourage even more people to learn and apply these ancient techniques. Our masterminding carried on for years, usually on his beloved Twitter, until he sadly passed away in April of 2019. I held a livestream in his honor, and struggled to hold back the tears. Death is the ultimate abandonment and I'm confident his teaching will ignite many minds for thousands of years to come. They are truly super nova.

The second reason this pin is so incredibly important is that I intentionally wore it when I asked my future wife's father for her hand in marriage in Mandarin Chinese after a few hours of small talk over dinner. Although I'm still far from fluent, I'd learned enough of the language to accomplish this feat in less than three months of study because I'd discovered the powerful memory secrets I've shared with you in this book. I've now assembled with the sober, grounded family I never dreamed possible and that pin has come to represent the transformation my life has undergone.

Every time I look at this "Warrior of the Mind" pin, I'm instantly reminded of those two life-altering events. When life gets hard and tries to distract me from my passion and purpose, these memories and the people who helped create them keep me focused on how far I've come. All of this is made possible because the brain remembers things *through* association. Whether it's Tony Buzan, Gary Weber or any other figure from a long list of teachers, so long as you can remember them, they are with you, in the "oneness" of that moment and the traces it makes. It just takes a special form of radical honesty and "awakeness" to realize that most of what you seek is already within you. The voices that might encourage you are available now for play on demand—even if these voices come from ancients who devised a means in Sanskrit to help them turn off the noise in their heads.

I shared some of my revelations with Weber and find that the "remote learning" process through abandonment generally aligns with what some people call the Feynman technique. Although people describe this technique in different ways, I believe that the core goal is to prevent yourself from falling into learned helplessness and relying on teachers to feed you information that won't help you anyway. Teachers often cannot help students because people learn through exploration, research, contemplation and expression. In many cases, the teacher willing to dole out an answer is only harming the student because data given easily all too often satisfy the itch of curiosity that kills the cat of accomplishment. The Feynman technique counters this by having you assume the mental model of being a teacher, in this case your own. It usually involves writing out what you're trying to learn on a piece of paper. Next, you write out an explanation in simpler terms. As you go through it, the process reveals the areas where your knowledge is lacking. Through your own initiative, you fill in the gaps as much as you can on your own.

I teach my memory students that they should also try answering questions on their own as part of completing the Magnetic Memory Method Masterclass. In fact, I suggest they write 250 words minimum, using a kind of self-inquiry to ask, "what exactly don't I understand about this?" Then I ask them to list out at least five things they could do to help answer the question on their own. The time to reach out is after these steps have been taken, not before—at least if they want the best possible answer. I teach them to come to me not so much with questions, but with the evidence of what they've done so I can better "laser target" the issue. Most of the time, having them take actions they've self-identified as the solution removes the need for my answers. Even better, these well-formulated questions teach me something new, or explain what they've done from an angle that triggers new ideas about how to use mnemonics. What could have been a disastrous situation that overwhelms the student with a bunch of data becomes a mutually rewarding situation that leads to collaborative teaching in our Mastermind group or on our public livestreams.

I feel that Weber's responses to my emails played a similar role: they gave me the opportunity to see that all the answers I already needed were staring me in the face. His books share numerous scholarly sources to follow up with and dialogues with his students. And the ultimate tool is the self-inquiry process of simply asking, "Who exactly experiences the feeling of need for more knowledge and a teacher?" Asking this question over approximately a week put out the sensation of seeking help from him or anyone else completely and I've been at peace with that particular sense of need ever since. The so-called Google Effect has trained us to type out questions so rapidly that we impoverish our creative capacity to search within for the answers, or hold ourselves to a standard of self-directed research and implementation. This leads to digital amnesia that often imprisons us in the ignorance we're trying to escape.

That is not to say that we shouldn't feel a keen interest in meeting other people who practice self-inquiry and memory training. If nothing else, from a brain science perspective, I will need to continue reading from other authors in this area to nourish the dendritic spines growing on the neuronal vines in the memory garden of my brain. Discussion about these topics with people in real time will potentially fortify the reading. By the same token, every person offers many lessons in what it means to be a human having an experience. If you dedicate yourself to a particular goal or realm of study that has no set destination, then everything you encounter teaches you along the way.

The hardest thing to contend with during the transformation is understanding that all of those teachers are "you" because they are occurring within the chemical bath of your brain. At first, this realization made me feel tremendously lonely and I felt that I would fall into the trap of solipsism. Then—and equally troubling—as my concern about this possibility started to dissolve through self-inquiry practice, the great warmth in my head made me wonder if perhaps there really is a god in the classic sense of a sentient entity guiding the universe. I understand why some people make this argument, and I understand it better than ever now that I've gone through many powerful hours of feeling connected to the entire universe. But here, self-inquiry questions of a different kind are instructive. I often ask myself:

If there really is a god or sentient character to the universe, what changes?

If there isn't a god or sentient character to the universe, what changes?

For all intents and purposes, the answer to both questions is simple: Nothing changes.

Yet, as we journey through life, we come up against many opposing views and contradictory terms about what this reality is all about. It is no different in even the best books on self-inquiry that I have found, where even the clearest passages are soon followed by complete contradictions. I imagine there are contradictions in the things I have to say too. In my view, all of these contradictions, if they are going to be solved, will sooner be solved through self-directed self-study than interaction with a teacher. Swami Dayananda deals with the problem of the teacher by focusing on the role of language: "A teacher can communicate only by words which are known to him as well as to the student."

There is great wisdom in this observation that gets to the core of so many problems in the learning of both memory techniques and meditation. In memory training, the student will encounter terms like *Memory Palace* and *method of loci*. Are they different? If so, how? Then what about linking, pegs and the Major Method?

In reality, all of these terms point to pretty much the same thing: the arrangement of different kinds of pre-existing mental imagery in the "space" of your mind for the purposes of association. How you arrange these elements will either help or hinder you based on your understanding of how these terms point at the goal and how clearly you've defined the reason you're using the memory techniques.

Likewise in meditation practices, we find an abundance of terms. Here, the exact terms matter more than in memory training, but their importance should be weighted with respect to your exact goals. In *The Teaching Tradition of Advaita Vedanta*, Dayananda tells us that the problem is not just a shared understanding of the lingo, but also an understanding of the game. Most people who come to spiritual practices like Advaita Vedanta are looking for bliss. Because many teachers let that word slide without qualification, all kinds of problems emerge. The same question mentioned previously is useful yet again:

If the teacher really does hold magical words and a magical understanding of those words, what changes?

If the teacher doesn't hold magical words and a magical understanding of those words, what changes?

In this case, perhaps the answer isn't "nothing," as before. But the only "something" I will be satisfied with is the one that comes free of self-delusion and what I've come to think of as SWAG—Spirituality Without Another God. Seriously. Human history has already suffered more than enough of them.

The consequences of getting confused by teachers without undertaking your own diligent self-study could be potentially even worse when you hear about creatures like Gary Weber enjoying a pleasant mental experience and then guys like myself talking about how I've managed to accelerate my own. But Dayananda takes care to point out that "bliss" is not what we're talking about in the sense of unending pleasure. As James Swartz (from whom I later discovered Dayananda's booklet) puts it, anything that comes into awareness ultimately leaves awareness, including pleasant states.

I can't speak for anyone else, but my states of pleasure do indeed come and go. I sometimes long for them when they are gone, but that longing keeps me focused on the knowledge I gained from them. When I stick with the awareness of my experience regardless of whether my head is bright and shiny or feeling "normal," I win. A day populated with more awareness than time lost in mindlessness is already a big improvement over the pain of being pummeled down by the endless shifting of thoughts.

So what then is this bliss, anyway? As Dayananda explains, *ananda*—the word usually translated as "bliss"—does not have just an experiential definition. When we define bliss in terms of experience, "the experience is only as good as one interprets it. And the interpretation is only as good as one's knowledge" (8). This is why self-study of the terminology is so important. All the teachers in the world cannot help you by dictating what the terminology means. You need to mingle the many potential meanings in the chemical bath of your brain so that your questions leave the realm of seeking and serve instead as points of discussion the open up an understanding *of* the now, *in* the now.

In my view, the proliferation of so many terms demonstrates where the market economy meets human evolution. What better way to harness curiosity about a product or service than having a crowd of humans around you who speak in code? As Swartz points out in the *Yoga of Love*: "It is not uncommon for Western seekers to pay through the nose for initiation into 'secret' mantras that daily blare incessantly from tens of thousands of temples throughout India."

Ultimately, the words themselves never produce the skill or the knowledge. Rather, these factors come from memory reserve and how it guides action. Knowledge is what we do to bring light into the darkness. Likewise, in memory, as David Berglas taught, "memory is a behavior." Treating these aspects of our experience as processes rather than outcomes or things creates a very special awareness: the awareness that you are a body with a brain engaged in an extended process of awareness being aware of itself.

This awareness is ultimately where I feel memory techniques and meditation meet. When you fine-tune your mind enough to be present and memorize a person's name in real time, you're not just aware of your memory. You have become the act of memory itself. I often talk about using a Memory Palace as being like a Zen archer. If you have all the skills of archery, the target on the wall is the station in your Memory Palace. The arrow is your Magnetic Imagery. How you judge the way you sling the arrow on the bow and gauge the wind is your skill. Then, the information flies by on the wind. You release the arrow. The arrow pierces the information and pins to the station in your Memory Palace. The archer, the arrow, the bow, the information and the target only *appear* to be different. But everything happens so fast when you're using memory techniques that, in that moment, everything is completely one. When I sit in a room of entrepreneurs and memorize all their names, it literally is as simple as firing off mnemonic areas. A woman says "Sarah Hazzard" and I fire off Sarah Ferguson waving her Daisy Dukes on top of the orange car from the *Dukes of Hazzard*. It happens instantly and something much like the self-inquiry of meditation happens next.

When I'm asked to recite the names of everyone in the room, I'm simply asking: "What happened there?" It is the question as much as the mnemonic that lets me pull the arrow back out of the target location in the Memory Palace. Then comes the answer.

"Oh yes, that was James Hetfield from Metallica smashing the Sonic Youth album called *Goo* to pieces"—these images may make no sense to you, but they are the arrows in my quiver. They helped me remember that the man's name is James Gooley. The answers will come back for you based on how well you selected the pre-prepared arrows from your quiver and hit the right mark in the Memory Palace. Incidentally, this process does not involve seeing pictures in my mind. There's really no time for creating anything even remotely like a mental picture when people are introducing themselves. It needs to be just as fast and automatic as nocking an arrow on the bow and letting it go with faith in your skill during the thick of life or death hunt. If I get these names wrong, my reputation is on the line. My ability to demonstrate how memory works is so close to survival that I really could wind up starving if I destroy my reputation with a mistake. This is living.

But anyone can experience this effect without nearly so much on the line. For now, the point is that your memory is happening all the time and you can craft an intimate relationship with it that opens your awareness of the present moment. We really do let so much slide by. This is the benefit of memorizing and using self-inquiry questions. If you can get out of the muck of so much competing terminology, the questions will help you stop getting lost in useless thoughts and "become" the experience of better thoughts that keep a watchful eye on the unfolding of you as a thinker. As Dayananda puts it: "By inquiry, the one who is aware of time is revealed to be that very awareness wherein the concept of time resolves."

And a few sentences later: "Self-knowledge is not another state of experience; it is the correction of an error about oneself, and the recognition of the invariable self as the truth and basis of all experiences."

I believe this "invariable self" is exactly what memorizing self-inquiry questions helps you find. The more you ask the questions, the more you find out that who you think you are is a constantly changing illusion with sharp hooks that create more pain than pleasure. The questions help you first remove these hooks and then put up a powerful shield between your real self and the snares of your ego.

The first self-inquiry questions are not difficult to remember. They simply involve questions like:

To whom is this experience happening?

Where is the "I" to which the experience is happening?

And when you look at another person, you can ask:

Where is the person I am currently perceiving?

Part IV

No More

Storms?

15 CRUISING ALTITUDE

D ID I EXPERIENCE THOUGHTS while writing this book? Of course. The words on these pages are evidence: this book is the *product of thought*. Read carefully, no one worth their bones in the spiritual world is *really* talking about eradicating thinking anyway. They're talking about helping us properly contextualize the appearance of thought in consciousness and separate operational and planning thoughts from useless, I-oriented thoughts that aren't useful most of the time. Although on some days I experience more I-thoughts than I would like, the majority of the time, my mental content is focused almost entirely outward—on helping people like you. I often talk about "karma yoga" on my podcast and livestreams, by which I mean showing up to serve the world with no particular expectation of any specific outcome.

Obviously, this body has to eat, and more hours than "I" might like are spent poring over "site speed" and "quality scores" as I work to keep magneticmemory-method.com compliant with Google and its endlessly shifting requirements. Anyone who still thinks free will exists needs to spend some time living life at the whim of search engine traffic in a world where none of the online platforms let you know how their algorithms connect your content with the individuals who want it. Some days these matters feel more like garbage on the ocean than meaningful wind in my sails.

Plus, the more I learned about non-duality and the more I meditated, the more poisonous the Internet started to feel. There is no doubt that it is filled with bad actors. Since the mind loves a good story, I sometimes find my mind tracking their battles more than necessary. I could see and understand the numbers, but competing in the game while experiencing such states of bliss sometimes raised (and still raises) a nearly Christ-like anger at the gamblers and merchants running amok in "the church of information" that is the Internet. I have no power to cast them out, and, due to the nature of my work, no particular means of playing the game any differently. And as they say, when you wrestle with a pig, you both get dirty and the pig likes it.

"Karma yoga" seems to be a great means of not turning the many "likes" and "dislikes" that arise into meaningful signals I used to respond to in ways that served no one. Constant meditation and sharing the memory training journey help me deal with some of the confusing emotions that arise while sailing the choppy seas of running a business online. As neurosurgeon James Doty points out in *Into the Magic Shop*:

> There's a reason stock traders are using meditation techniques; these techniques help them become not only more focused but, sadly, in some cases, more callous... They can increase focus and help us make decisions more quickly, but without wisdom and insight (opening the heart) the techniques can result in self-absorption, narcissism, and isolation.

My conclusion is that all the meditation and self-inquiry in the world can only take you so far. You need a moral compass. You need a means of separating the nonsense from what is true, all the more so as Persistent Non-Symbolic Experience floods your head with bliss. Science is itself a great and constant wake up call, and I cannot forget Ira Schepetin's video on his own journey with Vedanta, which emerged on YouTube in September 2018. In this video, the great bearded sage tells his story of awakening and concludes with the best of contemporary neuroscience. You can see regret in his eyes when he admits that the mysticism associated with the tradition cannot be true. All the "feel good" logic of being one with the universe is just more illusion.

Vedanta might be a great tool, but even this philosophical system is produced by a brain that follows rules. We may feel the presence of a great and intelligent "unified field" when we meditate and use self-inquiry effectively. But that doesn't mean there is one. Rather, the magical effects we experience in life have more to do with mirror neurons and the luck to be with positive people instead of negative ones. And to hell with luck: buy your way into rooms where happy neurons are firing that will rub off on you if that's what it takes. I have, and it's worth every penny. Assembling with others is the most likely path to lasting stability or what I like to think of as "cruising altitude." It's tricky finding people who can enjoy the headier ideas of the woo-woo without falling for it hook, line and sinker. But they're out there and you can find them.

16 THE VICTORIOUS MIND

WHEN I STARTED THIS journey, I did not believe I could experience a state free from thought. But I rapidly found increased well-being and probably wasted a ton of time second-guessing it all instead of just settling in to enjoy the ride. Then again, cross-referencing everything under the sun is part of the pleasure, and I was delighted when I checked back in with the work of Jeffrey Martin.

In his 2019 *Explorers Course*—"Where Finders Deepen"—PNSE (Persistent Non-Symbolic Experience) has been replaced with "Fundamental Wellbeing." This alternative struck me as wise, and PNSE had never sat well with me, as I had yet to experience anything that I would call "non-symbolic." If something even remotely like that occurred, I would start describing the state in my mind, thereby symbolizing. I even went so far as to coin SENSE (Sustaining, Enduring Neo-Symbolic Experience), which, if I'm honest, is even more unwieldy, even if more accurately representing the states I find myself enjoying.

Then, one day, I found my "like-dislike monster" (a.k.a. ego) mildly irritated with yet another sea change on the Internet. I took a walk and ran through some Sanskrit as I went. Seated on a bench in a park, thought completely disappeared. Nothing came in to fill the void or symbolize what was happening. It was exquisite.

A few months later, I wrote to Gary about my progress with this book:

> I need to shed, or at least update, a shoe-gazing, intellectual quibble with PNSE that no longer seems relevant. One afternoon while waiting for these photographs, I went to the park and, for lack of a better term, the world of thought disappeared more completely than before. I'm not sure how the next revision will reflect this experience, but the good news is that such periods continue to arise, leading to the best of both worlds: Almost entirely pleasing thoughts when they are around and sometimes, without a doubt in this mind, something resembling nothing at all. Maybe more like SENSE (Sustaining, Enduring Neo-Symbolic Experience). I don't know whether to laugh or cry at that one!

Gary replied:

> Your SENSE really captures the essence of Ramana's description of the ultimate objective as sahaja nirvikalpa samadhi, which means being without thoughts (*nirvikalpa samadhi*), naturally and effortlessly (*sahaja*). As he said re 'thoughts', *'If one wants to abide in the thought-free state, a struggle is inevitable. One must fight one's way through before regaining one's original primal state. If one succeeds in the fight and reaches the goal, the enemy, namely the thoughts, will all subside in the Self and disappear entirely.'*

So far so good.

Yet, as I hope to have shown in this book, the absence of thoughts is not the goal of a Victorious Mind that wants to learn, remember and participate in the world at the highest possible levels given the circumstances at hand. The world operates using many words and this isn't going to change any time soon. Even if achieving "no mind" is your goal, thought, as much as anything else, is what is likely to get you there. As James Swartz writes, Vedanta is *all about the words* and using them to inquire your way into freedom. I feel that Gary Weber is entirely on the same page when he recommends the memorization of Sanskrit verses for use in self-inquiry. Even if his teaching emerges in a different way, words combat words to help stillness find its way.

At this moment, it's unclear if I will ever reach the level of enduring mental emptiness Gary Weber describes. If I'm reading him correctly, thoughts still do appear for him, particularly when he's tired, in need of a meal or needs to be some place in the world. In the mental quietude and experiences of bliss I've been having, it's pretty much the same deal: any wavering on sleep or diet leads to just as many horrible thoughts and impulses as before. Meditation can help, but even then only to take the edge off. Weber is right that these tools help. I've been using them to dissolve the thoughts that aren't useful. Still, the best practice is to sleep and eat in ways that prevent these thoughts from knocking at the mental door in the first place.

I don't think I *want* thought to disappear *completely*. Martin talks about moving through his "locations" at will in order to show up and serve through his programs, and it sounds a lot like my own "karma yoga" on the Internet. There's another cool cat named Fred Davis who constantly tells you there is no Fred, and refers to the body you see on his YouTube channel as "the unit." He seems to be doing karma yoga too, and hams up the salesman shtick while paradoxically discouraging people from booking sessions with him because his calendar is too full to help "awareness over there" become aware of itself. Awareness produced by a "three pound brain," that is, another running joke that always makes me laugh when he says it. But his humor doesn't deprecate his message and it's not difficult to benefit from one of his sessions if you reach out and find he's booked out. Davis has published a replica of what they're like in *The Book of Undoing*, and it's a marvellous display of teaching what he calls "skillful behavior" using his own brand of abandonment and simply calling a spade a spade:

> 'We *shouldn't* have wars?' Is it true? I notice that we do. I know that we spend half our time and money preparing for them... Human beings *love* war. That's why we're always in them... That guy doesn't know how to drive?... 'He should signal when he changes lanes?' *Did he?* What's happening in the world is all that counts. All that shit in our heads? Worthless. Absolutely worthless. (89–90)

Listening to Davis or reading him is like spiritual stand-up comedy, minus god. If you're really into non-duality, you can't add a god because that would make you at least two, not one. It's a head trip, and probably not one worth stressing about. As Davis says, all that shit in our heads? Absolutely worthless. Unless it gets you somewhere. Or nowhere... they are probably the same place in the end.

To that end, remember these questions in whatever language you please:

How do my thoughts behave? Are they useful?

With the noise out of the way, you'll be pleasantly surprised by how much you can learn, remember and give back to the world that is appearing right now inside you. It *is* you. Let those self-inquiry questions dissolve your need to get anything in return. It's tough, but possible. As the quote in Gary Weber's email signature puts it:

> Why are you so unhappy?
> Because ninety-nine percent of what you think,
> And everything you do,
> Is for your self,
> And there isn't one.
>
> —*Wei Wu Wei*

* * *

"What the hell are you doing!" yelled that man so many years ago before pulling me back from certain death.

Back then I was just a body compelled, tossed and tormented by a defeated mind. I didn't have an answer for him. I let hospitals, medication of all kinds and control freakism speak to his efforts on my behalf.

Now, I do have an answer.

Whoever he was, this book outlines exactly what *this* assembling "I" has been doing: building a Victorious Mind. I hope it helps you build one too.

Brisbane, 2020

GRATITUDE

April, naturally.

Thanks also to The Outside, Haydee Windey, Ingrid Johnson and family, Cliff and Marta Wilde, Lars Rosenbaum, Nick Dorogavtsev, William Gordon, Brad Zupp, Barbara Oakley, Mark Channon, Alex Mullen, Lynne Kelly, Jamie Scott, Daniel Welsch, Nelson Dellis, John Graham, Peter Banerjea and Joy Ghose, Tansel Ali, Phil Chambers, Martin Faulks, Jimmy Naraine, Seph Fontane Pennock, Martin Rusis, Scott Gosnell, Amy Thomas, Dave Farrow, Jennie Gorman, Josie Thomson, Jonathan Levi, Jon Morrow, Tim Gary, everyone in Serious Bloggers Only, Ryan Holiday, the Jordan Peterson study group in Brisbane, the Magnetic Memory Method Mastermind Group, Stephanie Hughes, Allie Bayoco, Adolfo Artigas, Maricela Griffith, "Reclaiming Life," John Eric and, of course, the Magnetic Memory *Familia* at large. Decentralized or assembled for a YouTube livestream, you are truly one of a kind, and so kind, in being as One.

To Ben Fishel, for making the call to adventure. Keep those scientific papers coming.

To Gary Weber for offering the best possible "abandonment" answer to a lingering question and your gracious permission to use the selections, translations and transliterations from the *Ribhu Gita* in *Evolving Beyond Thought*:

Tat Tvam Asi.

Glossary

Bridging Figure: A figure such as a celebrity or historical person used in several associative images to help with recall along a Memory Palace journey.

Challenge-Frustration Curve: Finding a point between challenge and frustration is where optimal learning or progress happens; it is a curve, because this point shifts depending on a number of factors (familiarity, as well as your state of mind or body).

Forgetting Curve: The idea that if you do not practice information you have learned, over time you will forget it ("use it or lose it").

Journey: The path you take through your Memory Palace.

Long-term memory: The part of your memory system responsible for retaining information for great lengths of time.

Macro-Station: An entire room (i.e., bedroom, kitchen, living room, or bathroom) in a Memory Palace.

Magnetic Imagery: Mental imagery created in your imagination that lets you code and decode the sound and meaning of any item of information you want to memorize, such as foreign language words or phrases.

Magnetic Memory Method: Teaches you a systematic, 21st-century approach to memorizing foreign language vocabulary, dreams, names, music, poetry and much more in ways that are easy, elegant, effective and fun.

Magnetic Memory Method (MMM) LifeGrid: A list of all the buildings you know that are associated with your friends and relatives and which forms the basis of your Memory Palace Network.

Magnetic Modes: Multi sensory aspects of Magnetic Imagery; summed up in the acronym KAVE COGS for kinesthetic, auditory, visual, emotional, conceptual, olfactory, gustatory, and spatial.

Magnetic Word Division: The practice of breaking words down into components (usually syllables) that can be associated with Magnetic Imagery.

Major Method or the Major System: A method for memorizing numbers using PAO (Person Action Object) lists.

Memory Palace: The place you store your images and information. Usually based on a building or other structure, though not always. Memory Palace Networks are groups of Memory Palaces.

Micro-Station: A micro-station is an element inside of a room (e.g. a bookcase, bed, TV).

Mnemonic: A system or device that aids in remembering information. (As an adjective, aiding memory.)

N=1: There is only one test subject in this study: You. Experiment in the laboratory of your own body/mind.

PAO list: A collection of meaningful visualizations you associate with numbers using Persons, Actions, and/or Objects.

Pillar Technique: In a Memory Palace, the practice of starting at the ceiling and "writing" the Magnetic Imagery from the top down on imaginary pillars.

PNSE: An acronym for Persistent Non-Symbolic Experience (coined by Jeffrey Martin).

Predetermination: Predetermination involves charting out the memory locations and stations in your Memory Palace Network before making any single attempt to place the words you want to memorize.

Preparation: Preparation involves relaxing the mind.

Primacy Effect: The tendency to recall items at the beginning of a series more easily than those later in the series.

Recall Rehearsal: A specific means of practicing memorized information in order to place it your long-term memory.

Recency Effect: The tendency to recall things you experienced more recently than things experienced earlier.

Serial-Positioning Effect: The tendency to remember the first and last items in a series quite well, but struggle with recalling the middle items.

Short-term memory: The part of your memory system responsible for recalling information quickly, usually for only 20–30 seconds. Also called "working memory."

Spaced repetition: A means of repeating information in a sorted pattern. Software using this method automatically places information you tag as familiar out of frequency while making words you identify as less familiar appear more often.

Word Division: The practice of dividing words into component pieces and connecting each with associative imagery.

Ultimate Memorization Equation:
    Location = Vocabulary
    Image = Meaning/sound of the word
    Action = Meaning/sound of the word

NOTES

1. My friend Martin Rusis asked me if the Challenge-Frustration Curve relates to the "flow" state described by Mihály Csíkszentmihályi. (Mnemonic tip: to remember how to say his name, see yourself saying "hi!" and then sending your cheek up high to another version of yourself on your head, i.e., "Me-hi Cheek-sent-me-high!") The answer is a tentative maybe... leading to a definite no. Flow, as it has been defined in Csíkszentmihályi's work, involves:

- Intense and focused concentration on the present moment

- Merging of action and awareness

- A loss of reflective self-consciousness

- A sense of personal control or agency over the situation or activity

- A distortion of temporal experience—one's subjective experience of time is altered

- Experience of the activity as intrinsically rewarding, also referred to as autotelic experience.

Here's the key difference between the Challenge-Frustration Curve and flow. In the Magnetic Memory Method world, you're consciously monitoring and shifting things to make sure you're experiencing *both* intrinsic and extrinsic rewards with additional heterotelic experiences. You cannot enter a state of flow because you're always already assembled with a world that you experience entirely from *within* your own head. Everything you experience appears in your awareness because the chemical bath that makes up your brain makes it possible. The truth of this claim will become self-evident in your own experience if you use the techniques in the next section.

2. I practiced Systema a few times in Berlin, but never liked the club there. It felt different. In Vancouver, I undertook group and personal training with JP Gagliano for six months. We covered everything from blindfold work to knife-fighting and found we shared interests in Eriksonian hypnosis, accelerated learning and running a business.

3. Very little of the hypnosis and NLP training made it to the pages of my dissertation, where I wound up demonstrating that friendship is as much about "hypothetical consent" as it is about persuasion. Persuasion is important, but if we don't first assume that we have permission to say certain things and accept hearing certain things based on the idea of friendship, persuasion does not matter because it never takes place. Perhaps if I write a sequel to my dissertation, I'll build out a full thesis on the persuasion aspects of friendship. Despite not including much from the training in my scholarly writing, the study of friendship has helped me personally, and perhaps in the future, I'll turn that dusty tome into a work that might help you as well.

4. If you're interested in the neurochemistry that demonstrates why free will doesn't exist, writers like Sam Harris and Dan Dennett have held fascinating public debates about what the data demonstrate both in support of and against the conclusion that there is no free will. But please go beyond their debates! Read the accompanying material too.

5. Of course, Peterson and many others risk romanticizing the past, but that doesn't diminish the core point. We are forgetting the wisdom of the past, but not necessarily for the reasons people think. For example, Peterson strangely (at least in my mind), dismisses thinkers like Michel Foucault and Jacques Derrida as "postmodernists." Yet, Foucault has given us tools in *Madness and Civilization: A History of Insanity in the Age of Reason* and *The Birth of the Clinic: An Archaeology of Medical Perception* to see how Shakespeare, in Hamlet and King Lear, illuminates better ways we might have and did integrate "madness" into our society.

This is not the place to dive into an analysis of Poor Tom and King Lear and an argument about how society does have more than enough competence to take care of its ill far better (because that's what this book in total is trying to do), but it's been astonishing to me as a reader of *Maps of Meaning* to see Peterson himself shoot down the very scholars who bolster his own best arguments in that book. It shows us "digital amnesia" or "digital dementia" in effect when decent scholars "speed read" or "scroll read" through books and don't even remember what they've read. The scrolling itself is known to cause problems in reading comprehension. I aim to write more about this issue in the future, if the "laws governing reality" continue to persuade me in this direction. Since my writing on digital amnesia has generated the most shares on my site overall and this brain finds it alarming when other people invalidate books they haven't thoroughly read (but would substantiate them if they had), that may well be all the push I need. People think they are consuming more, and that may be, but that's no excuse for processing less and there are solutions. These solutions are in this book. You just need to find the triggers for change.

6. Counterfactuals are in fact a huge part of the art of sampling, remixing and mashups that mnemonists have been using in their minds for ages. You may have seen some of the videos where DJs and VJs create alternative versions of songs where, for example, the heavy metal band Slayer sings "War Ensemble" over "I need you tonight" by INXS to create "I need war ensemble". Is it not precisely in the mashup creator's ability to imagine counterfactual realities within the music of the song and singing of Tom Araya that led to its creation? Free will? Hardly. Both of those bands needed to exist in order for the creator to even have the sandbox of sounds and video to play in. Mnemonists create mashups like "I need war ensemble" all the time in their Memory Palaces. For example, when I was memorizing the Greek word *aletheia* for truth, I saw musician "Weird" Al Yankovic choking Al Pacino with a tie. "I'll tie ya!" he shouted to help me remember the sound of the word. Even though a past exists in which I created that Magnetic Imagery, I cannot go back in time and do anything differently.

7. Quote Investigator tracks it back to a 1974 quip by George Ludcke in the Wall Street Journal - *quoteinvestigator.com/2012/12/04/those-who-mind/*

8. If it helps you to know a bit of the phonology, consider what Jason Weaver shared on one of our community livestreams: D and T are "dentals" produced by touching tongue to teeth; F and V are "fricatives" made by forcing breath through a small passage; S and Z are "sibilant fricatives"; and B and P are "plosives" and so on.

9. For more on how disastrous false creations like the ones I've been invited and urged to create can be, see Orson Welles' compelling example of an early mockumentary, *F For Fake*. (Orson Welles is very real in my 00–99 as 87, built from a mental reference to this film.)

REFERENCES

Anderson, Neil T. (2006) *The Bondage Breaker*, Harvest House.

Aquinas, Thomas (1265–1274) *Summa Theologica*.

Augustine of Hippos (397–400) *Confessions*.

Berglas, David (1991) *A Question of Memory*, Jonathan Cape.

Brooks, Douglas Renfrew (2000). *Meditation Revolution: A History and Theology of the Siddha Yoga Lineage*. Delhi, India: Motilal Banarsidass Publishing.

Brown, Brenè. brenebrown.com/articles/2015/06/18/ own-our-history-change-the-story/

Chu, Chin-Ning (1994) *Thick Face, Black Heart*, Grand Central.

Clear, James (2018) *Atomic Habits*, Avery.

Coyle, Daniel (2009) *The Talent Code*, Bantam.

Csíkszentmihályi, Mihály (2008) *Flow*, Harper Perennial.

Dalgleish, Tim, et. al. "Method-of-loci as a mnemonic device to facilitate access to self-affirming personal memories for individuals with depression." Available at: https://psycnet.apa.org/record/2014-16937-006

Davis, Fred (2013) *The Book of Undoing*, Awakening Clarity Press.

Dayananda, Swami (1993) *The Teaching Tradition of Advaita Vedanta*, available at: https://www.shiningworld.com/site/files/pdfs/publications/articles/ The_Teaching_Tradition_of_Advaita_Vedanta.pdf.

Doty, James (2016) *Into the Magic Shop*, Avery.

Downman, Keith (2014) *The Flight of the Garuda: The Dzogchen Tradition of Tibetan Buddhism*.

Ebbinghaus, Hermann (1885) *Über das Gedächtnis* (Memory: A Contribution to Experimental Psychology)

Eyal, Nir (2019) *Indistractable: How to Control Your Attention and Choose Your Life*, BenBella Books.

Ferguson, Niall (2000) *Virtual History*, Basic Books.

Findley, Timothy (1994) *Headhunter*, Crown.

Foer, Joshua (2012) *Moonwalking with Einstein*, Penguin.

Harding, Douglas (2002) *On Having No Head*, Inner Directions.

Hardy, Benjamin (2018) *Willpower Doesn't Work*, Hatchette Books.

Harris, Sam (2013) *Lying*, Four Elephants Press.

Harris, Sam (2015) *Waking Up*, Simon & Schuster.

Harris, Sam, *Making Sense* Podcast.

Haskell, Robert (2008) *Deep Listening: Hidden Meanings in Everyday Conversation* and *Between the Lines: Unconscious Meaning in Everyday Conversation*, Information Age.

Hawking, Stephen (2018) *Brief Answers to Big Questions*, Bantam.

Heuman, Linda (2018) "Whose Buddhism Is Truest?" in *Shifting the Ground We Stand On*, Tricycle.

Jameson, Kay Redfield (2000) *Night Falls Fast: Understanding Suicide*, Vintage.

Jha, A.P., Krompinger, J. and Baime, M.J. (2007) "Mindfulness training modifies subsystems of attention." *Cognitive, Affective, and Behavioral Neuroscience*, 7(2), 109–119. Available at: www.amishi.com/lab/assets/pdf/2007_JhaKrompingerBaime.pdf

Kozhevnikov, Maria, James Elliott, Jennifer Shephard, and Klaus Gramann. "Neurocognitive and somatic components of temperature increases during g-tummo meditation: legend and reality." Available at: https://dash.harvard.edu/handle/1/11180396

Kapleau, Philip (1989) *Three Pillars of Zen*, Anchor.

Greenberg, Gary, (2018) "What if the Placebo Effect Isn't a Trick?" https://www.nytimes.com/2018/11/07/magazine/placebo-effect-medicine.html)

Kelly, Lynne (2017) *The Memory Code*, Pegasus.

Kelly, Lynne, (2020) *Memory Craft*, Pegasus.

Kleiner, Art, Schwartz, Jeffrey M., and Thomson, Josie (2019) *The Wise Advocate*, Columbia Business School.

Kosslyn, Stephen (2009) *The Case for Mental Imagery*, Oxford.

Kreutz G., Bongard S., Rohrmann S., Hodapp V., Grebe D. (2004) "Effects of choir singing or listening on secretory immunoglobulin A, cortisol, and emotional state." DOI: 10.1007/s10865-004-0006-9. Available at: https://link.springer.com/article/10.1007%2Fs10865-004-0006-9.

Langs, Robert (1997) *Death Anxiety and Clinical Practice*, Routledge.

Langs, Robert (2008) "Unconscious Death Anxiety and the Two Modes of Psychotherapy." *The Psychoanalytic Review* Vol. 95, No. 5, October: 791–818.

Maclean, K.A., Ferrer, E., Aichele, S.R., Bridwell, D.A., Zanesco, A.P., Jacobs, T.L., King, B.G., Rosenberg, E.L., Sahdra, B.K., Shaver, P.R., Wallace, B.A., Mangun, G.R., and Saron, C.D. (2015) "Intensive Meditation Training Improves Perceptual Discrimination and Sustained Attention." *Psychological Science* (2010): 829–39. Upaya. Web. 29 December.

Maharshi, Ramana *Upadesa Saram*

Martin, Jeffrey (ND) "Clusters of Individual Experiences Form a Continuum of Persistent Non-Symbolic Experiences in Adults." http://www.nonsymbolic.org/PNSE-Article.pdf

MeaningofLife.tv, "The Path to Enlightenment."

Metivier, Anthony (2013) *Mother Love*.

Metivier, Anthony *The Memory Connection*

Ministry (1989) *The Mind is a Terrible Thing to Taste*, Sire Records.

Mrazek, M.D., Franklin, M.S., Phillips, D.T., Baird, B., and Schooler, J.W. (2013) "Mindfulness Training Improves Working Memory Capacity and GRE Performance While Reducing Mind Wandering." *Psychological Science*: 776–81. Sage Pub. Psychological Science. Web. 29 December.

Mueller, Pam A. and Oppenheimer, Daniel M. (2014) "The Pen Is Mightier than the Keyboard." Available at: https://linguistics.ucla.edu/people/hayes/Teaching/papers/MuellerAndOppenheimer2014OnTakingNotesByHand.pdf

Newberg, Andrew and Mark Waldman (2017) *How Enlightenment Changes Your Brain*, Avery.

Osbourne, Ozzy (1980) "Suicide Solution," *Blizzard of Ozz*, Jet—Epic.

Peterson, Jordan (1999) *Maps of Meaning*, Routledge.

Peterson, Jordan (2018) *Twelve Rules for Life*, Random House.

Pinker, Steven (2012) *The Better Angels of Our Nature*, Penguin.

Pinker, Steven (2018) *Enlightenment Now*, Viking.

Plato, *The Republic*.

Quach, Dianna, Jastrowski Mano, Kristen E., and Alexander, Kristi (2015) "A Randomized Controlled Trial Examining the Effect of Mindfulness Meditation on Working Memory Capacity in Adolescents." *Journal of Adolescent Health*. Science Direct. Elsevier. Web. 29 December.

Rowland, Ian (2005) *The Full Facts Book of Cold Reading*, Ian Rowland.

Russell, Peter (1976) *The TM Technique: An Introduction to Transcendental Meditation and the Teachings of Maharishi Mahesh Yogi*. Routledge and Kegan Paul.

Shankaracharya, Adi, *Atma Bodha*.

Segal, Suzanne (1996) *Collision with the Infinite: A Life Beyond the Personal Self*, Blue Dove.

Shermer, Michael (2017) *Skeptic: Viewing the World with a Rational Eye*, St. Martin's Griffin.

Suzuki, Shunryu

Swartz, James (2012) *Mystic by Default*, Shining World Press.

Swartz, James (2019) *The Yoga of Love*, Shining World Press.

Thomas, John W., and Cohen, Marc (2014) "A Methodological Review of Meditation Research." Frontiers in Psychiatry Front. Psychiatry. PMC. Web. 29 December.

Tolle, Eckhart (2004) *The Power of Now*, Namaste.

Unknown (c. 90 BCE) *Rhetorica Ad Herennium*.

Wachowski, Lana and Wachowski, Lilly (1999) *The Matrix*, Warner Bros.

Weber, Gary (2007) *Happiness Beyond Thought*, iUniverse.

Weber, Gary (2018) *Evolving Beyond Thought*, CreateSpace.

Wiseman, Richard (2010) *59 Seconds: Change Your Life in Under a Minute*, Anchor.

Young, Shinzen (2016) *The Science of Enlightenment*, Sounds True.

Zeidan, Fadel, Susan K. Johnson, Bruce J. Diamond, Zhanna David, and Paula Goolkasian (2010) "Mindfulness Meditation Improves Cognition: Evidence of Brief Mental Training." Consciousness and Cognition: 597-605. Print.

ABOUT THE AUTHOR

Anthony Metivier is the founder of the Magnetic Memory Method, a systematic, 21st-century approach to memorizing foreign language vocabulary, dreams, names, music, poetry and much more in ways that are easy, elegant, effective and fun.

Anthony writes his books and creates video courses for a variety of people who need help with a number of different memory needs. What separates Anthony from others in the memory training world is that he doesn't focus on long strings of digits or training for memory championships. He offers simple techniques for memorizing the information that improves your daily life: foreign language vocabulary, names and faces, material for tests and exams. There's no hype in his training, just techniques that work.

INDEX

H

I

J

K

L

M

CPSIA information can be obtained
at www.ICGtesting.com
Printed in the USA
LVHW021444260623
750808LV00013B/247